Microsoft Azure Administrator – Exam Guide AZ-103

Your in-depth certification guide in becoming Microsoft Certified Azure Administrator Associate

Sjoukje Zaal

BIRMINGHAM - MUMBAI

D1211157

Microsoft Azure Administrator – Exam Guide AZ-103

Commissioning Editor: Karan Sadawana
Acquisition Editor: Rahul Nair
Content Development Editor: Nithin George Varghese
Technical Editor: Komal Karne
Copy Editor: Safis Editing
Project Coordinator: Nusaiba Ansari
Proofreader: Safis Editing
Indexer: Tejal Daruwale Soni
Graphics: Jisha Chirayil
Production Coordinator: Jyoti Chauhan

First published: May 2019

Production reference: 1300519

Published by Packt Publishing Ltd.
Livery Place
35 Livery Street
Birmingham
B3 2PB, UK.

ISBN 978-1-83882-902-5

www.packtpub.com

`mapt.io`

Mapt is an online digital library that gives you full access to over 5,000 books and videos, as well as industry leading tools to help you plan your personal development and advance your career. For more information, please visit our website.

Why subscribe?

- Spend less time learning and more time coding with practical eBooks and Videos from over 4,000 industry professionals

- Improve your learning with Skill Plans built especially for you

- Get a free eBook or video every month

- Mapt is fully searchable

- Copy and paste, print, and bookmark content

Packt.com

Did you know that Packt offers eBook versions of every book published, with PDF and ePub files available? You can upgrade to the eBook version at `www.packt.com` and as a print book customer, you are entitled to a discount on the eBook copy. Get in touch with us at `customercare@packtpub.com` for more details.

At `www.packt.com`, you can also read a collection of free technical articles, sign up for a range of free newsletters, and receive exclusive discounts and offers on Packt books and eBooks.

Contributors

About the author

Sjoukje Zaal is a Microsoft Principal Architect and Microsoft Azure MVP with over 15 years' experience providing architecture, development, consultancy, and design expertise. She works at Ordina, a system integrator based in the Netherlands.

She loves to share her knowledge and is active in the Microsoft community as a co-founder of the Dutch user groups SP&C NL and MixUG. She is also a board member of Azure Thursdays. Sjoukje is a public speaker and is involved in organizing events. She has written several books, writes blogs and is active on the Microsoft Tech Community. Sjoukje is also part of the Diversity and Inclusion Advisory Board.

About the reviewers

Sander Rossel is a Microsoft-certified professional developer with experience and expertise in .NET and .NET Core (C#, ASP.NET, and Entity Framework), SQL Server, Azure, Azure DevOps, JavaScript, and other technologies. He has an interest in various technologies including, but not limited to, cloud computing, NoSQL, continuous integration/continuous deployment, functional programming, and software quality in general. In his spare time, he writes articles for MSDN, CodeProject, and his own blog, as well as books about object-oriented programming, databases, and Azure.

I'd like to thank Sjoukje Zaal for having me as a reviewer. She's achieved great work by getting this book written and published. It was, again, a pleasure working together!

Steef-Jan Wiggers is all in on cloud technology. He works as an Azure technology consultant in the Netherlands and has over 20 years' experience in a wide variety of scenarios, including custom .NET solution development, overseeing complex enterprise integrations, mentoring, and consulting. He loves challenges in the Microsoft arena, building his approach to tackling them on his domain knowledge in the utilities, insurance, healthcare, agriculture, (local) government, bio-sciences, retail, travel, and logistics sectors. Furthermore, he is an InfoQ editor for cloud and a global public speaker, and also is very active in the community as a blogger. For these efforts, Microsoft has recognized him a Microsoft MVP for the past nine years. He can be found on Twitter as @steefjan.

I want to thank Packt for providing me with the opportunity to review this excellent exam guide on Azure administration. Sjouke Zaal, the author, has done a fantastic job writing this guide to help those who want to pass the AZ-103 exam.

Packt is searching for authors like you

If you're interested in becoming an author for Packt, please visit authors.packtpub.com and apply today. We have worked with thousands of developers and tech professionals, just like you, to help them share their insight with the global tech community. You can make a general application, apply for a specific hot topic that we are recruiting an author for, or submit your own idea.

Table of Contents

Preface

Azure is an ever-evolving platform. It offers an environment on the cutting edge of technology that suits many different industry requirements. New capabilities and features are coming out fast, which makes it difficult to stay up to date. This book will give you a complete overview of all the current features and capabilities that Azure has to offer from an administrative perspective, and is a complete guide to preparing for the AZ-103 exam.

This book will cover all the exam objectives. It will start with how to manage Azure subscriptions and resources, where you will learn how to manage Azure subscriptions and resource groups, analyze resource utilization and consumption, and manage **role-based access control** (**RBAC**). In the second part, you will learn how to implement and manage storage by creating and configuring storage accounts, how to import and export data to Azure, and how to configure Azure Files and implement Azure Backup. The third part will cover how to deploy and manage **virtual machines** (**VMs**), where you will learn how to create and configure VMs for Windows and Linux and how to manage Azure VMs and VM backups. The fourth part of this book will cover how to configure and manage virtual networks, by covering implementing and managing virtual networking; how to integrate on-premise networks with Azure virtual networks; how to monitor and troubleshoot virtual networking; how to create and manage Azure Security Groups and Azure DNS; and how to implement Azure Load Balancer. The last part of this book will cover how to manage identities, where you will learn how to manage Azure **Active Directory** (**AD**), how to implement and manage hybrid identities, and how to implement **multi-factor authentication** (**MFA**).

Each chapter will conclude with a *Further reading* section, which is a very important part of each chapter, as it will give you extra, and sometimes crucial, information for passing the AZ-103 exam. As the questions on the exam will change slightly over time and this book will eventually become outdated, the *Further reading* sections will be the place that will provide you with all the updates.

Who this book is for

This book targets experienced administrators who want to pass the *Exam AZ-103: Microsoft Azure Administrator* and broaden their knowledge of Azure from an administrative perspective.

What this book covers

Chapter 1, *Managing Azure Subscriptions and Resource Groups*, covers how to configure Azure subscriptions and resource groups, assign administrator permissions, configure Azure subscription policies, implement and set tagging on resource groups, configure cost center quotas, configure resource locks, move resources across resource groups, and remove resource groups.

Chapter 2, *Analyzing Resource Utilization and Consumption*, covers Azure Monitor, including how to create and analyze metric and alerts, create action groups, configure diagnostic settings on resources, use Azure Log Analytics, and utilize Log Search Query functions.

Chapter 3, *Managing Role-Based Access Control*, covers RBAC, configuring access to Azure resources by assigning roles, configuring management access to Azure, creating a custom role, Azure Policy, and implementing and assigning Azure policies.

Chapter 4, *Creating and Configuring Storage Accounts*, covers Azure storage accounts, how to create and configure a storage account, install and use Azure Storage Explorer, configure network access to the storage account, generate and manage SAS, and implement Azure storage replication.

Chapter 5, *Importing and Exporting Data to Azure*, covers how to configure and use Azure Blob storage, how to import into and export from Azure jobs, how to use **Azure Content Delivery Network (CDN)**, how to configure Azure CDN endpoints, and how to use Azure Data Box.

Chapter 6, *Configuring Azure Files and Implementing Azure Backup*, covers how to create Azure file share and Azure file share sync services, how to use Azure Backup, how to use Azure Site Recovery, how to perform a backup and restore operation, how to create Recovery Services vaults, and creating and configuring a backup policy.

Chapter 7, *Creating and Configuring VMs for Windows and Linux*, covers VMs, how to deploy Windows and Linux VMs, configuring high availability, deploying and configuring scale sets, and modifying and deploying **Azure Resource Manager (ARM)** templates.

Chapter 8, *Managing Azure VMs and VM Backups*, covers how to manage VM sizes, redeploying VMs, moving VMs, adding data disks and network interfaces, automating configuration management, and configuring VM backup and restore.

Chapter 9, *Implementing and Managing Virtual Networking*, covers Azure VNet, IP addresses, how to configure subnets and VNets, configuring private and public IP addresses, and creating and configuring VNetpeering.

Chapter 10, *Integrating On-Premise Networks with Azure Virtual Networks*, covers Azure **Virtual Private Network (VPN)** Gateway, creating and configuring an Azure VPN gateway, creating and configuring a site-to-site VPN, verifying on-premises connectivity, and VNet-to-VNet functionality.

Chapter 11, *Monitoring and Troubleshooting Virtual Networking*, covers Network Watcher, network resource monitoring, managing virtual network connectivity, monitoring and troubleshooting on-premises connectivity, and managing external networking.

Chapter 12, *Azure Security Groups and Azure DNS*, covers **Network Security Groups (NSGs)**, how to create and configure an NSG, associating an NSG to a subnet or network interface, creating and evaluating security rules, using Azure DNS, and how to configure private and public DNS zones.

Chapter 13, *Implementing Azure Load Balancer*, covers Azure Load Balancer, configuring an internal load balancer, creating health probes, creating load balancing rules, and configuring a public load balancer.

Chapter 14, *Managing Azure Active Directory*, covers Azure AD, how to create and manage users and groups, adding and managing guest accounts, performing bulk user updates, configuring self-service password reset, Azure AD Join, how to manage device settings, and adding custom domains.

Chapter 15, *Implementing and Managing Hybrid Identities*, covers Azure AD Connect, how to install Azure AD Connect, managing Azure AD Connect, and managing password sync and password writeback.

Chapter 16, *Implementing Multi-Factor Authentication*, covers Azure MFA, configuring user accounts for MFA, configuring verification methods, configuring fraud alerts, configuring bypass options, and configuring trusted IPs.

To get the most out of this book

This book assumes that you are already familiar with managing cloud services that use storage, security, networking, and cloud compute capabilities. You should have a deep understanding of each service across the full IT life cycle. You should also have experience using PowerShell, the command-line interface, the Azure portal, ARM templates, operating systems, virtualization, cloud infrastructure, storage structures, and networking.

Download the example code files

You can download the example code files for this book from your account at www.packt.com. If you purchased this book elsewhere, you can visit www.packt.com/support and register to have the files emailed directly to you.

You can download the code files by following these steps:

1. Log in or register at www.packt.com.
2. Select the **SUPPORT** tab.
3. Click on **Code Downloads & Errata**.
4. Enter the name of the book in the **Search** box and follow the onscreen instructions.

Once the file is downloaded, please make sure that you unzip or extract the folder using the latest version of:

- WinRAR/7-Zip for Windows
- Zipeg/iZip/UnRarX for Mac
- 7-Zip/PeaZip for Linux

The code bundle for the book is also hosted on GitHub at https://github.com/ PacktPublishing/Microsoft-Azure-Administrator-Exam-Guide-AZ-103. In case there's an update to the code, it will be updated on the existing GitHub repository.

We also have other code bundles from our rich catalog of books and videos available at https://github.com/PacktPublishing/. Check them out!

Download the color images

We also provide a PDF file that has color images of the screenshots/diagrams used in this book. You can download it here: https://www.packtpub.com/sites/default/files/ downloads/9781838829025_ColorImages.pdf.

Conventions used

There are a number of text conventions used throughout this book.

CodeInText: Indicates code words in text, database table names, folder names, filenames, file extensions, pathnames, dummy URLs, user input, and Twitter handles. Here is an example: "Open the PacktNetworkWatcher resource group and select VM1 from the list."

A block of code is set as follows:

```
{
"Name": "Packt Custom Role",
    "Id": null,
    "IsCustom": true,
    "Description": "Allows for read access to Azure Storage, Network and
Compute resources and access to support"
}
```

When we wish to draw your attention to a particular part of a code block, the relevant lines or items are set in bold:

```
{
"Name": "Packt Custom Role",
    "Id": null,
    "IsCustom": true,
    "Description": "Allows for read access to Azure Storage, Network and
Compute resources and access to support"
}
```

Any command-line input or output is written as follows:

```
Connect-AzAccount
```

Bold: Indicates a new term, an important word, or words that you see onscreen. For example, words in menus or dialog boxes appear in the text like this. Here is an example: "Click **Assign** in the top menu."

Warnings or important notes appear like this.

Tips and tricks appear like this.

Get in touch

Feedback from our readers is always welcome.

General feedback: If you have questions about any aspect of this book, mention the book title in the subject of your message and email us at customercare@packtpub.com.

Errata: Although we have taken every care to ensure the accuracy of our content, mistakes do happen. If you have found a mistake in this book, we would be grateful if you would report this to us. Please visit www.packt.com/submit-errata, selecting your book, clicking on the Errata Submission Form link, and entering the details.

Piracy: If you come across any illegal copies of our works in any form on the Internet, we would be grateful if you would provide us with the location address or website name. Please contact us at copyright@packt.com with a link to the material.

If you are interested in becoming an author: If there is a topic that you have expertise in and you are interested in either writing or contributing to a book, please visit authors.packtpub.com.

Reviews

Please leave a review. Once you have read and used this book, why not leave a review on the site that you purchased it from? Potential readers can then see and use your unbiased opinion to make purchase decisions, we at Packt can understand what you think about our products, and our authors can see your feedback on their book. Thank you!

For more information about Packt, please visit packt.com.

Section 1: Managing Azure Subscriptions and Resources

In this section, you will learn how to manage Azure subscriptions and resources.

The following chapters will be covered in this section:

- Chapter 1, *Managing Azure Subscriptions and Resource Groups*
- Chapter 2, *Analyzing Resource Utilization and Consumption*
- Chapter 3, *Managed Role-Based Access Control*

Managing Azure Subscriptions and Resource Groups

1

This book will cover all the exam objectives for the AZ-103 exam. When relevant, we will provide you with extra information and further reading guidance about the different topics in this book.

The first chapter of this book will introduce the first objective, which is how to manage Azure subscriptions and resources. In this chapter, we are going to focus on assigning permissions for administrators so that they can manage your Azure subscriptions and resource groups. You will learn how to configure policies for your Azure subscriptions and resources in order to stay compliant with your organizational standards and SLAs. We are also going to set tagging on resource groups, and you'll learn how to configure cost center quotas and resource locks. To finish this chapter, we will cover how to move resources across different resource groups after creation, and how to completely remove resource groups from your Azure subscription.

In brief, the following topics will be covered in this chapter:

- Azure subscriptions and resource groups
- Assigning administrator permissions
- Configuring Azure subscription policies
- Implementing and setting tagging on resource groups
- Configuring cost center quotas
- Configuring resource locks
- Moving resources across resource groups
- Removing resource groups

Azure subscriptions and resource groups

Before we start with the objectives that are required for the exam, which involves how to manage the Azure subscriptions and resource groups, we will cover some high-level information about Azure subscriptions and resource groups.

Azure subscriptions

Azure subscriptions are basically the billing accounts in Azure. Aside from billing, access to the Azure portal and the creation of the different Azure services in the portal are done through the use of Azure subscriptions.

If you look at the Azure account hierarchy, you will see where Azure subscriptions actually fit in. In the following diagram, the account hierarchy is shown:

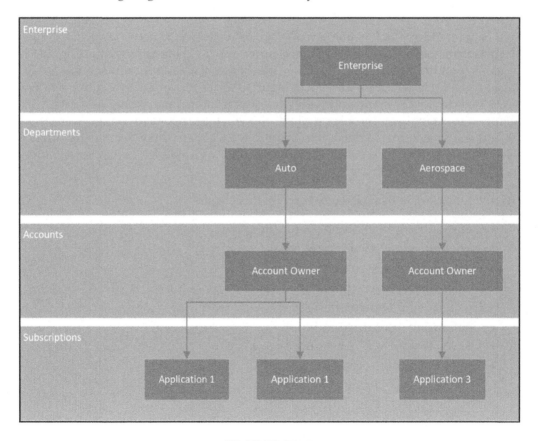

Account hierarchy in Azure

It is divided into **Enterprise**, **Department**, **Accounts**, and **Subscriptions** levels. In the following overview, you'll get an idea of what these different levels are for:

- **Enterprise**: This is also called the **Enterprise Agreement**, and is only used by organizations. It can be accessed from a separate portal (`https://ea.azure.com`) and is used for the whole organization to create the different departments.
- **Departments**: At the department level, sub-accounts for the different departments in your organization are created. You can also group your departments in a functional way, like an IT and finance department, or group them in a geographical way, like North America and Europe, for instance. You can add a department owner here, which will be the person in charge of owning the budget for the department, for instance.
- **Accounts**: This is where the different departments can create multiple accounts within their department. They can also add additional owners to manage these accounts. When you create a personal account in Azure, this is the starting point for creating the subscriptions. The Microsoft account that you use to log in to the Azure portal is then added to this account as the owner.
- **Subscriptions**: You can create multiple subscriptions in an account. This is the level where the actual billing takes place and where the different Azure resources are created. You can add additional subscription owners that can manage the subscriptions, create the different resources, and assign other users to the subscription. Subscriptions always have a trust relationship with an Azure Active Directory instance.

Inside the Azure subscription, you can create multiple resource groups. This will be covered in the next section.

Azure resource groups

Each resource that you create inside Azure must belong to a resource group. It is a logical container that groups multiple resources together. An example would be all the resources that share a similar life cycle, like all the different resources for a particular application; this can be a virtual machine, an Azure Database, a virtual network in Azure, and more, grouped inside the same resource group. They can then be managed and deleted as a single entity.

If you don't have an Azure account yet and you want to get started, you can refer to the following site to create an Azure trial account: `https://azure.microsoft.com/en-us/free/`.

In the next section, we'll assign administrator permissions to a user.

Assigning administrator permissions

There are two ways to assign administrator permissions to your users. The first is done inside Azure Active Directory and is used to assign global administrator permissions. The second is done by using **role-based access control (RBAC)** and can be set from the subscription level.

In the following sections, we'll look at both possibilities.

Assigning global administrator permissions

With global administrator permissions, you can manage all subscriptions and management groups. A management group provides a level of scope above permissions and can be used to manage multiple subscriptions together.

When a user is assigned to the global administrator role, it is able to see all Azure subscriptions and management groups in an organization, allow an automation app to access all Azure subscriptions and management groups, regain access to an Azure subscription or management group when a user has lost access, and grant another user (or themselves) access to an Azure subscription or management group.

To assign administrator permissions to a user on the subscription level, take the following steps:

1. Navigate to the Azure portal by opening `https://portal.azure.com`.
2. In the left-hand menu, select **Azure Active Directory** to open the **Azure AD** blade.
3. Then, under **Manage**, select **Properties**.
4. In the **Directory properties** blade, enable **Access management for Azure resources**:

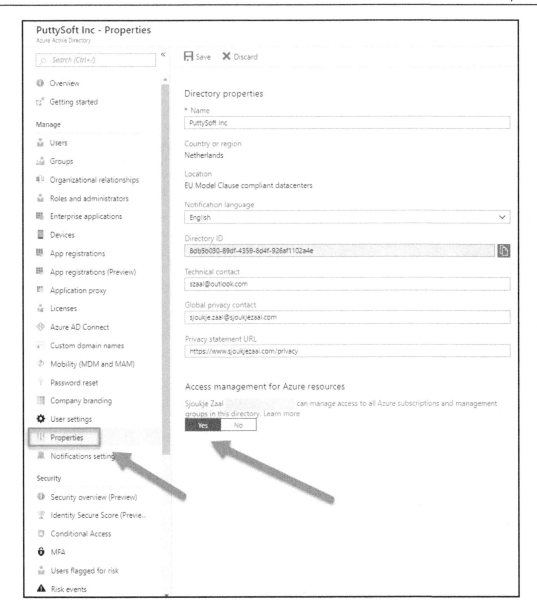

Selecting Properties

5. Click on **Save**.

In the next section, we're going to assign owner permissions to a user on the subscription level.

Assigning owner permissions

The owner of a subscription has full access to all the resources inside the subscription and is able to delegate the access to others. To assign owner permissions to a user on the subscription level using RBAC, perform the following steps:

1. Navigate to the Azure portal by opening `https://portal.azure.com`.
2. In the left-hand menu, select **All services** and select **Subscriptions** (you can also add it to your favorites so that's displayed in the left-hand menu):

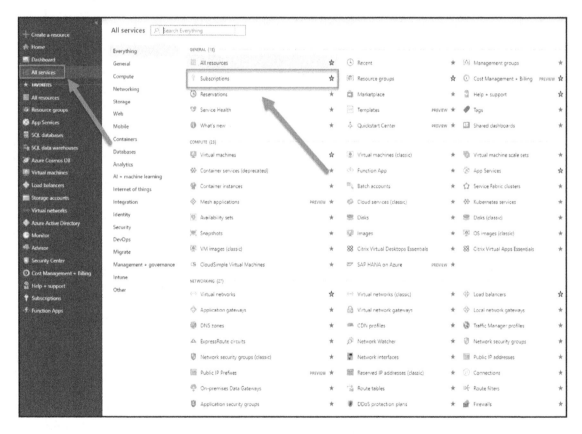

Selecting the subscription

3. Select your subscription, and in the **Subscription** overview blade, click **Access control (IAM)**:

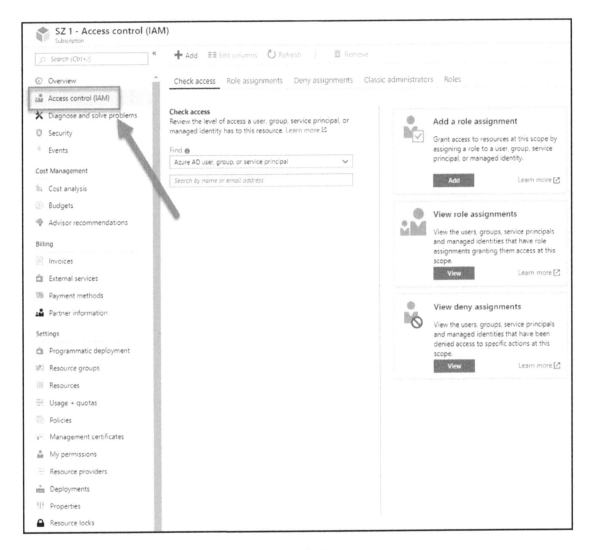

Access control settings

4. To add a user with administrator permissions, click **Add** | **Add role assignment** to open the **Add role assignment** pane.
5. In the **Role** drop-down list, select the **Owner** role.

6. Then, in the **Select** list, select the user. If you don't see the user in the list, you can search for it in the textbox by name and email address:

Selecting the user

7. Click on **Save** to add the user to the owner role.

In this demonstration, we added administrator permissions to a user. In the next section, we're going to configure Azure subscription policies.

Configuring Azure subscription policies

With Azure Policy, you can create, assign, and manage policies. These policies can be used so that you stay compliant with your corporate standards and SLAs by enforcing different rules and effects over your Azure resources. Your resources are evaluated by the assigned policies for non-compliance. For instance, you can create a policy that only allows virtual machines from a certain SKU size in your environment. When this policy is assigned, all new and existing resources are evaluated for compliance with this policy.

To configure subscription policies, perform the following steps:

1. Navigate to the Azure portal by opening `https://portal.azure.com`.
2. In the left-hand menu, select **Subscriptions** (this is if you added it to your favorites; otherwise, take the steps that we described in the previous demonstration).
3. In the **Subscriptions** overview blade, in the left-hand menu under **Settings**, select **Policies**:

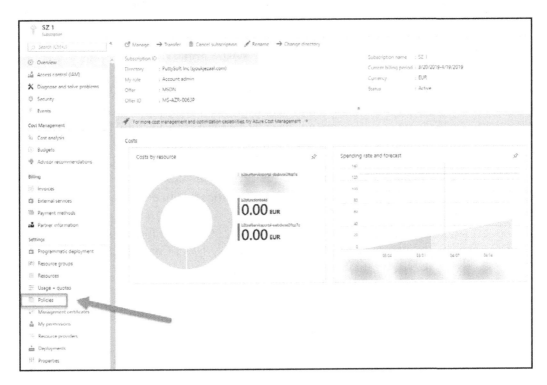

Selecting subscription policies

4. In the **Policies** overview blade, select **Assign policy** to create a new policy:

Creating a new policy

5. On the next screen, we're going to create a definition for our policy. Add the following values to create the policy so that resources for this subscription can only be created in selected regions:
   - **Scope**: The subscription name.
   - **Exclusions**: Leave this blank; we are going to create a policy that applies to the entire subscription.
   - **Policy definition**: When you select this, you can choose from a number of available policies that you can apply to your subscription. Microsoft has created these JSON templates for you, based on the best practices from different enterprises. You can create your own templates here as well. Select a policy from the list (for instance, **Allowed locations**), and then click **Select**.
   - **Assignment name**: This is automatically filled in after selecting the policy.
   - **Parameters**: Here, you can select the allowed locations where users can deploy their resources. For instance, select **Central US**, **East US**, **East US 2**, **West US**, and **West US 2**.

6. After selecting the different regions, click the **Assign** button:

Assigning a new policy

After applying this policy, resources for this subscription can only be created in the selected regions. If you want to add additional regions or remove regions from this policy, you can edit this later.

 You can apply policies at the resource group level as well. This works exactly the same as adding policies at the subscription level. Once you have created a resource group, you can go to the overview blade and select **Policies** from the left-hand menu. In there, you can apply policies at the resource group level.

In the next section, we're going to implement a resource group and add a tag to it.

Implementing and setting tagging on resource groups

You can apply tags to all of your Azure resources. This way, you add extra metadata to the resource group, which can be used to logically organize them into a taxonomy. Each tag consists of a name and a value pair. For instance, you can set the name to Environment and the value to Demo, or you can set the name to Maintenance Window and the value to Saturday 9 AM. After applying these tags, you can easily retrieve all the resources with the same tag name and value. This can be a useful feature for billing or management purposes.

For billing based on your tags, you can use the assigned tags to group the billing for certain resources; for example, if you run VMs and databases for different environments (test, pre-production, and production), you can use tags to categorize the costs. These tags will then show up in the different cost reporting views. For instance, they are visible in the cost analysis view immediately after they are created, and in the detail usage .csv after the first billing period.

You can create resource groups in Azure using the Azure portal, PowerShell, and the CLI. In this demonstration, we are going to create an Azure resource group in our subscription from the Azure portal. You can also set tagging on the resource group level, so we are going to do that, as well. Therefore, perform the following steps:

1. Navigate to the Azure portal by opening `https://portal.azure.com`.
2. In the left-hand menu, select **Resource groups**:

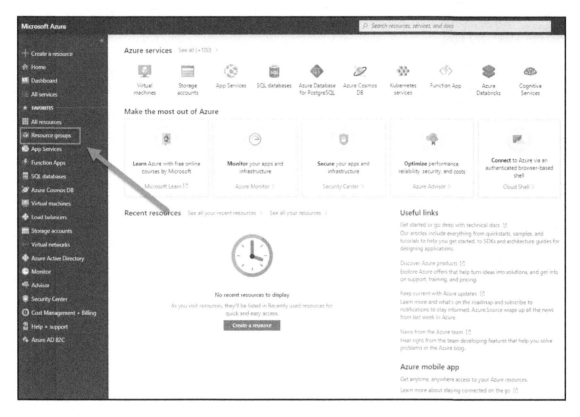

Azure portal overview page

3. In the **Resource groups** blade, click on the **Add** button in the top menu:

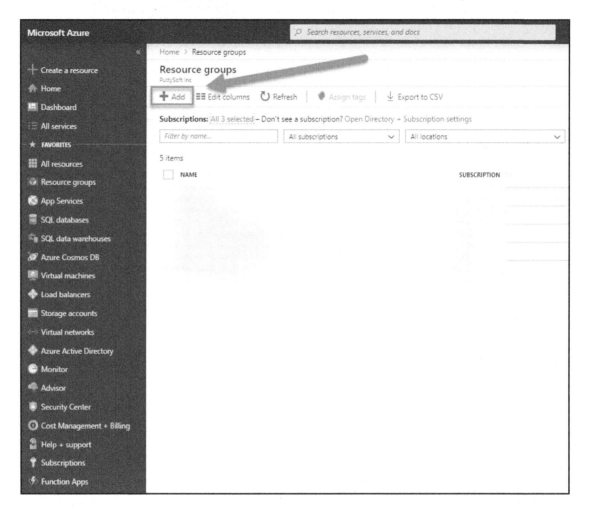

Creating a new resource group

4. Fill in the following values:
    - **Subscription**: Select the subscription to which you want to add the resource group.
    - **Name**: PacktResourcegroup.
    - **Region**: Keep the default (**Central US**, in my case). You can also select another region, if you prefer.

5. Next, select **Tags** in the top menu:

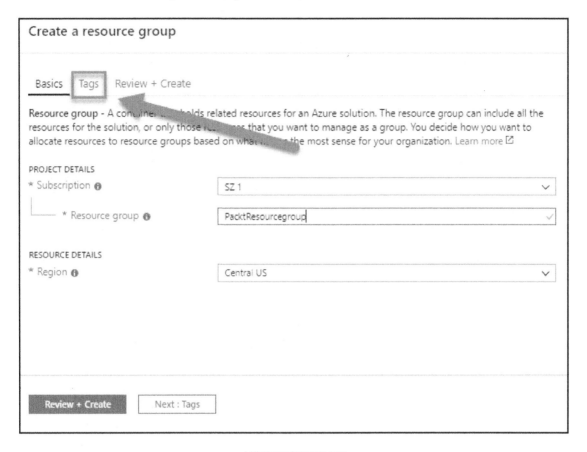

Adding tags to the resource group

6. Add the following values to create a tag for this resource group:
   - **Name**: Environment
   - **Value**: Demo

7. Click on **Review + Create**, and then **Create**.

8. Repeat these steps for some of the resources inside the subscription. In my case, I've added the same tag to the VM.

We have now created a new resource group and applied a tag to it. You can also manage your tags from the **Tags** blade of the resource group. In the next section, we're going to look at how to configure cost center quotas.

Configuring cost center quotas

Quotas in Azure are basically the limits of creating an amount of resources in Azure. For example, there is a limit of 2,000 availability sets that can be created inside an Azure subscription. However, you can contact Microsoft support if you wish to increase this quota. We need to perform the following steps:

1. Navigate to the Azure portal by opening `https://portal.azure.com`.
2. In the left-hand menu, select **Subscriptions**.
3. Select the right subscription. In the **Subscriptions** overview blade, under **Settings**, select **Usage + quotas**. There, you can select a provider:

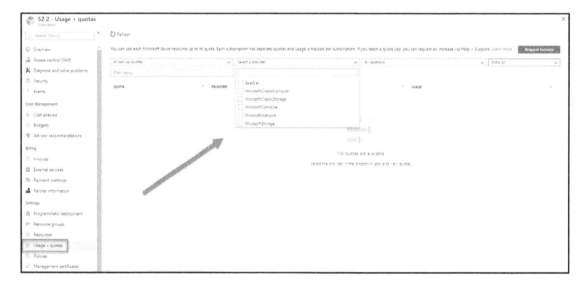

Usage and quotas overview

4. Select **Microsoft.Compute**.
5. You will see the amount of available availability sets for this subscription. If you want to increase this, select the **Request Increase** button on the right-hand side of the screen:

Increasing quotas

6. A new blade will open, where you can create a new support request for increasing the quota of an Azure resource.

In the next section, we're going to configure resource locks and resource policies.

Configuring resource locks

Administrators can set locks on your Azure resources to prevent other users from deleting the resource or making any changes to it. You can set two different lock levels on your subscriptions, resource groups, or resources:

- **CanNotDelete**: This level prevents authorized users from deleting the resource. They can still read and modify the resource.
- **ReadOnly**: Within this level, authorized users can read a resource, but they cannot delete or update it. This level is similar to assigning all authorized users to the reader role using RBAC.

To apply a lock on your resource group, you have to perform the following steps:

1. Navigate to the Azure portal by opening `https://portal.azure.com`.
2. In the left-hand menu, select **Resource groups**. Select the resource group that we created in the previous demonstration.

3. In the **Resource Group** overview blade, under **Settings**, select **Locks**:

Resource group overview

4. On the next screen, click **Add** in the top menu to create a new lock for this resource.

5. Add the following values:
    - **Name:** No-Deletion
    - **Lock type:** **Delete:**

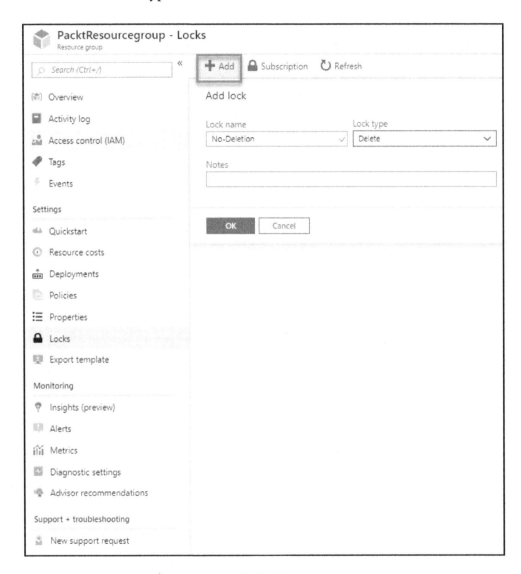

Creating a lock

6. Click on **OK** to create the lock.

We have created a lock for this resource group to prevent authorized users from deleting it. In the next section, we are going to look at how we can move resources across different resource groups.

Moving resources across resource groups

You can easily move your resources across different resource groups and subscriptions by using the Azure portal, PowerShell, the CLI, and the REST API. During the move operation, both the source group and the target group are locked. This blocks all write and delete operations on the resource group until the movement is complete. This means that you cannot update, add, or delete resources in the resource group, but the resources aren't frozen. There will be no downtime for these resources. However, the location of the resources will remain the same, even when the new resource group is created in a different location.

 There are limitations for moving resources across different resource groups and subscriptions. For instance, a VM with managed disks that is deployed inside an availability zone cannot be moved. For more information about these limitations, you can refer to the following article: https://docs.microsoft.com/en-us/azure/azure-resource-manager/resource-group-move-resources.

In the following demonstration, we are going to move resources from a resource group to another resource group using the Azure portal. For this demonstration, I've added a VM to this resource group and created a new resource group called PacktResourceGroup1. To move this VM, perform the following steps:

1. Navigate to the Azure portal by opening https://portal.azure.com.

2. In the left-hand menu, select **Resource groups**. Select the `PacktResourceGroup` that we created in the previous demonstration. Select all the VM resources from the list, and in the top menu, select **Move**:

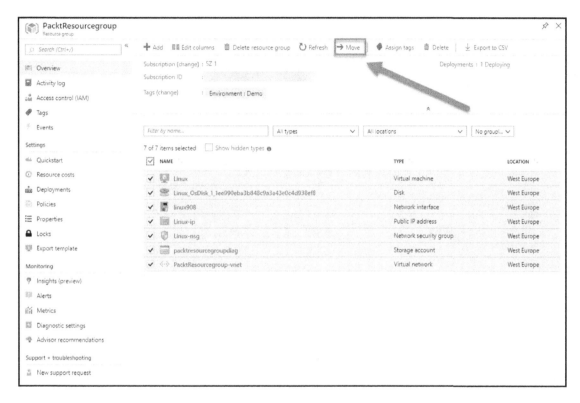

Moving resources

3. You have two possibilities: **Move to another resource group** and **Move to another subscription**. Click on **Move to another resource group**, and in the next screen, select `PacktResourceGroup1` as the resource group, and check the checkbox underneath:

Moving resources

4. Click on **OK** to move the resources to the other resource group.

After moving the resources, you can open the overview blade of `PacktResourceGroup1`. You will see that all the resources have been moved.

In the next (and final) section of this chapter, we are going to remove the resource group.

Removing resource groups

Resource groups can be removed using the Azure portal, PowerShell, the CLI, and the REST API. You can remove the resource group and all the resources inside of it at once.

In the following demonstration, we are going to remove `PacktResourceGroup1`, which we used for the previous demonstration:

1. Navigate to the Azure portal by opening `https://portal.azure.com`.
2. In the left-hand menu, select **Resource groups**. Select `PacktResourceGroup1`. In the top menu, select **Delete resource group**:

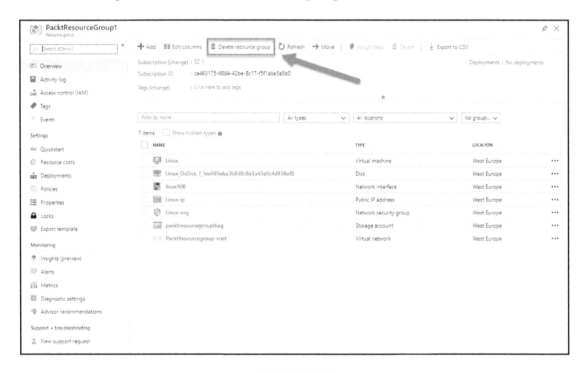

Deleting a resource group

3. To confirm that you want to delete the resource group, you have to specify the name. Enter the name of the resource group and select **Delete**:

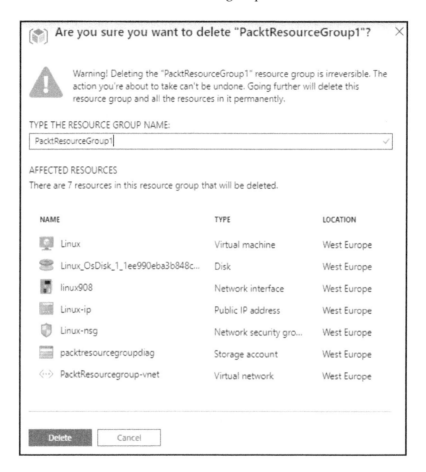

Confirm deletion

The resource group will now be deleted.

Summary

In this chapter, we introduced the various aspects of Azure subscriptions and resource groups. We assigned administrator permissions and described how to create policies to stay compliant. We also covered cost center quotas and resource locks. At the end of this chapter, we moved and removed resource groups completely.

In the next chapter, we'll cover the second part of this exam objective by describing how to analyze resource utilization and consumption.

Questions

Answer the following questions to test your knowledge of the information in this chapter. You can find the answers in the *Assessments* section at the end of this book:

1. Suppose that you have a VM using managed disks that is deployed inside an availability set, and you want to move resources to another resource group. Is this possible?
    - Yes
    - No

2. Suppose that you want to create a resource group using PowerShell. Is this possible?
    - Yes
    - No

3. Suppose that you want to delete a resource group using the CLI. Is this possible?
    - Yes
    - No

Further reading

You can check out the following links for more information about the topics that were covered in this chapter:

- *Associate or add an Azure subscription to your Azure Active Directory tenant*: `https:/
/docs.microsoft.com/en-us/azure/active-directory/fundamentals/active-
directory-how-subscriptions-associated-directory`
- *Resource access management in Azure*: `https://docs.microsoft.com/en-us/
azure/architecture/cloud-adoption/getting-started/azure-resource-
access`
- *Elevate access to manage all Azure subscriptions and management groups*: `https://
docs.microsoft.com/en-us/azure/role-based-access-control/elevate-
access-global-admin`
- *Understand Azure Policy effects*: `https://docs.microsoft.com/en-us/azure/
governance/policy/concepts/effects`
- *Prevent unexpected charges with Azure billing and cost management*: `https://docs.
microsoft.com/en-us/azure/billing/billing-getting-started`
- *Use tags to organize your Azure resources*: `https://docs.microsoft.com/en-us/
azure/azure-resource-manager/resource-group-using-tags`
- *Lock resources to prevent unexpected changes*: `https://docs.microsoft.com/en-us/
azure/azure-resource-manager/resource-group-lock-resources`
- *Move resources to new resource group or subscription*: `https://docs.microsoft.
com/en-us/azure/azure-resource-manager/resource-group-move-resources`

Analyzing Resource Utilization and Consumption

2

In the previous chapter, we covered how to create and manage the different aspects of Azure subscriptions and resources.

This chapter will cover the second part of *Managing Azure Subscriptions and Resources* objective. In this chapter, we are going to illustrate how to monitor your different Azure resources using Azure Monitor. You will learn about the different capabilities of Azure Monitor and how to create and analyze different metrics and alerts, thereby using Azure Monitor to provide valuable insights about the performance and behavior of all your Azure resources. To finish this chapter, we're going to look at Azure Log Analytics and how it's integrated inside Azure Monitor. You'll also learn how to create Log Search Query functions.

The following topics will be covered in this chapter:

- Azure Monitor
- Creating and analyzing metrics and alerts
- Creating action groups
- Configuring diagnostic settings on resources
- Azure Log Analytics
- Utilizing Log Search Query functions

Azure Monitor

Azure Monitor is a monitoring solution in the Azure portal that delivers a comprehensive solution for collecting, analyzing, and acting on telemetry from cloud and on-premises environments. It can be used to monitor various aspects (for instance, the performance of applications) and identify issues affecting those applications and other resources that depend on them.

The data that is collected by Azure Monitor fits into two fundamental types: metrics and logs. Metrics describe an aspect of a system at a particular point in time and are displayed in numerical values. They are capable of supporting near real-time scenarios. Logs are different from metrics. They contain data that is organized into records, with different sets of properties for each type. Data like events, traces, and performance data are stored as logs. They can then be combined for analysis purposes.

Azure Monitor supports data collection from a variety of Azure resources, which are all displayed in the overview page in the Azure portal. Azure Monitor provides the following metrics and logs:

- **Application monitoring data**: This will consist of data about the functionality and performance of the application and the code that is written, regardless of its platform.
- **Guest OS monitoring data**: This will consist of data about the operating system on which your application is running. This could be running in any cloud or on-premises.
- **Azure resource monitoring data**: This will consist of data about the operation of an Azure resource.
- **Azure subscription monitoring data**: This will consist of data about the operation and management of an Azure subscription, as well as data about the health and operation of Azure itself.
- **Azure tenant monitoring data**: This will consist of data about the operation of tenant-level Azure services, such as Azure Active Directory.

Azure Monitor now integrates the capabilities of Log Analytics and Application Insights together. You can also keep using Log Analytics and Application Insights on their own.

Now that we have some basic knowledge about Azure Monitor, we are going to look at how to analyze alerts and metrics across subscriptions.

Creating and analyzing metrics and alerts

To analyze alerts and metrics across Azure Monitor, we need to go to the monitoring resource inside the Azure portal. In the upcoming sections, we will set up metrics and alerts and show you how to analyze them.

Metrics

Metrics describe an aspect of a system at a particular point in time and are displayed in numerical values. They are capable of supporting near real-time scenarios.

Creating a metric

To display the metrics for the various Azure resources in Azure Monitor, perform the following steps:

1. Navigate to the Azure portal by opening `https://portal.azure.com`.

2. In the left-hand menu, select **Monitoring** to open the **Azure Monitor** overview blade:

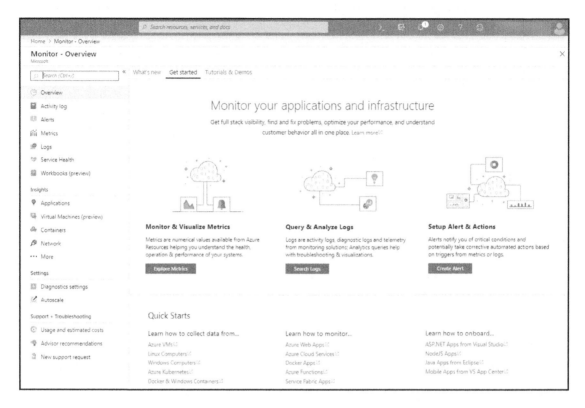

Azure Monitor overview

3. First, we're going to look at metrics. Therefore, in the left-hand menu, select **Metrics**, or select the **Explore Metrics** button from the overview blade.

4. In the **Metrics** overview blade, click on the **+ Select a resource** button. A new blade will open up where you can select the subscription, the resource group, and the resource type. Select the subscription that was used for the demonstration of the previous chapter, select PacktResourceGroup, and then select the VM (in my case, Linux). You can filter by other resource types, as well:

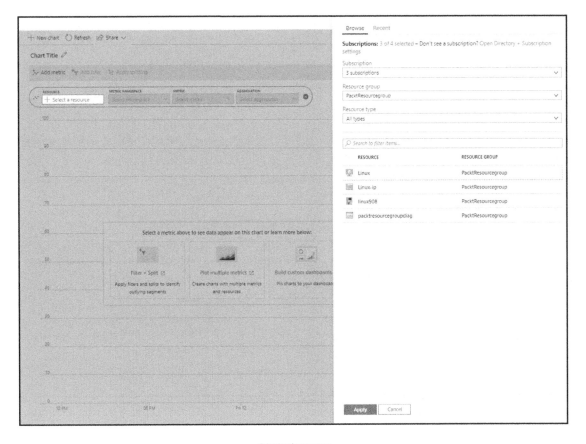

Selecting the resources

5. Click on **Apply**.

6. Then, you can select the metric type. Select **CPU Credits Consumed**, for instance:

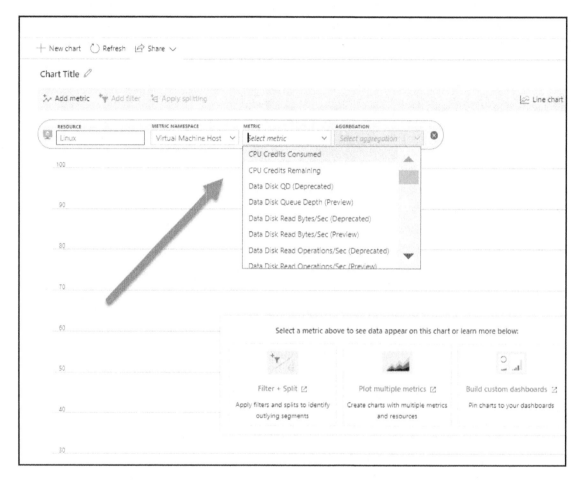

Metric type

Take some time to look at the different metrics that you can choose from. This may be a part of the exam questions.

7. You can select a different type of aggregation as well, like the count, average, and more, in the filter box. In the top-right of the blade, you can select a different time range for your metric as well:

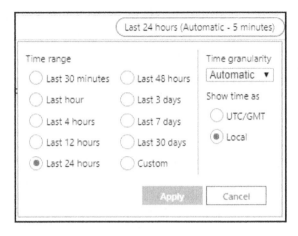

Time ranges

8. You can also pin this metric to the overview dashboard in the Azure portal. Therefore, click on the **Pin to dashboard** button, and then choose to pin it to the current dashboard or create a new dashboard for it. For now, select **Pin to current dashboard**:

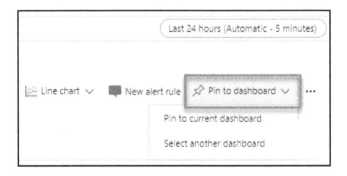

Pin metric to dashboard

9. If you now select **Dashboard** from the left-hand menu, you'll see that this metric is added to it. This way, you can easily analyze this metric without the need to open Azure Monitor.

 Metrics are also available directly from the Azure resource blades. So, for instance, if you have a VM, go to the VM resource by selecting it. Then, in the left-hand menu, under **Monitoring**, you can select **Metrics**.

In the next section, we're going to look at how to set up and analyze alerts in Azure Monitor.

Alerts

With alerts, Azure can proactively notify you when critical conditions occur in the Azure or on-premises environment. Alerts can also attempt to take corrective actions automatically. Alert rules that are based on metrics will provide near real-time alerting, based on the metric. Alerts that are created based on logs can merge data from different resources together.

The alerts in Azure Monitor use action groups, which are unique sets of recipients and actions that can be shared across multiple rules. These action groups can use Webhooks to start external actions, based on the requirements that are set up for this alert. These external actions can then be picked up by different Azure resources, like runbooks, functions, or logic apps. Webhooks can also be used for adding these alerts to external **IT Service Management** (**ITSM**) tools.

You can also set alerts for all the different Azure resources. In the following sections, we are going to create an alert.

Creating an alert

To create an alert, perform the following steps:

1. From the **Azure Monitor** overview blade, in the left-hand menu, select **Alerts**. You can also go to the alerts settings by clicking on **Create alert** in order to create an alert directly**.**

2. In the **Alerts** blade, click on **+ New alert rule** in the top menu:

Creating a new alert

3. The **Create rule** blade is displayed. Here, you can create the rule and action groups. To create a new rule, you need to first select the resource. Click on the **Select** button under the **RESOURCE** section:

Creating a new rule

4. In the next blade, you can filter by the subscription and resource type. Select
   Virtual machines:

Filtering by subscription and resource type

5. Select the VM that we created in the previous chapter from the list and click **Done**.

6. Now that we have a resource selected, we're going to set up the condition. Click on **Add condition**.

7. The condition blade is open, and so we can filter by a certain signal. Select **Percentage CPU** and click **Done**:

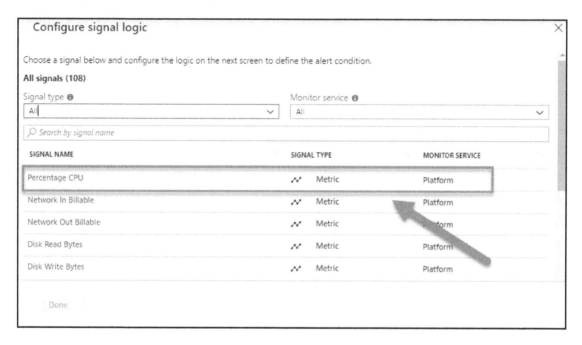

Filtering on a signal

8. Next, you can set the alert logic for this alert. You can choose multiple operators, set the aggregation type, and set the threshold value for this alert. Set the following:
   - **Operator: Greater than**
   - **Aggregation type: Average**
   - **Threshold Value: 90%**

9. Leave **Evaluated based on** with its default settings.

10. This alert will notify you when the CPU of the virtual machines is greater than 90% over a five minute period of time. Azure Monitor will check this every minute:

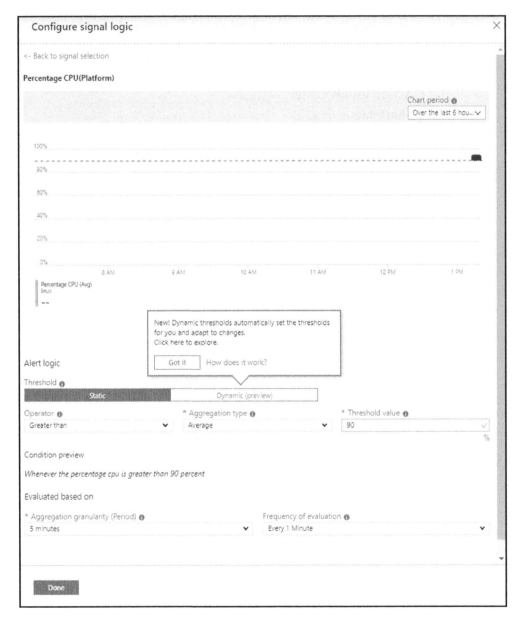

Setting condition values

11. Click on **Done** to create this condition.

12. Now, we have to create an action group to send the alert to. This is then responsible for handling the alert and taking further action on it. The action group that you create here can be reused across other alerts as well. So, in our case, we will create an email action group that will send out an email to a certain email address. After its creation, you can add this existing action group to other alerts. Under **Action group**, select the **Create new** button.

13. In the **Action Group** blade, add the following settings:
    - **Action group name**: Send email
    - **Short name**: email
    - **Subscription**: Select the subscription where the VM is created, as well
    - **Resource group**: Select **Default-ActivitiyLogAlerts** (to be created)

14. Then, we have to provide the actual action. Add the following values:
    - **Action name**: email
    - **Action type**: **Email/SMS/Push/Voice**

15. Then, select **Edit details** and select the **Email** checkbox. Provide an email address and click on the **OK** button:

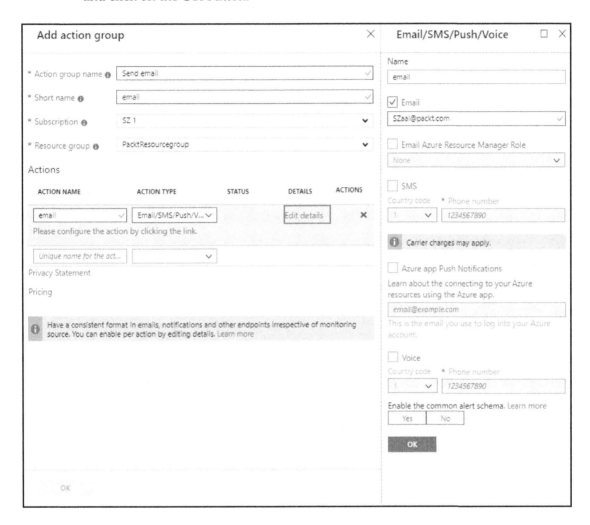

Creating an action group

16. Click on **OK** again.

17. Finally, you have to specify an alert name, set the severity level of the alert, and click on **Create alert rule**:

Alert settings

We have now created an alert and an action group that will alert a user via email when the CPU goes over 90%. In the next section, we're going to configure diagnostic settings on resources.

Configuring diagnostic settings on resources

You can also configure diagnostic settings on different Azure resources. There are two types of diagnostic logs available in Azure Monitor:

- **Tenant logs**: These logs consist of all the tenant-level services that exist outside of an Azure subscription. An example of this is the Azure Active Directory logs.
- **Resource logs**: These logs consist of all the data from the resources that are deployed inside an Azure subscription; for example, virtual machines, storage accounts, and network security groups.

The contents of these logs are different for every Azure resource. These logs differ from guest OS-level diagnostic logs. To collect OS-level logs, an agent needs to be installed on the virtual machine. The diagnostic logs don't require an agent to be installed; they can be accessed directly from the Azure portal.

The logs that can be accessed are stored inside a storage account and can be used for auditing or manual inspection purposes. You can specify the retention time in days by using the resource diagnostic settings. You can also stream the logs to event hubs to analyze them in PowerBI, or insert them into a third-party service. These logs can also be analyzed with Azure Monitor. Then, there will be no need to store them in a storage account first.

Enabling diagnostic settings

To enable the diagnostic settings for resources, perform the following steps:

1. Navigate to the Azure portal by opening `https://portal.azure.com`.
2. Go to the VM that we created in the previous chapter again. Make sure that the VM is running, and in the left-hand menu, under **Monitoring**, select **Diagnostic settings**.
3. The **Diagnostic Settings** blade will open up. You will need to select a storage account where the metrics can be stored.

4. Click on the **Enable guest-level monitoring** button to update the diagnostic settings for the virtual machine:

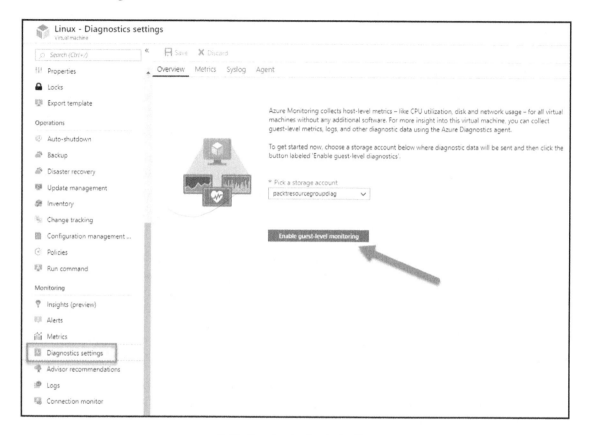

Enabling diagnostic settings for a virtual machine

5. When the settings are updated, you can go to **Metrics** in the top menu to set the metrics that are collected. The **syslog** blade is used for setting the minimum log level.
6. New metrics will be available from the metrics blade after enabling diagnostic logging in Azure Monitor. You can analyze them in the same way that we did earlier in this chapter, in the *Metrics* section.

In the next section, we're going to look at the Azure Log Analytics service, which is now a part of Azure Monitor as well.

Viewing alerts in Log Analytics

Azure Log Analytics is a service that collects telemetry data from various Azure resources and on-premises resources. All of that data is stored inside a Log Analytics workspace, which is based on the Azure Data Explorer. It uses the Kusto Query Language, which is also used by Azure Data Explorer to retrieve and analyze the data.

Analyzing this data can be done from Azure Monitor. All the analysis functionalities are integrated in there. The term **Log Analytics** now primarily applies to the blade in the Azure portal where you can analyze metric data.

Before we are able to display, monitor, and query the logs from Azure Monitor, we need to create a Log Analytics workspace. For that, we have to perform the following steps:

1. Navigate to the Azure portal by opening `https://portal.azure.com`.
2. Click on **Create a new resource**.
3. Type `Log Analytics` in the search box and create a new workspace.
4. Add the following values:
    - **Log Analytics workspace**: `PacktWorkspace`
    - **Subscription**: Select a subscription
    - **Resource group**: Create a new one and call it `PacktWorkspace`
    - **Location**: **West US**
    - **Pricing tier**: Keep the default one, which is **per GB**
5. Click on the **OK** button to create the workspace.

 You can also create this workspace from Azure Monitor. Go to the **Azure Monitor** blade, and under **Insights** in the left-hand menu, select **More**. When no workspace has been created, Azure will ask to create one.

Now that we have created a Log Analytics workspace, we can use it inside Azure Monitor to create some queries to retrieve data. We will do this in the next section.

Utilizing Log Search Query functions

Azure Monitor is now integrated with the features and capabilities that Log Analytics was offering. This also includes creating search queries across the different logs and metrics by using the Kusto Query Language.

To retrieve any type of data from Azure Monitor, a query is required. Whether you are configuring an alert rule, analyzing data in the Azure portal, retrieving data using the Azure Monitor Logs API, or being notified of a particular condition, a query is used.

The following list provides an overview of all the different ways queries are used by Azure Monitor:

- **Portal**: From the Azure portal, an interactive analysis of log data can be performed. In there, you can create and edit queries and analyze the results in a variety of formats and visualizations.
- **Dashboards**: The results of a query can be pinned to a dashboard. This way, results can be visualized and shared with other users.
- **Views**: By using the View Designer in Azure Monitor, you can create custom views of your data. This data is provided by queries as well.
- **Alert rules**: Alert rules are also made up of queries.
- **Export**: Exports of data to Excel or PowerBI are created with queries. The query defines the data to export.
- **Azure Monitor Logs API**: The Azure Monitor Logs API allows any REST API client to retrieve log data from the workspace. The API request includes a query to retrieve the data.
- **PowerShell**: You can run a PowerShell script from a command line or an Azure Automation runbook that uses `Get-AzOperationalInsightsSearchResults` to retrieve log data from Azure Monitor. You need to create a query for this cmdlet to retrieve the data.

In the following section, we are going to create some queries to retrieve data from the logs in Azure Monitor.

Querying logs in Azure Monitor

To query logs in Azure monitor, perform the following steps:

1. Navigate to the Azure portal by opening `https://portal.azure.com`.
2. In the left-hand menu, select **Monitoring** to open the **Azure Monitor** overview blade. Under **Insights**, select **More**. This will open the Log Analytics workspace that we created in the previous step.

3. On the overview page, click on **Logs** in the top menu. This will open the Azure Monitor query editor:

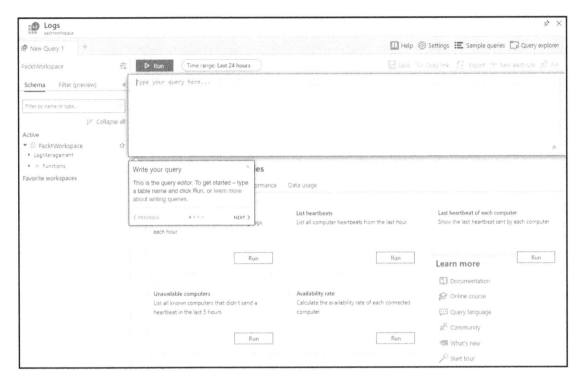

Azure Monitor query editor

4. Here, you can select some default queries. They are displayed at the bottom part of the screen. There are queries for retrieving unavailable computers, the last heartbeat of a computer, and much more. Add the following queries to the query editor window to retrieve data:

- This query will retrieve the top 10 computers with the most error events over the past day:

```
Event | where (EventLevelName == "Error") | where
(TimeGenerated > ago(1days)) | summarize ErrorCount =
count() by Computer | top 10 by ErrorCount desc
```

- This query will create a line chart with the processor utilization for each computer from last week:

```
Perf | where ObjectName == "Processor" and CounterName
== "% Processor Time" | where TimeGenerated between
(startofweek(ago(7d)) .. endofweek(ago(7d)) ) |
summarize avg(CounterValue) by Computer,
bin(TimeGenerated, 5min) | render timechart
```

 A detailed overview and tutorial on how to get started with the Kusto Query Language is beyond the scope of this book. If you want to find out more about this query language, you can refer to https:// docs.microsoft.com/en-us/azure/azure-monitor/log-query/get-started-queries.

Summary

In this chapter, we covered the second part of the *Managing Azure Subscriptions and Resources* objective. We covered the various aspects of Azure Monitor and how you can use metrics to monitor all of your Azure resources and alerts in order to get notified when certain things are happening with your Azure resources. We also used Azure Log Analytics and created queries so that we could get valuable data out of the logs.

In the next chapter, we will cover the third (and final) part of this exam objective. In that chapter, we will cover how to manage **role-based access control (RBAC)**.

Questions

Answer the following questions to test your knowledge of the information in this chapter. You can find the answers in the *Assessments* section at the end of this book:

1. Is Azure Log Analytics now a part of Azure Monitor?
   - Yes
   - No

2. Suppose that you want to create a query to retrieve specific log data from a virtual machine. Do you need to write a SQL statement to retrieve this?
   - Yes
   - No

3. Are action groups used to enable metrics for Azure Monitor?
    - Yes
    - No

Further reading

You can check out the following links for more information about the topics that were covered in this chapter:

- *Azure Monitor overview*: `https://docs.microsoft.com/en-us/azure/azure-monitor/overview`
- *Collect and consume log data from your Azure resources*: `https://docs.microsoft.com/en-us/azure/azure-monitor/platform/diagnostic-logs-overview`
- *Analyze log data in Azure Monitor*: `https://docs.microsoft.com/en-us/azure/azure-monitor/log-query/log-query-overview`
- *Create custom views by using View Designer in Azure Monitor*: `https://docs.microsoft.com/en-us/azure/azure-monitor/platform/view-designer`
- *Azure Monitor naming and terminology changes*: `https://docs.microsoft.com/en-us/azure/azure-monitor/terminology`

Managing Role-Based Access Control

3

In the previous chapter, we covered the second part of this book's objective by covering how to analyze resource utilization and consumption in Azure. We've covered how to monitor different Azure resources using Azure Monitor, and how to use Azure Log Analytics to query the logs.

This chapter will cover the last part of the *Managing Azure Subscriptions and Resources* objective by covering **role-based access control** (**RBAC**). You'll learn how to configure access to Azure resources by assigning RBAC roles from the Azure portal. You'll also learn how to configure management access by assigning global administrators to your Azure subscription and other resources. You'll learn how to create custom roles, which you can apply when custom permissions are needed for your users. This chapter will finish by covering Azure policies and how you can apply them to your Azure resources.

The following topics will be covered in this chapter:

- RBAC
- Configuring access to Azure resources by assigning roles
- Configuring management access to Azure
- Creating a custom role
- Azure Policy
- Implementing and assigning Azure policies

Technical requirements

This chapter will use the Azure PowerShell (`https://docs.microsoft.com/en-us/powershell/azure/install-az-ps?view=azps-1.8.0`) for the examples.

The source code for the sample application can be downloaded from `https://github.com/PacktPublishing/Microsoft-Azure-Administrator-Exam-Guide-AZ-103/tree/master/Chapter03`.

RBAC

With RBAC, you can manage who has access to the different Azure resources inside of your tenant. You can also set what the users can do with different Azure resources.

A best practice for assigning permissions is using the principle of least permissions; this involves giving users the exact permissions they need to do their jobs properly. Users, groups, and applications are added to roles in Azure, and those roles have certain permissions. You can use the built-in roles that Azure offers, or you can create custom roles in RBAC.

The roles in Azure can be added to a certain scope. This scope can be an Azure subscription, an Azure resource group, or a web application. Azure then uses access inheritance; roles that are added to a parent resource give access to child resources automatically. For instance, a group that is added to an Azure subscription gets access to all the resource groups and underlying resources that are in that subscription as well. A user that is added to a **virtual machine** (**VM**) only gets access to that particular VM.

Let's start looking at RBAC in detail by first looking at built-in roles.

Built-in roles

Azure offers various built-in roles that you can use for assigning permissions to users, groups, and applications. RBAC offers the following three standard roles that you can assign to each Azure resource:

- **Owner**: Users in this role can manage everything, and can create new resources.
- **Contributor**: Users in this role can manage everything, just like users in the owner role, but they can't assign access to others.
- **Reader**: Users in this role can read everything, but they are not allowed to make any changes.

Aside from the standard roles, each Azure resource also has roles that are scoped to particular resources. For instance, you can assign users, groups, or applications to the SQL security manager, from which they can manage all security-related policies of the Azure SQL Server, or you can assign them to the VM contributor role, where they can manage the VMs, but not the VNet or storage accounts that are connected to a VM.

 For an overview of all the built-in roles that Azure offers, you can refer to `https://docs.microsoft.com/en-us/azure/role-based-access-control/built-in-roles`.

While these built-in roles usually cover all possible use cases, they can never account for every requirement in an organization. To allow for flexibility in role assignment, RBAC provides the ability to make custom roles. Let's look at this feature.

Custom roles

You can also create custom roles in RBAC when none of the built-in roles suit your needs. Custom roles can be assigned to the exact same resources as built-in roles and can only be created using PowerShell, the CLI, and the REST API. You can't create them in the Azure portal. In each Azure tenant, you can create up to 2,000 roles.

Custom roles are defined in JSON, and after deployment, they are stored inside the Azure AD tenant. By storing them inside the Azure AD tenant, they can be used in all the different Azure subscriptions that are connected to the Azure AD tenant.

Configuring access to Azure resources by assigning roles

If a user in your organization needs permissions to access Azure resources, you need to assign the user to the appropriate role in Azure. In this demonstration, we are going to assign administrator access to a user for a VM. To configure access to the VM for the user, you have to perform the following steps:

1. Navigate to the Azure portal by opening `https://portal.azure.com`.
2. Open the `PacktNetworkWatcher` resource group and select **VM1** from the list:

The PacktNetworkWatcher resources

3. You will be redirected to the VM settings blade.

4. In the settings blade, select **Access control (IAM)** and click on **Add | Add role assignment** in the top menu:

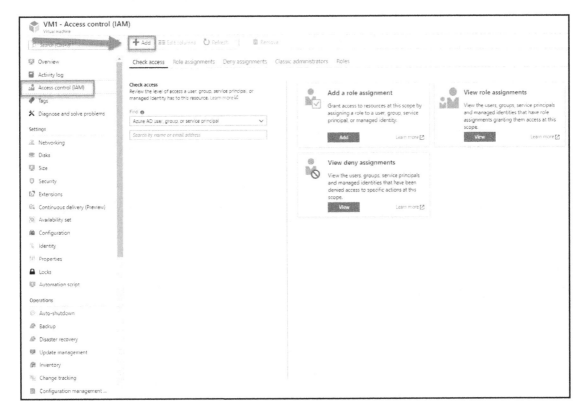

Access control settings

5. In the **Add role assignment** blade, specify the following values:

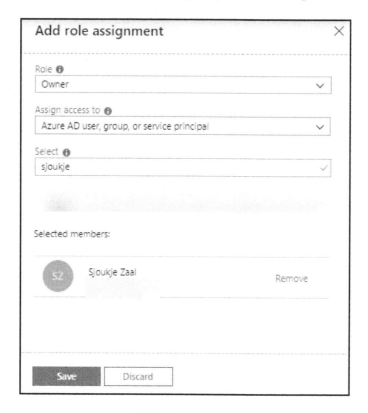

The Add role assignment blade

6. Click on **Save**.
7. The user now has administrator permissions on the VM.

In this demonstration, we assigned administrator access to a user for a VM. We are now going to look at how to configure management access to Azure.

Configuring management access to Azure

Management access to Azure can be configured at the subscription level. To do this, perform the following steps:

1. Navigate to the Azure portal by opening `https://portal.azure.com`.
2. Select **All services** and type `subscriptions` in the search box. Then, select **Subscriptions**, as highlighted in the following screenshot:

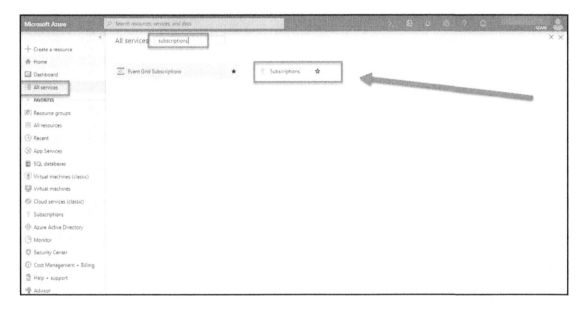

Selecting subscriptions

3. Select the subscription that you want to grant management access to from the list.

4. In the subscription settings blade, select **Access control (IAM)** and click on **Add | Add co-administrator** in the top menu:

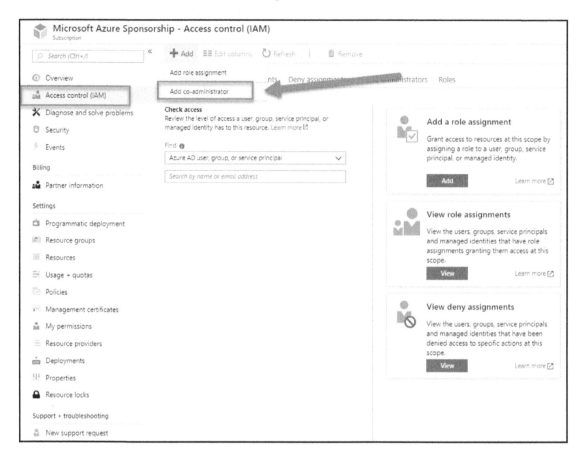

The access control settings

5. In the **Add co-administrator** blade, specify the following values:

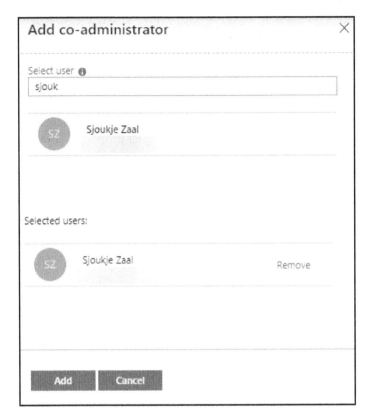

Adding a co-administrator

6. Click on **Add**.

Now that we have configured management access to Azure, we are going to look at how to create a custom role for your users.

Creating a custom role

In the following example, we will create a custom role that can only restart VMs in Azure. For this, you need to create a JSON file that will be deployed using PowerShell. We are assigning that role to a user account inside the JSON file, as follows:

1. You can define the custom role by using the following JSON code. You should set the Id to null because the custom role gets an ID assigned to it at creation. We will add the custom role to two Azure subscriptions, as follows (replace the subscriptions in the AssignableScopes part with your subscription IDs):

```
{
"Name": "Packt Custom Role",
 "Id": null,
 "IsCustom": true,
 "Description": "Allows for read access to Azure Storage, Network
and Compute resources and access to support",
    "Actions": [
        "Microsoft.Compute/*/read",
        "Microsoft.Storage/*/read",
        "Microsoft.Network/*/read",
        "Microsoft.Resources/subscriptions/resourceGroups/read",
        "Microsoft.Support/*"
    ],
    "NotActions": [
    ],
    "AssignableScopes": [
    "/subscriptions/********-****-****-****-***********",
    "/subscriptions/********-****-****-****-***********"
    ]
}
```

2. Save the JSON file in a folder named CustomRoles on the C: drive of your computer. Then, run the following PowerShell script to create the role. First, log in to your Azure account, as follows:

   Connect-AzAccount

3. If necessary, select the right subscription:

   Select-AzSubscription -SubscriptionId "******-****-****-****-***********"**

4. Then, create the custom role in Azure by importing the JSON file into PowerShell:

```
New-AzRoleDefinition -InputFile
"C:\CustomRoles\PacktCustomRole.json"
```

In this demonstration, we created a custom role that can only restart VMs in Azure. Now, we're going to take a look at how you can create policies using Azure Policy.

Azure Policy

With Azure Policy, you can create policies that enforce rules over your Azure resources. This way, resources stay compliant with service-level agreements and corporate standards. With Azure Policy, you can evaluate all the different Azure resources for non-compliance. For example, you can create a policy to allow only a certain size of VM in your Azure environment. When the policy is created, Azure will check all the new and existing VMs to see whether they apply to this policy.

Azure Policy is different than RBAC because Azure Policy focuses on resource properties for existing resources and during deployment. RBAC focuses on user actions at different scopes. A user can be added to the owner role in a resource group, for instance, which will give the user full rights to that resource group.

Azure offers built-in policies and custom policies. Some examples of these built-in policies are as follows:

- **Allowed VM SKUs**: This policy specifies a set of VM sizes and types that can be deployed in Azure.
- **Allowed locations**: This policy restricts the available locations where resources can be deployed.
- **Not allowed resource types**: This policy prevents certain resource types from being deployed.
- **Allowed resource types**: This policy defines a list of resource types that you can deploy. Resource types that are not on the list can't be deployed inside the Azure environment.
- **Allowed storage account SKUs**: This policy specifies a set of storage account SKUs that can be deployed.

If the built-in policies don't match with your requirements, you can create a custom policy instead. Custom policies are created in JSON and look like the following example. The first part of the code sets the different properties:

```json
{
    "properties": {
        "displayName": "Deny storage accounts not using only HTTPS",
        "description": "Deny storage accounts not using only HTTPS. Checks
the supportsHttpsTrafficOnly property on StorageAccounts.",
        "mode": "all",
        "parameters": {
            "effectType": {
                "type": "string",
                "defaultValue": "Deny",
                "allowedValues": [
                    "Deny",
                    "Disabled"
                ],
                "metadata": {
                    "displayName": "Effect",
                    "description": "Enable or disable the execution of the
policy"
                }
            }
        },
```

In this part of the code, we are looking at the policy rule:

```json
        "policyRule": {
            "if": {
                "allOf": [
                    {
                        "field": "type",
                        "equals": "Microsoft.Storage/storageAccounts"
                    },
                    {
                        "field":
"Microsoft.Storage/storageAccounts/supportsHttpsTrafficOnly",
                        "notEquals": "true"
                    }
                ]
            },
            "then": {
                "effect": "[parameters('effectType')]"
            }
        }
    }
}
```

Policies are assigned at the management group level, the subscription level, or the resource group level.

Implementing and assigning Azure policies

To implement Azure policies, you have to assign them. In this demonstration, we are going to assign an **Allowed location** policy to an Azure resource group. Therefore, you have to perform the following steps:

1. Navigate to the Azure portal by opening `https://portal.azure.com`.
2. Open the `PacktNetworkWatcher` resource group.
3. Then, under **Settings**, select **Policies**:

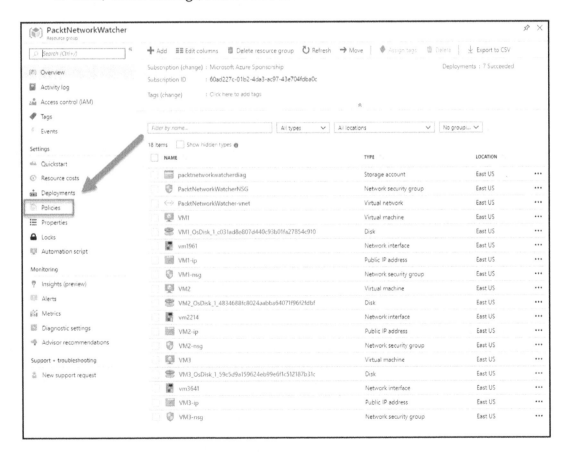

Policies

4. Click on the **Getting started** menu item. You will see a page that is similar to the following:

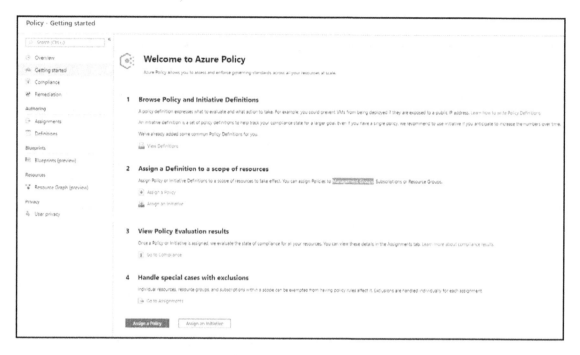

Getting started with Azure policies

5. The first step is to view and select the policy definition. Select the **View Definitions** link on the page.

6. You will go to the available built-in and custom policies inside your subscription. On the right-hand side, type `Locations` in the search bar:

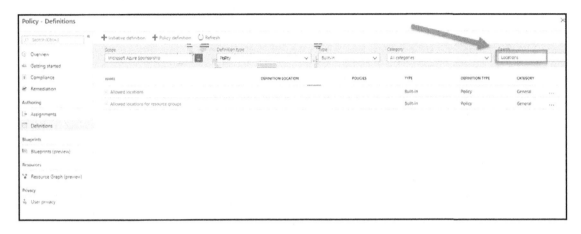

Searching for a locations policy

7. Then, select the **Allowed locations** policy; you will be redirected to the blade where you can see the policy definition in JSON and assign the policy:

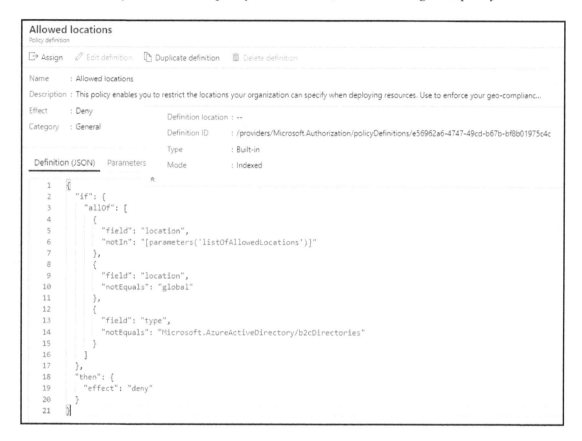

Allowed locations
Policy definition

⟶ Assign   ✎ Edit definition   ⧉ Duplicate definition   🗑 Delete definition

Name : Allowed locations
Description : This policy enables you to restrict the locations your organization can specify when deploying resources. Use to enforce your geo-complianc...

Effect : Deny
Category : General

Definition location : --
Definition ID : /providers/Microsoft.Authorization/policyDefinitions/e56962a6-4747-49cd-b67b-bf8b01975c4c
Type : Built-in

Definition (JSON)   Parameters   Mode : Indexed

```
 1  {
 2    "if": {
 3      "allOf": [
 4        {
 5          "field": "location",
 6          "notIn": "[parameters('listOfAllowedLocations')]"
 7        },
 8        {
 9          "field": "location",
10          "notEquals": "global"
11        },
12        {
13          "field": "type",
14          "notEquals": "Microsoft.AzureActiveDirectory/b2cDirectories"
15        }
16      ]
17    },
18    "then": {
19      "effect": "deny"
20    }
21  }
```

Policy definition

8. Click on **Assign** in the top menu.
9. To assign the policy, you have to fill in the following values:
   - **Scope**: Select a subscription, and, optionally, a resource group. I've selected the `PacktNetworkWatcher` resource group for this demonstration.

- **Allowed locations**: Only select **West Europe**, as demonstrated in the following screenshot:

Assigning the policy definition

10. Click on **Assign**. The policy will be assigned to the resource group.

11. Now, when we add a new resource to the resource group (such as a new VM, for instance) and set the location to **East US**, we will notice a validation error on the top-left of the screen. When you click on it, you will see the following details on the right-hand side of the screen:

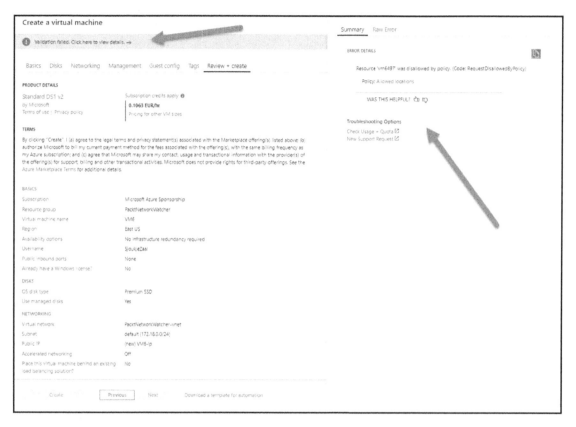

Validation error

In this section, we covered how to assign a policy in Azure.

Summary

In this chapter, we covered the third part of the *Managing Azure Subscriptions and Resources* objective by covering how to configure access to Azure resources by assigning roles, how to configure management access, how to create a custom role, how to assign RBAC roles, and how to implement and assign Azure policies.

In the next chapter, which will introduce a new objective for implementing and managing storage, we are going to cover how to create and configure storage accounts.

Questions

Answer the following questions to test your knowledge of the information in this chapter. You can find the answers in the *Assessments* section at the end of this book:

1. With Azure Policy, can you assign permissions to users, giving them access to your Azure resources?
    * Yes
    * No

2. Suppose that you want to check whether all the VMs inside your Azure subscription use managed disks. Can you use Azure Policy for this?
    * Yes
    * No

3. Are custom policies created in XML?
    * Yes
    * No

Further reading

You can checkout the following links for more information about the topics that were covered in this chapter:

* *What is role-based access control (RBAC) for Azure resources?*: https://docs.microsoft.com/en-us/azure/role-based-access-control/overview
* *Troubleshoot RBAC for Azure resources*: https://docs.microsoft.com/en-us/azure/role-based-access-control/troubleshooting
* *Overview of the Azure Policy service*: https://docs.microsoft.com/en-us/azure/governance/policy/overview
* *Create a custom policy definition*: https://docs.microsoft.com/en-us/azure/governance/policy/tutorials/create-custom-policy-definition

Section 2: Implementing and Managing Storage

2

In this section, you will learn how to implement and manage storage in Azure.

The following chapters will be covered in this section:

- Chapter 4, *Creating and Configuring Storage Accounts*
- Chapter 5, *Importing and Exporting Data to Azure*
- Chapter 6, *Configuring Azure Files and Implementing Azure Backup*

4
Creating and Configuring Storage Accounts

In the previous chapter, we covered how to configure **role-based access control** (**RBAC**) in Azure, how to create custom roles, and how to implement and assign Azure policies.

This chapter will introduce a new objective in terms of implementing and managing storage. In this chapter, we are going to cover the different types of storage account, and you will learn which types are available for storing your data in Azure. We will also cover how to install Azure Storage Explorer, which can be used to manage data inside Azure storage accounts. We are going to look at how to secure data using **shared access signatures** (**SAS**) and how to implement storage replication to keep data safe.

The following topics will be covered in this chapter:

- Azure storage accounts
- Creating and configuring a storage account
- Installing and using Azure Storage Explorer
- Configuring network access to the storage account
- Generating and managing SAS
- Implementing Azure storage replication

Technical requirements

This chapter will uses Azure PowerShell (`https://docs.microsoft.com/en-us/powershell/azure/install-az-ps?view=azps-1.8.0`) for examples.

The source code for our sample application can be downloaded from `https://github.com/PacktPublishing/Microsoft-Azure-Administrator-Exam-Guide-AZ-103/tree/master/Chapter04`.

Azure storage accounts

Azure offers a variety of types of storage accounts that can be used to store all sorts of files in Azure. You can store files, documents, and datasets, but also blobs and **virtual hard disks (VHDs)**. There is even a type of storage account for archiving, specifically. In the next section, we are going to look at the different types of storage accounts, and storage account replication types, that Azure has to offer.

Storage account types

Azure storage offers three different account types, which can be used for blob, table, file, and queue storage.

General-purpose v1

The **general-purpose v1 (GPv1)** storage account is the oldest type of storage account. It offers storage for page blobs, block blobs, files, queues, and tables, but it is not the most cost-effective storage account type. It is the only storage account type that can be used for the classic deployment model. It doesn't support the latest features, such as access tiers.

Blob storage

The blob storage account offers all the features of `StorageV2` accounts, except that it only supports block blobs (and append blobs). Page blobs are not supported. It offers access tiers, which consist of hot, cool, and archive storage, and which will be covered later in this chapter.

General-purpose v2 (GPv2)

`StorageV2` is the newest type of storage account, and it combines the V1 storage with blob storage. It offers all the latest features, such as access tiers for blob storage, with a reduction in costs. Microsoft recommends using this account type over the V1 and blob storage account types.

V1 storage accounts can easily be upgraded to V2.

For more information on pricing and billing for these different account types, you can refer to the following pricing page: `https://azure.microsoft.com/en-us/pricing/details/storage/`.

Storage replication types

Data that is stored in Azure is always replicated to ensure durability and high availability. This way, it is protected from unplanned and planned events, such as network or power outages, natural disasters, and terrorism. It also ensures that, during these types of events, your storage account still meets the SLA. Data can be replicated within the same data center, across zonal data centers within the same region, and across different regions. These replication types are named **locally redundant storage (LRS)**, **zone redundant storage (ZRS)**, **geo-redundant storage (GRS)**, and **read-access geo-redundant storage (RA-GRS)**, and they will be covered in more detail in the upcoming sections.

You choose a replication type when you create a new storage account. Storage accounts can be created inside the Azure portal, as well as from PowerShell or the CLI.

LRS

LRS is the cheapest option, and replicates the data three times within the same data center. When you make a write request to your storage account, it will be synchronously written during this request to all three replicas. The request is committed when the data is completely replicated. With LRS, the data will be replicated across multiple update domains and fault domains within one storage scale unit.

ZRS

ZRS is currently in preview, and is only available in US East 2 and US Central. It replicates three copies across two or three data centers. The data is written synchronously to all three replicas, in one or two regions. It also replicates the data three times inside the same data center where the data resided, just like LRS.

GRS

GRS replicates the data three times within the same region, like ZRS, and also replicates three copies to other regions asynchronously.

RA-GRS

RA-GRS provides georeplication across two regions, with read-only access to the data in the secondary location. This will maximize the availability for your storage account. When you enable RA-GRS, your data will be available on a primary and a secondary endpoint for your storage account as well. The secondary endpoint will be similar to the primary endpoint, but it appends the **secondary** suffix to it. The access keys that are generated for your storage account can be used for both endpoints.

Now that we have covered the different storage replication types that are set when you create a storage account, we can look at the different storage accounts that Azure has to offer.

Azure blob storage

Azure blob storage offers unstructured data storage in the cloud. It can store all kinds of data, such as documents, VHDs, images, and audio files. There are two types of blobs that you can create. One type is page blobs, which are used for the storage of disks. So, when you have a VHD that needs to be stored and attached to your VM, you will have to create a page blob. The maximum size of a page blob is 1 TB.

The other type is block blobs, which basically cover all the other types of data that you can store in Azure, such as files and documents. The maximum size of a block blob is 200 GB. However, there is also a third blob type named append blob, but this one is used internally by Azure and can't be used in order to store actual files. There are a couple of ways that you can copy blobs to your blob storage account. You can use the Azure portal (only one at a time) or Azure Storage Explorer, or you can copy your files programmatically by using .NET, PowerShell, the CLI, or by calling the REST API.

Access tiers

Blob storage accounts use access tiers to determine how frequently the data is accessed. Based on this access tier, you will get billed. Azure offers three storage access tiers: hot, cool, and archive.

Hot

The hot access tier is most suitable for storing data that's accessed frequently and data that is in active use. For instance, you would store images and style sheets for a website inside the hot access tier. The storage costs for this tier are higher than for the other access tiers, but you pay less for accessing the files.

Cool

The cool access tier is the most suitable for storing data that is not accessed frequently (less than once in 30 days). Compared with the hot access tier, the cool tier has lower storage costs, but you pay more for accessing the files. This tier is suitable for storing backups and older content that is not viewed often.

Archive

The archive storage tier is set on the blob level and not on the storage level. It has the lowest costs for storing data and the highest cost for accessing data compared to the hot and cool access tiers. This tier is for data that will remain in the archive for at least 180 days, and it will take a couple of hours of latency before it can be accessed. This tier is most suitable for long-term backups or compliance and archive data. A blob in the archive tier is offline and cannot be read (except for the metadata), copied, overwritten, or modified.

Azure file storage

With Azure files, you can create file shares in the cloud. You can access your files using the **Server Message Block** (**SMB**) protocol, which is an industry standard and can be used on Linux, Windows, and macOS devices. Azure files can also be mounted as if it is a local drive on these same devices as well, and they can be cached for fast access on Windows Server using Azure File Sync.

File shares can be used across multiple machines, which makes them suitable for storing files or data that are accessed from multiple machines, such as tools for development machines, or configuration files or log data. Azure File Share is part of the Azure storage client libraries and offers an Azure storage REST API, which can be leveraged by developers in their solutions.

 Details on how to configure Azure file storage will be covered in more detail in `Chapter 6`, *Configuring Azure Files and Implementing Azure Backup*.

Azure disk storage

The disks that are used for virtual machines are stored in Azure blob storage as page blobs. Azure stores two disks for each virtual machine: the actual operating system (VHD) of the VM, and a temporary disk that is used for short-term storage. This data is erased when the VM is turned off or rebooted.

There are two different performance tiers that Azure offers: standard disk storage and premium disk storage.

Standard disk storage

Standard disk storage offers HDD drives to store the data on, and it is the most cost-effective storage tier that you can choose. It can only use LRS or GRS in order to support high availability for your data and applications.

Premium disk storage

With premium disk storage, your data is stored on SSDs. Not all Azure virtual machines series can use this type of storage. It can only be used with DS, DSv2, GS, LS, or FS series Azure virtual machines. It offers high-performance and low-latency disk support.

Unmanaged versus managed disks

Managed disks automatically handle the storage account creation for you. With unmanaged disks, which are the traditional disks used for VMs, you need to create a storage account manually, and then select that storage account when you create the VM. With managed disks, this burden is handled for you by Azure. You select the disk type and the performance tier (standard or premium), and the managed disk is created. It also handles scaling automatically for you.

Managed disks are recommended by Microsoft over unmanaged disks.

Now that we have covered all the background information that you need to know about the different storage accounts, we are going to create a new storage account.

Creating and configuring storage accounts

Before you can upload any data or files to Azure storage, a storage account needs to be created. This can be done using the Azure portal, PowerShell, the CLI, ARM templates, or Visual Studio.

In this demonstration, we are going to create a storage account with PowerShell:

1. First, we need to log in to the Azure account:

   ```
   Connect-AzAccount
   ```

2. If necessary, select the right subscription:

   ```
   Select-AzSubscription -SubscriptionId "********-****-****-****-
   ***********"
   ```

3. Create a resource group:

   ```
   New-AzResourceGroup -Name PacktPubStorageAccount -Location EastUS
   ```

4. Create the storage account:

   ```
   New-AzStorageAccount -ResourceGroupName PacktPubStorageAccount -
   AccountName packtpubstorage -Location "East US" -SkuName
   Standard_GRS -Kind StorageV2 -AccessTier Hot
   ```

In this demonstration, we created a new storage account using PowerShell. If you are new to storage accounts, I highly recommend creating a storage account from the Azure portal as well. That way, you will see all the available storage account types, storage replication types, access tiers that you can choose from, the different performance tiers (standard or premium), and how this is all connected to each other.

Now that we have created a new storage account, we can install the Azure Storage Explorer tool.

Installing and using Azure Storage Explorer

Azure Storage Explorer is a standalone application that can be used to easily work with the different types of data that are stored in an Azure storage account. You can upload, download, and manage files, queues, tables, blobs, data lake storage, and Cosmos DB entities using Azure Storage Explorer. Aside from that, you can also use the application to configure and manage **cross-origin resource sharing (CORS)** rules for your storage accounts. This application can be used on Windows, Linux, and macOS devices.

To install the application, you have to perform the following steps:

1. Navigate to `https://azure.microsoft.com/en-us/features/storage-explorer/` to download the application.
2. Once it has been downloaded, install the application.
3. When the application is installed, open the application. You will be prompted to connect to your Azure environment. There are a couple of options to choose from. You can add an Azure account by connecting to your Azure environment using your administrator credentials, use a shared access signature (which will be covered later in this chapter), use a storage account name and key, and you can select the **Attach to a local emulator** option if you so desire. For this demonstration, keep the default option selected and click on **Sign in**:

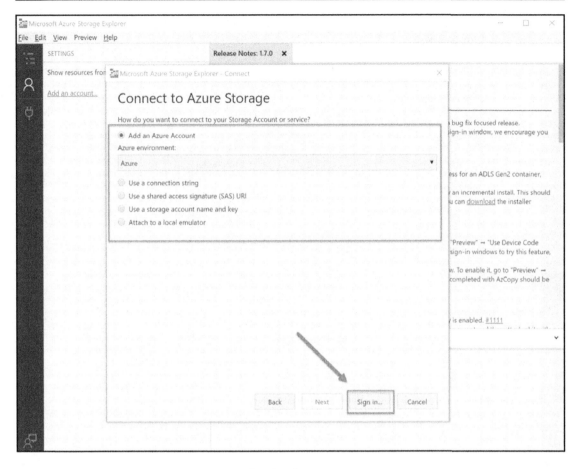

Connecting to Azure storage

4. Provide your credentials and log in.

5. All of your subscriptions will be added to the left-hand pane. Once this is done, click on **Apply**:

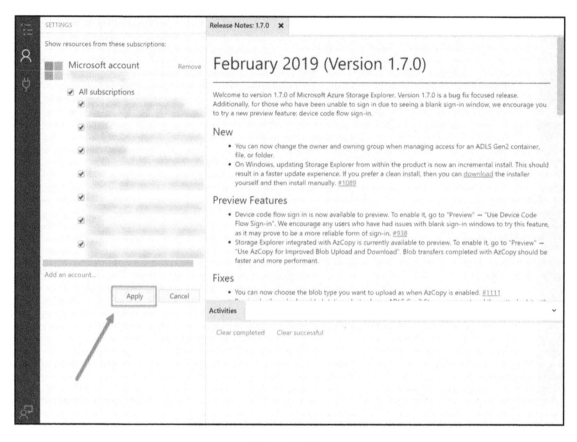

Applying the subscriptions

6. You can now drill down to the subscription and the storage account that we created in the first demonstration from the left-hand pane. Select the storage account. From there, you can access the blob containers, file shares, queues, and tables:

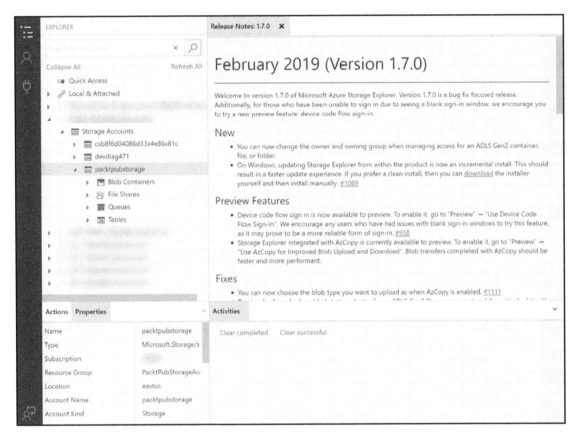

Storage account settings

7. To add some files to a blob container, we need to create a blob container in the storage account. Therefore, right-click on **Blob Containers** in the left-hand menu and select **Create Blob Container.** Call the container `packtblobcontainer`; now, you can upload files to that container. Click on the **Upload** button in the top menu, click on **Upload files**, and select some files from your local computer:

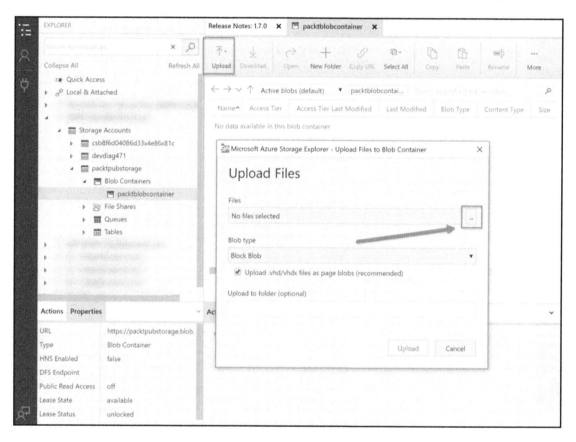

Uploading files to the blob container

You will see that the files will be uploaded to the blob container.

 If you navigate to the overview blade of the storage account in the Azure portal, you will see a button on the top menu that says **Open in explorer**. This will open the Azure Storage Explorer, which can then be used to easily manage all the data that resides in the storage account.

Now that we have installed the Azure Storage Explorer tool and uploaded some files to a blob container, we can configure the network access to the storage account.

Configuring network access to the storage account

You can secure your storage account to a specific set of supported networks. For this, you have to configure network rules so that only applications that request data over the specific set of networks can access the storage account. When these network rules are effective, the application needs to use proper authorization on the request. This authorization can be provided by Azure Active Directory credentials for blobs and queues, with an SAS token or a valid account access key.

In the following demonstration, we are going to configure network access to the storage account that we created in the previous step. You can manage storage accounts through the Azure portal, PowerShell, or CLIv2. We are going to set this configuration from the Azure portal. Therefore, we have to perform the following steps:

1. Navigate to the Azure portal by opening `https://portal.azure.com`.
2. Go to the storage account that we created in the previous step.

3. From the overview blade, in the left-hand menu, select **Firewalls and virtual networks**:

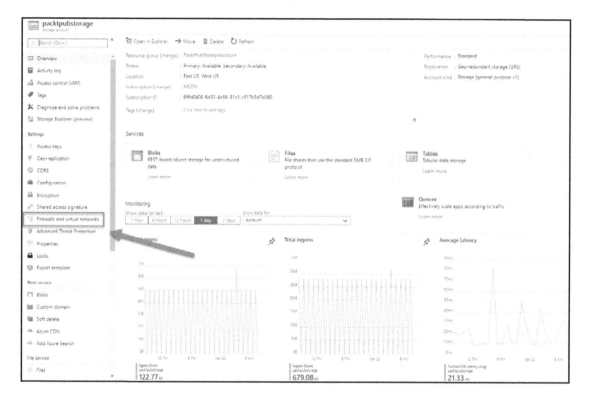

Storage account overview blade

4. To grant access to a virtual network with a new network rule, under **Virtual Networks**, there are two options to choose from: **All networks**, which allows traffic from all networks (both virtual and on-premises) and the internet to access the data, and **Selected networks**. If you select this option, you can configure which networks are allowed to access the data from the storage account. Select **Selected networks**. Then, you can select whether you want to add an existing virtual network or create a new one. For this demonstration, click on + **Add new virtual network**:

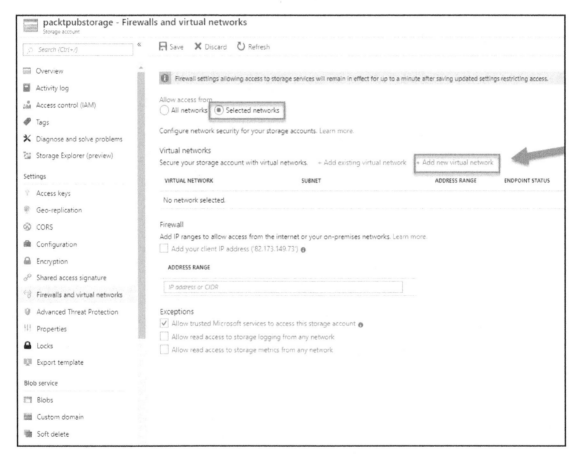

Creating a new network

5. A new blade will open, where you will have to specify the network configuration. Specify the configuration that's shown in the following screenshot:

Network configuration settings

6. Click on **Create.**
7. The virtual network will be added to the overview blade. This storage account is now secure and can be accessed only from applications and other resources that use this virtual network. In this same blade, you can also configure the firewall and only allow certain IP ranges from the internet or your on-premises environment:

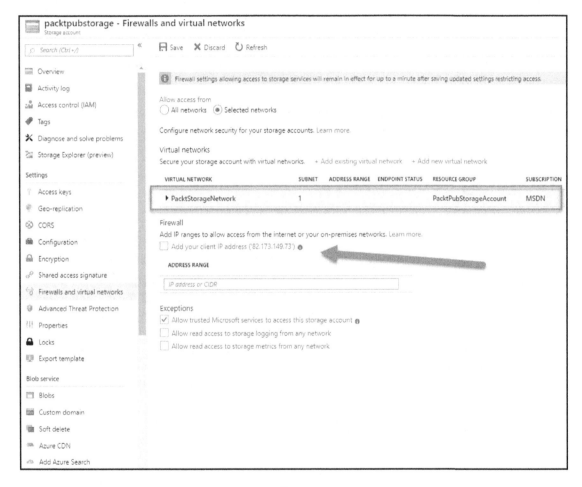

IP ranges

This concludes this demonstration. In the next demonstration, we are going to generate and manage SAS.

SAS and access keys

By using an SAS, you can provide a way to grant limited access to objects and data that are stored inside your storage account to the clients that connect to it. Using an SAS, you don't have to expose your access keys to the clients.

When you create a storage account, primary and secondary access keys are created. Both of these keys can grant administrative access to your account and all the resources within it. Exposing those keys can also open your storage account to negligent or malicious use. SAS provides a safe alternative to this that will allow clients to read, write, and delete data in your storage account according to the permissions you've explicitly granted, and without the need for an account key.

In the next section, we're going to look at how to manage our access keys and how to generate an SAS for our storage account.

Managing access keys

To manage access keys, perform the following steps:

1. Navigate to the Azure portal by opening `https://portal.azure.com`.
2. Again, go to the storage account that we created in the previous step.
3. Once the overview blade is open, under **Settings**, select **Access keys**.
4. Here, you can see both of the access keys that were generated for you when the storage account was created. The reason that Azure created two access keys for you is because if you regenerate a new key, all of the SAS that you created for this key will no longer work. You can then let applications access that data using the secondary key, and once the key is regenerated, you can share the new key with your clients. You can generate new keys by clicking on the buttons next to both keys:

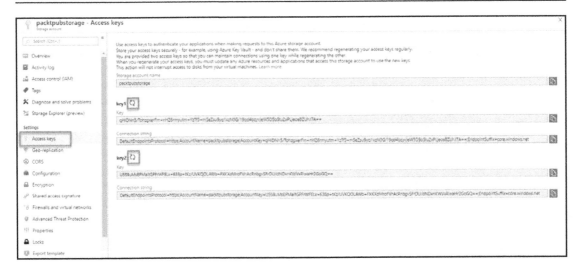

Access keys

5. There is also a connection string provided for each key which can be used by client applications to access the storage account.

In the next section, we're going to generate an SAS for the access keys.

Generating an SAS

In this demonstration, we are going to generate an SAS for our blob store. To generate an SAS, perform the following steps:

1. Navigate to the Azure portal by opening `https://portal.azure.com`.
2. Again, go to the storage account that we created in the previous step.

3. Once the overview blade is open, under **Settings**, select **Shared access signature**:

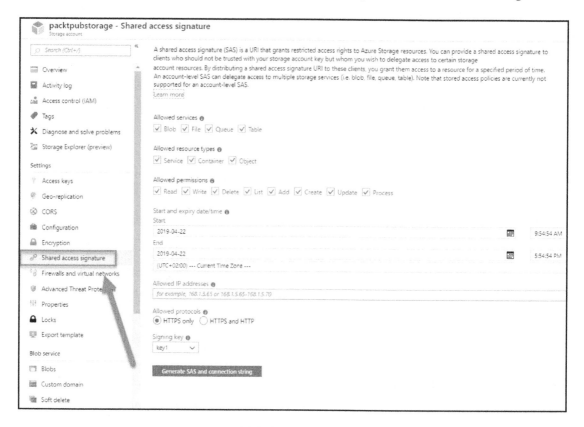

Selecting Shared access signature

4. To only allow the blob storage to be accessed, disable the file, queue, and table. Keep the default permissions, and then select an expiration date and time. You can also set the allowed protocols in here. At the bottom of the screen, you can apply these permissions to the different keys. Keep **key1** selected and click on **Generate SAS and connection string**:

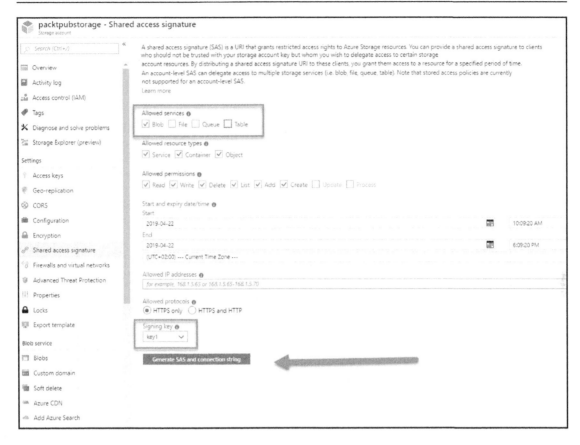

Generating SAS and connection string

5. You can now use this token to request the data from the blob storage.

This concludes this demonstration. In the next section, we are going to look at how to implement Azure storage replication.

Implementing Azure storage replication

The data in Azure is always replicated to ensure durability and high availability. Azure storage copies your data so that it is protected from planned and unplanned events, including transient hardware failures, network or power outages, and massive natural disasters. We have already covered the different replication types that Azure offers for your storage accounts.

Storage replication can be set during the creation of the storage account. You can change the type of replication later as well by using Azure portal, PowerShell, or the CLI. To change this in the Azure portal, you have to perform the following steps:

1. Navigate to Azure portal by opening `https://portal.azure.com`.
2. Go to the storage account that we created in the previous step.
3. Under **Settings**, select **Configuration**. In this blade, under **Replication**, you can change the type of replication:

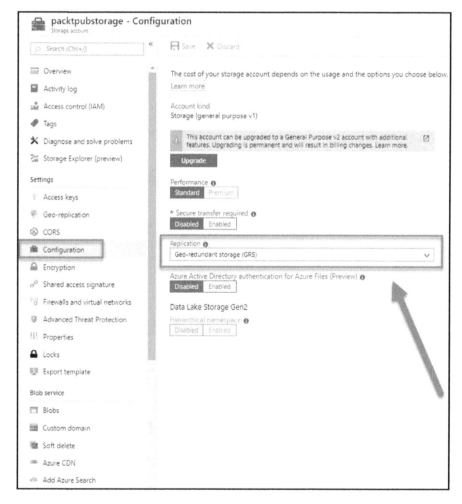

Changing the type of replication

Summary

In this chapter, we covered the first part of the *Implementing and Managing Storage* objective. We covered the different types of storage that are available to us in Azure, and when we should use them. We also covered how we can manage our data using Azure Storage Explorer, and how we can secure our data using SAS. Finally, we covered how to replicate data from storage accounts.

In the next chapter, we'll cover the second part of this exam objective. In that chapter, we will cover how to import and export data to Azure.

Questions

Answer the following questions to test your knowledge of the information in this chapter. You can find the answers in the *Assessments* section at the end of this book:

1. Can the Azure Storage Explorer application only be used on Windows devices?
   - Yes
   - No

2. Can you configure storage accounts to be accessed from specific virtual networks, and not from on-premises networks?
   - Yes
   - No

3. Can you only set the type of replication for your storage accounts during the creation of the storage account?
   - Yes
   - No

Further reading

You can check out the following links for more information about the topics that were covered in this chapter:

- *Azure Storage Documentation*: `https://docs.microsoft.com/en-us/azure/storage/`
- *Get started with Storage Explorer*: `https://docs.microsoft.com/en-us/azure/vs-azure-tools-storage-manage-with-storage-explorer?tabs=windows`
- *Configure Azure Storage firewalls and virtual networks*: `https://docs.microsoft.com/en-us/azure/storage/common/storage-network-security`
- *Azure Storage redundancy*: `https://docs.microsoft.com/en-us/azure/storage/common/storage-redundancy`

Importing and Exporting Data to Azure

5

In the previous chapter, we covered the different types of storage that are available to you in Azure and when you should use them. We also covered how to install and use Azure Storage Explorer for to manage your data.

This chapter proceeds with the second part of *Implementing and Managing Storage* objective. In the first part of this chapter, we are going to create storage accounts, by configuring Azure Blob Storage. The second part of this chapter is going to cover how you can import and export data to and from Azure. You will learn how to import and export data using Azure Job. The third part of this chapter is focused on **content delivery networks (CDNs)** in Azure. You will learn how to create and configure a CDN, which can be used for caching your static content on the edge servers in Azure. In the last part of this chapter, we will briefly look at Azure Data Box.

The following topics will be covered in this chapter:

- Configuring and using Azure Blob Storage
- Creating import into, and export from Azure Job
- Azure CDN
- Configuring Azure CDN endpoints
- Azure Data Box

Technical requirements

This chapter uses Azure PowerShell (`https://docs.microsoft.com/en-us/powershell/azure/install-az-ps?view=azps-1.8.0`) for our examples.

The source code for our sample application can be downloaded from `https://github.com/PacktPublishing/Microsoft-Azure-Administrator-Exam-Guide-AZ-103/tree/master/Chapter05`.

Configuring and using Azure Blob Storage

In the previous chapter, we created an Azure storage account using PowerShell and from the Azure Storage Explorer, we created a blob container for that storage account and uploaded some files to it as well.

In this section, we are going to configure Azure Blob Storage from PowerShell. We are going to use the same storage account that we created in the previous chapter, but now we will use PowerShell to add a blob container to it. We will also provide an example to create multiple blob containers at once. Therefore, take the following steps:

1. First, we need to log in to the Azure account as follows:

   ```
   Connect-AzAccount
   ```

2. If necessary, select the right subscription as follows:

   ```
   Select-AzSubscription -SubscriptionId "********-****-****-****-
   ***********"
   ```

3. Select the storage account that we created in the previous chapter and add it to a variable as follows:

   ```
   $accountObject = Get-AzStorageAccount -ResourceGroupName
   "PacktPubStorageAccount" -AccountName "packtpubstorage"
   ```

4. Then retrieve the context of the storage account:

```
$Context = $accountObject.Context
```

5. Create a blob container to it with public access as `Blob` as follows:

```
new-AzStoragecontainer -Name "packtblobcontainerps" -Context
$Context -Permission blob
```

We are going to use this blob container in the next section, where we will create an import into and an export using Azure Job.

Creating import into, and export from Azure Job

You can create an import and export job for your Azure Blob Storage (and Azure file storage) account to upload data from on-premises data disks to Azure. This service can be used to import large amounts of data into your Azure Blob Storage. It does require you to ship encrypted disk drives with the data on it to an Azure Datacenter.

The disk drives that are going to be shipped to the Azure Datacenter need to be prepared before shipment. BitLocker encryption needs to be enabled and, once the volume is encrypted, you can copy the data to it. After encryption, the disk needs to be prepared using the `WAImportExport.exe` tool. By running this tool, there is automatically a *journal file* created in the same folder that you ran the tool. There are two other files created as well, an `.xml` file and a `drive-manifest.xml` file. You need these files later for creating the import/export job. The disk is now ready to be shipped to Azure.

After the disks are shipped to Azure, you can create an import or export job from the Azure portal. Therefore, you have to take the following steps:

1. Navigate to the Azure portal by opening `https://portal.azure.com/`.
2. From the left menu, click **All services** | **Storage** | **Import/export jobs**.

3. As shown in the following screenshot, click **Create import/export job**:

Creating an import/export job

4. In the next blade, you can choose between creating an import or an export job. Select **Import into Azure**, give the job a name, and select a resource group or create a new resource group as follows:

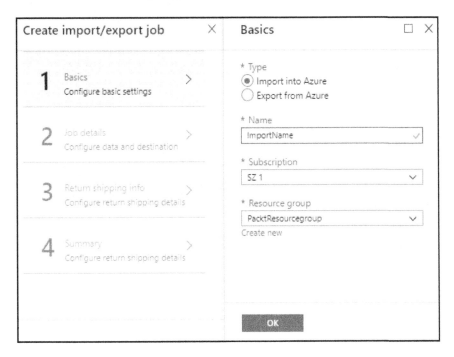

Defining the job type

5. Click **OK**.

6. In the next blade, you need to upload the journal files that are created when you prepared the disks. Select the journal files from your local computer and select the import destination as follows:

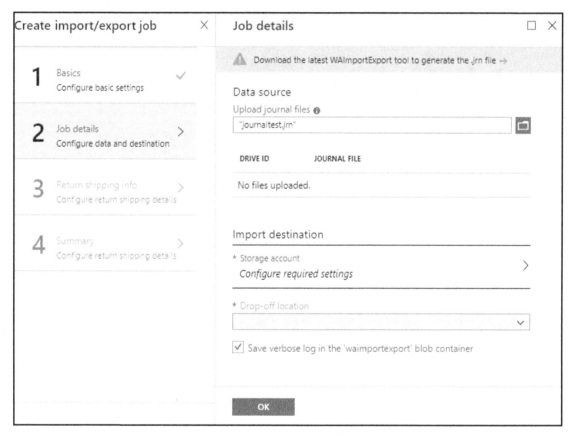

Upload journal files

7. Click **OK**.

8. In the last two steps, you can provide the return shipping information for your disks and configure them. The data can now be uploaded to the storage account that you have selected in the previous step.

9. The steps for creating an export job are similar to those for creating the import job. Just select export job in the first step and fill in the required fields. You don't have to upload the journal files, just select the storage account from where you want to export the data as follows:

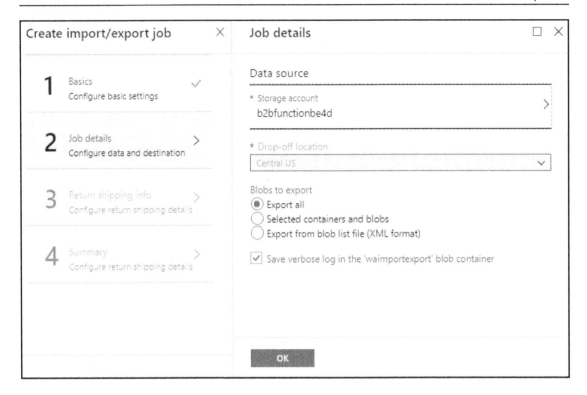

Export job settings

10. Then provide the shipping details again, and Microsoft will copy the data to the drive and ship it back to you.

This concludes the import and export Azure Job objective. In the next section, we are going to look at Azure CDN and how to configure it.

Azure CDN

A CDN is a service that can be used to scale your apps globally. It caches your static content, such as HTML pages, style sheets, images, documents, files, and client-side scripts on edge servers in different regions. This way, it will take less time to download them because the content is physically closer to the user, which increases the performance of your apps.

Azure CDN offers the following pricing tiers: Azure CDN Standard from Microsoft, Azure CDN Standard from Akamai, Azure CDN Standard from Verizon, and Azure CDN Premium from Verizon.

Azure CDN offers the following key features:

- **Dynamic site acceleration**: Normally, CDNs have the ability to cache files closer to the end users to speed up the performance of loading the files. However, with dynamic web applications, the content is generated in response to the user behavior. Speeding up the loading process is more complex in these situations and requires a different solution, where each content element is fine-tuned along the full data path from inception to delivery. This feature is part of *Azure CDN from Akamai* and *Azure CDN from Verizon*.
- **CDN caching rules**: By using caching rules, the default cache expiration can be set or modified globally, and by using custom conditions, such as URL path and file extension. Azure CDN provides the following two different ways of controlling how files are cached:
    - **Caching rules**: The following global and custom caching rules are available:
        - **Global caching rules**: For each endpoint in your CDN profile, you can set one global caching rule. This will affect all requests that are made to that endpoint. If set, this global rule will override any HTTP cache-directive headers.
        - **Custom caching rules**: You can set one or more custom caching rules for each endpoint in your CDN profile. These rules match specific file extensions and paths, are processed in order, and override the global caching rule, if set.
    - **Query string caching**: How Azure CDN treats caching for requests with query strings can be adjusted as well. The query string caching setting has no effect if the file itself is not cacheable based on caching rules and CDN default behaviors.
- **HTTPS custom domain support**: If you are using the HTTPS protocol on your custom domain (for instance, `https:az-103.com`) for your apps (by installing an SSL certificate), a secure connection is made over TLS/SSL. Azure CDN supports HTTPS on a CDN endpoint host name by default. So, if you create a CDN endpoint (for instance, `https://https:az-103.azureedge.net`), HTTPS is enabled automatically. This feature is not available with Azure CDN Standard from Akamai products.

- **Azure diagnostics logs**: You can view core analytics and save them to a variety of different sources. Azure diagnostics logs give you the ability to export the basic usage metrics from the CDN endpoints to an Azure storage account and then to a CSV, where you can create graphs in Excel to Azure Event Hubs and correlate data from other Azure services to Log Analytics workspace, and view data in there as well. This feature is available for all the pricing tiers.
- **File compression**: File compression is an effective way to speed up the transferring of files and increasing the performance of the page load of your app. The file size is reduced before it is sent from the server. This can provide a more responsive experience for your app and can reduce the bandwidth costs. There are the following two options of file compression available:
    - **Enable compression on the origin server**: Azure CDN passes on the files that are already compressed at the server and delivers them to the client.
    - **Enable compression on the CDN POP servers (compression on the fly)**: The CDN compresses the files itself and delivers them to the client.
- **Geo-filtering**: With Azure CDN, you can restrict access to content by country. You can create rules on specific paths on your CDN endpoint to block or allow content in selected countries. This feature is not supported by Azure CDN Standard from Microsoft.

> For comparing the features and capabilities of the different CDN products that are available for Azure, you can refer to the following article: `https:/ /docs.microsoft.com/en-us/azure/cdn/cdn-features`.

In the next section, we are going to configure Azure CDN endpoints.

Configuring Azure CDN endpoints

In this demonstration, we are going to set up an Azure CDN by creating a new CDN profile and CDN endpoint from the Azure portal. Therefore, we have to perform the following steps:

1. Navigate to the Azure portal by opening `https://portal.azure.com/`.
2. From the left menu, click **Create a resource**. In the search box, type `CDN` and click the **Create** button.

3. Add the following values, as shown in the next screenshot:

- **Name:** PacktCDN.

- **Subscription**: Select the same subscription as we used for creating the blob storage account. We are going to use this to store the images that can be accessed by the CDN.

- **Resource group**: Create a new one and call it PacktCDNResourcegroup.

- **Resource group location: East US**.

- **Pricing tier**: Select **Standard Verizon** from the drop-down list.

- **Create a new CDN endpoint now**: Leave unselected; we will do this later:

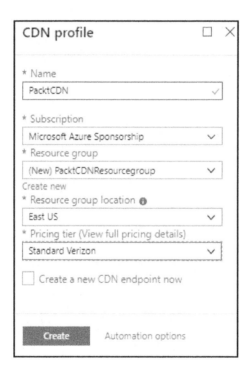

Creating a new CDN profile

4. Click **Create**.

5. The CDN profile will now be created. After creation, we can configure a new CDN endpoint for it.

6. Open the CDN overview blade and select **Endpoint** from the top menu as follows:

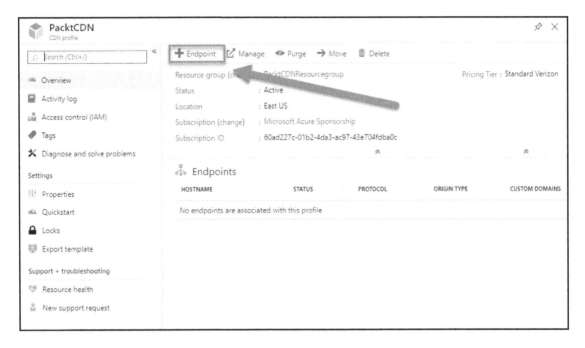

Creating a new CDN endpoint

7. For the endpoint, specify the following values, as shown in the next screenshot:
   - **Name:** `PacktCDNEndpoint`.
   - **Origin type: Storage**.
   - **Origin hostname:** This name must be unique. Pick the storage account that is used in the previous section; in my case, this is `packtpubstorage.blob.core.windows.net`.
   - **Origin path:** Leave blank.
   - **Origin host header:** Leave the default generated value.
   - **Protocol:** Leave the default HTTP and HTTPS options selected.
   - **Origin port:** Leave the default here.

- **Optimized for**: Leave the default here, which is **General web delivery**:

Adding an endpoint

8. Click **Add** to add the endpoint to the profile.
9. We have now created a CDN profile and an endpoint that can be used to access the images or other files that are stored inside the blob container in the storage account. You can request the images and other files using the endpoint that is generated for you as follows:

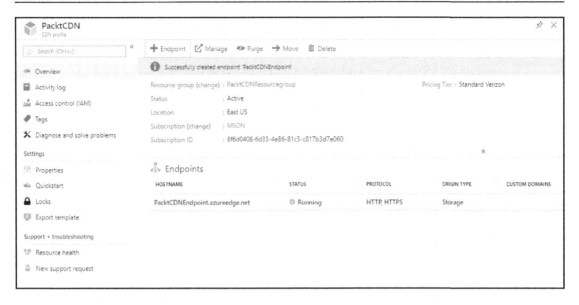

Generated endpoint

10. An example of requesting an image from the endpoint that we generated will look like the following:

```
https://PacktCDNEndpoint.azureedge.net/images/image.png
```

11. This can be tested inside a browser window.

In the next section, we are going to cover Azure Data Box.

Azure Data Box

Data that is moved to Azure over the network isn't always as fast as required for organizations. With the Azure Data Box solution, you can send terabytes of data into Azure quickly. You can order this Data Box solution from the Azure portal. You will then receive a Data Box storage device with a storage capacity, which can be used to transfer the data securely.

Azure offers the following three different types of storage device:

- **Data Box**: This device, with 100 TB of capacity, uses standard **network attached storage (NAS)** protocols and common copy tools. It features AES 256-bit encryption for safer transit.
- **Data Box Disk**: This device had a capacity of 8 TB with SSD storage (with packs of up to 5 for a total of 40 TB). It has a USB/SATA interface and has 128-bit encryption.
- **Data Box Heavy (Preview)**: This is a self-contained device that is designed to lift 1 PB of data to the cloud.

You can copy this data from your servers to one of the devices and ship this back to Azure. Microsoft will then upload this data in the Azure Datacenter from the device. This entire process is tracked by the Data Box service in the Azure portal to deliver insights in all the steps of this data migration process.

This Data Box solution is well suited for scenarios where there is no or limited network connectivity and where data sizes larger than 40 TB need to be migrated. It is also an ideal solution for one-time migrations, and for initial bulk transfers, followed by incremental transfers over the network.

For the incremental transfers over the network, Azure offers the following two different services:

- **Azure Data Box Gateway:** Data Box Gateway is a virtual device based on a virtual machine provisioned in your virtualized environment or hypervisor. The virtual device resides in your on-premises environment and you write data to it using the **Network File System (NFS)** and **Server Message Block (SMB)** protocols. The device then transfers your data to Azure block blobs, page blobs, or Azure Files.
- **Azure Data Box Edge:** Azure Data box Edge is a physical device supplied by Microsoft for secure data transfer. This device resides in your on-premises environment, and you can write data to it using the NFS and SMB protocols. Data Box Edge has all the gateway capabilities of Data Box Gateway. Data Box is additionally equipped with AI-enabled edge computing capabilities that help analyze, process, or filter data as it moves to Azure block blobs, page blobs, or Azure Files.

The following diagram gives you an overview of the steps that are taken to store the data onto the device and ship it back to Azure:

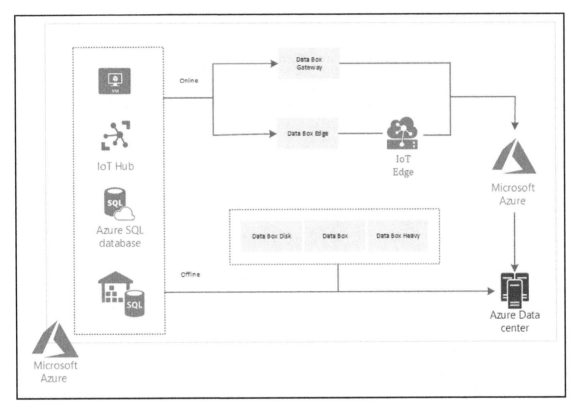

Azure Data Box

We have now looked at Azure Data Box and the different methods that you can use to ship your data to Azure. This concludes this chapter.

Summary

In this chapter, we covered the second part of the *Implementing and Managing Storage* objective. We covered the different ways of migrating large amounts of data to Azure, using disks and Azure Data Box. We also covered how to set up Azure Blob Storage, and we covered how to configure an Azure CDN.

In the next chapter, we will cover the third and last part of this exam objective. In this chapter, we will cover how to configure Azure Files and implement Azure Backup.

Questions

Answer the following questions to test your knowledge of the information in this chapter. You can find the answers in the *Assessments* section at the end of this book:

1. If you want to import data using an Azure import job, you first need to enable BitLocker on the disk.
    - Yes
    - No

2. Azure CDN doesn't support HTTPS on a CDN endpoint host name by default.
    - Yes
    - No

3. Azure Data Box is a physical device that can be used to upload large amounts of data. This box is then shipped to Azure, where Microsoft will upload the data inside an Azure Datacenter.
    - Yes
    - No

Further reading

You can check out the following links for more information about the topics that were covered in this chapter:

- *What is a content delivery network on Azure?*: https://docs.microsoft.com/en-us/azure/cdn/cdn-overview

- *Dynamic site acceleration via Azure CDN*: https://docs.microsoft.com/en-us/azure/cdn/cdn-dynamic-site-acceleration

- *Tutorial: Configure HTTPS on an Azure CDN custom domain*: https://docs.microsoft.com/en-us/azure/cdn/cdn-custom-ssl?tabs=option-1-default-enable-https-with-a-cdn-managed-certificate

- *Improve performance by compressing files in Azure CDN*: https://docs.microsoft.com/en-us/azure/cdn/cdn-improve-performance

- *Restrict Azure CDN content by country/region*: https://docs.microsoft.com/en-us/azure/cdn/cdn-restrict-access-by-country

- *Compare Azure CDN product features*: https://docs.microsoft.com/en-us/azure/cdn/cdn-features

- *Content delivery networks (CDNs)*: https://docs.microsoft.com/en-us/azure/architecture/best-practices/cdn

- *What is Azure Data Box?*: https://docs.microsoft.com/en-us/azure/databox/data-box-overview

- *What is Azure Data Box Gateway?*: https://docs.microsoft.com/en-us/azure/databox-online/data-box-gateway-overview

- *What is Azure Data Box Edge?*: https://docs.microsoft.com/en-us/azure/databox-online/data-box-edge-overview

- *Use the Azure Import/Export service to import data to Azure Blob Storage*: https://docs.microsoft.com/en-us/azure/storage/common/storage-import-export-data-to-blobs?toc=%2fazure%2fstorage%2fblobs%2ftoc.json

6
Configuring Azure Files and Implementing Azure Backup

In the previous chapter, we covered the different ways of migrating large amounts of data to Azure using disks and Azure Data Box. We also covered how to configure an Azure **Content Delivery Network (CDN)** to cache static and dynamic content and deliver it more quickly to your users.

This chapter proceeds with the last part of the *Implementing and Managing Storage* objective. In this chapter, we are going to cover how you can create Azure file share and how to troubleshoot them. We are also going to look at the backup and restore capabilities in Azure. You will learn about Azure Backup and Azure Site Recovery, and we are going to perform a backup and restore operation for our Azure file share.

The following topics will be covered in this chapter:

- Creating an Azure file share and Azure file share sync service
- Azure Backup
- Azure Site Recovery
- Performing a backup and restore operation
- Creating a Recovery Services vault
- Creating and configuring a backup policy

Technical requirements

This chapter uses Azure PowerShell (https://docs.microsoft.com/en-us/powershell/azure/install-az-ps?view=azps-1.8.0) for our examples.

The source code for this chapter can be downloaded from `https://github.com/PacktPublishing/Microsoft-Azure-Administrator-Exam-Guide-AZ-103/tree/master/Chapter06`.

Azure file share and Azure file share sync service

Azure Files was briefly covered in `Chapter 4`, *Creating and Configuring Storage Accounts*. In this chapter, we are going to create and configure an Azure file share.

With Azure Files, you can create file shares in the cloud. You can access your files using the **Server Message Block** (**SMB**) protocol, which is an industry standard that can be used on Linux, Windows, and macOS devices. Azure Files can also be mounted as if it is a local drive on these same devices, and they can be cached for fast access on Windows Server using Azure File Sync.

In the following section, we are going to create an Azure file share from the Azure portal.

Creating an Azure file share

To create an Azure file share, we first need to create a new storage account from the Azure portal. We created a storage account in `Chapter 4`, *Creating and Configuring Storage Accounts.* In this demonstration, we are going to create one from the Azure portal as follows:

1. Navigate to the Azure portal by opening `https://portal.azure.com`.
2. In the left menu, click **+ Create a resource** | **Storage** | **Storage Account**.
3. Add the following values:
   - **Subscription**: Select the subscription where you want to create the storage account.
   - **Resource group**: Create a new one, and call it `PacktFileShareResourceGroup`.
   - **Storage account name**: `packtfileshare`.
   - **Location**: **East US**.
   - **Performance**: **Standard**.
   - **Account type**: **StorageV2**.

- **Replication**: Select **Read-access geo-redundant Storage (RA-GRS)**.
  This will make six copies of the data distributed over different Azure
  regions.
- **Access tier**: **Hot**, because this data is going to be accessed frequently.

These values are shown in the following screenshot:

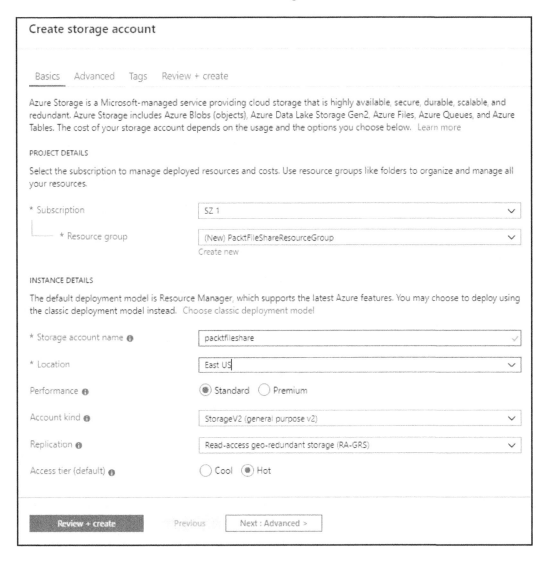

Creating a new storage account

4. Click **Review + create**. After the review, click the **Create** button.

5. After creation, open the resource and you will be redirected to the overview blade of the storage account. In there, we can create our file share. In the left menu, under **File service**, select **Files**. And in the **Files** blade, click **+ File share** in the top menu as shown in the following screenshot:

Creating a new file share

6. Add the following values as shown in the following screenshot:
   - **Name:** `packtfileshare`
   - **Quota:** `10`

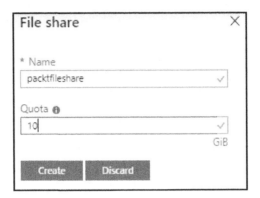

Setting the file share properties

7. Click **Create**.
8. After creation, in the overview blade, click the context menu button. After that, select **Connect** as follows:

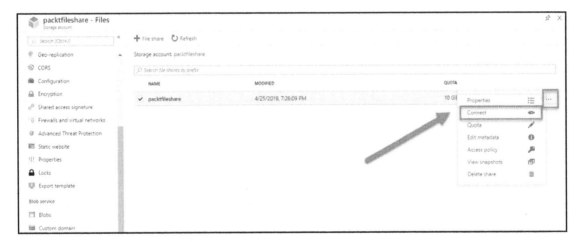

Connect to the file share

9. A new blade will be opened with the details to connect to this file share from a **Windows**, **Linux**, and **MacOS** machine as shown in the following screenshot:

Connection information

10. Let's now connect this file share to our local computer using the command line prompt. Copy and paste the command highlighted in the preceding screenshot in a command line prompt window. When you run that command, the following output will be generated:

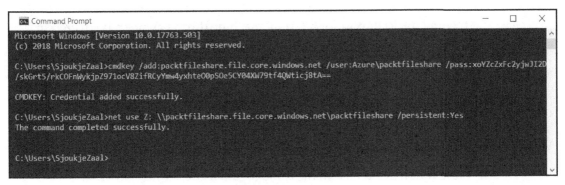

Adding the drive to the local filesystem

The drive is now added to your local filesystem.

Now that we have created a file share and added it to our local machine, we can proceed with the Azure file share sync service.

Azure file share sync service

The Azure file share sync service is a service that can synchronize the data from on-premises file shares with Azure Files. This way, you can keep the flexibility, compatibility, and performance of an on-premises file server, but also store a copy of all the data on the file share in Azure. You can use any protocol that's available on Windows Server to access your data locally, including **Server Message Block (SMB)**, **Network File System (NFS)**, and **File Transfer Protocol over TLS (FTPS)**.

In the next demonstration, we are going to configure Azure File Sync. For this, the following couple of things need to be in place:

- Windows Server. For this, I created a Windows Server 2016 VM in Azure. Make sure that you enable **Remote Desktop** (**RDP**) on the server.

> Opening the RDP port for a virtual machine during creation is covered in *chapter 7: Creating and Configuring VMs for Windows and Linux*, in the "Deploying a Windows VM from the Azure portal" section.

- A storage account (this storage account needs to be created in one of the supported regions for Azure File Sync). You can refer to the following website for the available regions: `https://docs.microsoft.com/en-us/azure/storage/files/storage-sync-files-planning#region-availability`.
- An Azure file share created in the same region as the storage account.

Once the preceding resources are created, we can start with the creation of the Azure File Sync service in Azure and the installation of Azure File Sync on the Windows Server.

First, we will create the Azure File Sync service in Azure. Therefore, take the following steps:

1. Navigate to the Azure portal by opening `https://portal.azure.com`.
2. In the left menu, click **+ Create a resource**, and in the search box, type `Azure File Sync`. Create a new service.
3. Add the following values:
   - **Name:** `PacktFileSync`.
   - **Subscription:** Pick the same subscription as where the storage account and file share are created.
   - **Resource group:** Pick the same subscription as where the storage account and file share are created.
   - **Location:** Pick the same location as where the storage account and file share are created.

These values are shown in the following screenshot:

Creating a file sync service

4. Click **Create**.

5. After deployment, open the Storage Sync Service and click **+ Sync group** in the top menu. We are going to create this group to connect the sync service to the file share as follows:

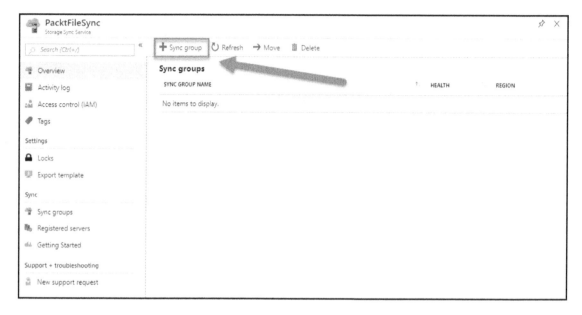

Creating a sync group

6. Add the following values:
   - **Name**: packtsyncgroup.
   - **Subscription**: Select the subscription where the storage account and file share are created.
   - **Storage account**: Select the storage account where the file share is created.

These values are shown in the following screenshot:

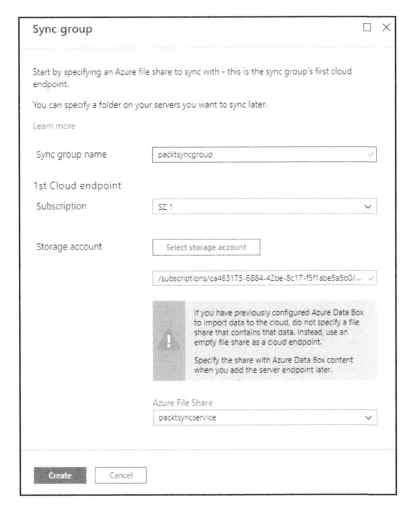

Configuring the sync group

7. RDP to the Windows Server and log in. We first need to disable **IE Enhanced Security Configuration**. Open **Server Manager | Local Server** and disable it for both administrators and users.

8. Download the Azure File Sync agent from the following website: `https://www.microsoft.com/en-us/download/details.aspx?id=57159`.

9. Install the agent on the server. Keep the default path to install the agent. In the next screen, enable **Use the existing proxy settings configured on the server** as shown in the following screenshot:

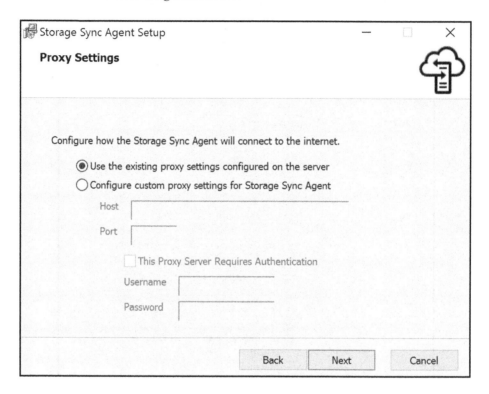

Proxy Settings

10. Click **Next**.
11. Enable Windows updates and install the tool.
12. Once the tool is installed, open the installation folder, which will be `C:\Program Files\Azure\StorageSyncAgent`.
13. Run the `ServerRegistration` tool from the installation folder.

14. Now, we can register the server. First, we need to sign in. Click the **Sign In** button as follows:

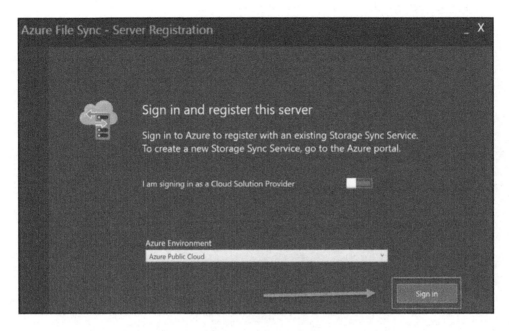

Selecting a Azure Environment

15. Log in using your Azure administrator credentials.

16. We can now select the Storage Sync Service that we created in the Azure portal earlier. Therefore, you need to select the subscription, resource group, and the actual Storage Sync Service as follows:

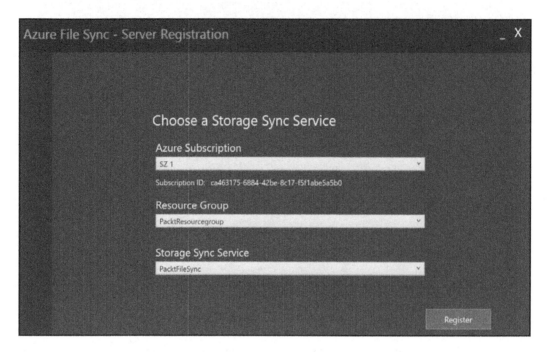

Selecting a Storage Sync Service

17. Click **Register**.
18. After the registration is successful, there is a trust relationship established between the on-premises server and the Storage Sync Service in Azure. Click **OK**.

19. Now, we need to go back to the sync service in the Azure portal to create an endpoint. Go to the Storage Sync Service again and select the sync group that we created earlier. In the sync group settings blade, select **Add server endpoint** in the top menu as follows:

Adding a server endpoint

20. Select the registered server and provide the following path: D:\Data. Keep **Cloud Tiering** and **Offline Data Transfer** disabled and click **Create** as follows:

Endpoint values

The server endpoint is now created.

21. If you now go back to the VM where we installed the sync agent and open the D drive, you will see that there is a folder added called `Data`. You can copy files to it as shown in the following screenshot:

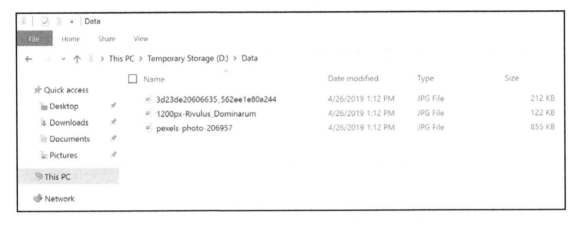

Images stored in the Data folder

22. When you switch back to the file share in Azure, you will see that all the files are synced to the storage account in Azure as shown in the following screenshot:

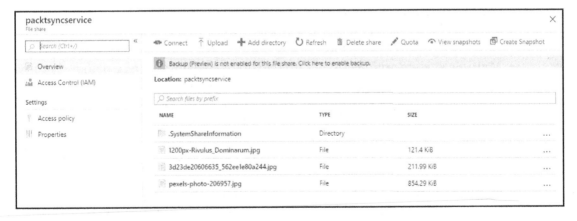

Synced files to Azure file storage

This concludes the section about Azure file storage and the Azure file share sync service. In the next section, we are going to look at Azure Backup and recovery.

Azure Backup

The Azure Backup service is used to back up resources and data in Azure. This can be used for cloud only or hybrid scenarios where you want to back up your on-premises VMs to Azure. Your on-premises backup solution can also be extended to the cloud in conjunction with Azure Backup. Azure Backup is capable of creating backups for VMs, files, folders, applications, workloads, system states, and volumes.

Azure Backup consists of the following features and capabilities:

- **Back up on-premises resources to Azure**: Azure Backup offers short and long-term backup. This can be a replacement for tape and off-site backup.
- **Back up Azure VMs**: Azure Backup offers independent and isolated backups. These backups are stored in a Recovery Services vault. This vault has built-in management for recovery points.
- **Automatic scaling**: You can get unlimited scale without maintenance overheads. Alerts can be set for delivering information about events.
- **Unlimited data transfer**: There is no limit to the amount of inbound and outbound traffic that can be transferred during the backup process. However, if you use the Azure import/export service for importing large amounts of data, then there is a cost associated with inbound data.
- **Data encryption**: Data can be encrypted using an encryption passphrase. This is stored locally and is then needed to restore the data.
- **Short and long-term retention**: Recovery Services is where the backups are stored and provides short and long-term backups. Azure doesn't limit the time or length that data can be stored in a Recovery Services vault.
- **Multiple storage options**: Azure Backup offers two types of replication—**Locally redundant storage (LRS)**, where your data is replicated three times by creating three copies of the data within the same region, and **Geo-redundant storage (GRS)**, which is the default option, where the data is replicated to a secondary region.

You can use Azure Backup to back up data that is protected by the following products:

- **System Center Data Protection Manager (DPM)**: DPM can run on-premises or in Azure on physical servers or virtual servers. The DPM server can be backed up to Recovery Services as well. The DPM server and its machines need to be in the same network. On-premises machines can only be protected by an on-premises DPM server, while Azure machines can only be protected by a DPM server that is running in Azure.

- **Microsoft Azure Backup Server (MABS)**: MABS can run on-premises or in Azure on physical servers or virtual servers. It offers similar capabilities to DPM, except that MABS can be backed up to tape and you don't need to have a system center license for it. Just like DPM, on-premises machines can only be protected by an on-premises MABS server, while Azure machines can only be protected by an MABS server that is running in Azure.

Azure Site Recovery

Azure Site Recovery can be replicated from Azure VMs and other workloads, such as Azure file storage between different Azure regions, as well as on-premises VMs, physical (file) servers, and Azure Stack VMs.

Azure Recovery Services offers the following features:

- **Site Recovery service**: Site Recovery makes sure that your VMs, apps, and workloads are still running during outages. It replicates the workloads running on the machines, both virtual and physical, from a primary to a secondary location. You can fail over to a secondary location when an outage occurs at the primary site. When the primary location is up again, you can fail back to it.
- **Backup service**: This service keeps your data safe by backing it up to Azure.

You can also use Azure Site Recovery for migration from on-premises machines to Azure VMs. This differs from disaster recovery in the following ways:

- **Disaster recovery**: With disaster recovery, machines are replicated regularly. In the case of an outage, the machines are failed over from the primary to the secondary site in Azure. The machines can then be accessed from the secondary site. When the primary site is available again, you fail back from the secondary site to the primary again.
- **Migration**: On-premises machines are replicated to Azure, or Azure VMs to a secondary region. After that, the VM is failed over from the primary site to the secondary site, which completes the migration process without a failback process.

In the next section, we are going to perform a backup and restore operation for an Azure file share.

Performing a backup and restore operation

In this demonstration, we will be performing a backup and restore operation for an Azure file share. We are going to back up the file share that we created in this chapter and restore it from a Recovery Services vault.

 In Chapter 8, *Managing Azure VMs and VM Backups*, we are going to set up backup and restore for a virtual machine in Azure from the Azure portal. You can refer to this chapter for more information about backup and restore.

Creating a Recovery Services vault

We are going to create the Recovery Services vault in Azure. You can create this using the Azure portal, PowerShell, and CLI. We are going the create the vault using PowerShell. To create this, perform the following steps:

1. First, we need to log in to the Azure account as follows:

   ```
   Connect-AzAccount
   ```

2. If necessary, select the right subscription as follows (make sure that you use the same subscription here as that you've used to create the file share in):

   ```
   Select-AzSubscription -SubscriptionId "********-****-****-****-************"
   ```

3. Create a resource group for the Recovery Services Vault as follows:

   ```
   New-AzResourceGroup -Name PacktRecoveryServicesGroup -Location EastUS
   ```

4. Create a new Recovery Services vault as follows:

   ```
   New-AzRecoveryServicesVault -Name PacktFileVault -ResourceGroupName PacktRecoveryServicesGroup -Location EastUS
   ```

5. You can now set the type of redundancy to use for the vault storage as follows:

   ```
   $vault1 = Get-AzRecoveryServicesVault `
    -Name PacktFileVault

   Set-AzRecoveryServicesBackupProperties -Vault $vault1 `
    -BackupStorageRedundancy GeoRedundant
   ```

We have now created the Recovery Services vault. In the next part, we are going to create a backup policy for the Azure file share.

Configuring a backup policy

A backup policy specifies the schedule for backups, and how long backup recovery points should be kept. It is associated with at least one retention policy, which defines how long a recovery point will be kept before it is deleted.

In the following example, we are going to create a backup policy in PowerShell, which will take a daily backup and will retain for 30 days:

1. First, we need to store the vault ID in a variable to pass it on creating the policy later as follows:

```
$vaultID = Get-AzRecoveryServicesVault `
    -ResourceGroupName PacktRecoveryServicesGroup `
    -Name PacktFileVault `
    | select -ExpandProperty ID
```

2. Next, we are going to set two variables for storing the schedule and retention policies. Then we will create a new backup policy using these values:

```
$packtSchPol = Get-AzRecoveryServicesBackupSchedulePolicyObject -
WorkloadType "AzureFiles"
$packtRetPol = Get-AzRecoveryServicesBackupRetentionPolicyObject -
WorkloadType "AzureFiles"

$afsPol = New-AzRecoveryServicesBackupProtectionPolicy -Name
"PacktFSPolicy" `
    -WorkloadType "AzureFiles" `
    -RetentionPolicy $packtRetPol `
    -SchedulePolicy $packtSchPol `
    -VaultId $vaultID `
    -BackupManagementType AzureStorage
```

3. And lastly, we can enable this policy for the Azure files storage account as follows:

```
Enable-AzRecoveryServicesBackupProtection -VaultId $vaultID `
    -Policy $afsPol `
    -Name "packtfileshare" `
    -StorageAccountName "packtfileshare"
```

We have now created a backup policy to back up our file share that we created at the beginning of this chapter. This backup policy will create a daily backup. You can also trigger an on-demand backup. For this, leave PowerShell open, because we need the Vault ID in to trigger an on-demand job. We will cover this in the next section.

Trigger an on-demand backup

In this demonstration, we are going to trigger an on-demand backup using PowerShell. With your PowerShell session still open, take the following steps:

1. First, we need to retrieve the backup container:

```
$afsPacktContainer = Get-AzRecoveryServicesBackupContainer -
FriendlyName "packtfileshare" `
   -ContainerType AzureStorage `
   -VaultId $vaultID
```

2. Then we need to retrieve the backup item from the container:

```
$afsPacktBackupItem = Get-AzRecoveryServicesBackupItem `
   -Container $afsPacktContainer `
   -WorkloadType "AzureFiles" `
   -Name "packtfileshare" `
   -VaultId $vaultID
```

3. At last, we can schedule the job:

```
$job = Backup-AzRecoveryServicesBackupItem -Item
$afsPacktBackupItem -VaultId $vaultID
```

Now that we have created a backup, we can restore it using PowerShell. We will do this in the next section.

Restore the backup

To restore the backup that we created in the previous demonstration from PowerShell, we have to take the following steps:

1. Generate a list of available recovery points:

```
$startDate = (Get-Date).AddDays(-7)
$endDate = Get-Date
$rp = Get-AzRecoveryServicesBackupRecoveryPoint -Item
$afsPacktBackupItem `
```

```
        -StartDate $startdate.ToUniversalTime ()  `
        -EndDate $enddate.ToUniversalTime ()  `
        -VaultId $vaultID

$rp[0] | fl
```

2. Restore the backup. In this example we are going to restore the backup in the original destination. You can also use an alternative destination, like another storage account for instance. We first need to set the vault context again before we can restore the backup:

```
Get-AzRecoveryServicesVault -Name "PacktFileVault" | Set-
AzRecoveryServicesVaultContext

Restore-AzRecoveryServicesBackupItem `
    -RecoveryPoint $rp[0] `
    -TargetStorageAccountName "packtfileshare" `
    -TargetFileShareName "packtfileshare" `
    -TargetFolder "AzureFS_restored" `
    -ResolveConflict Overwrite
```

Summary

In this chapter, we covered the third and last part of the *Implementing and Managing Storage* objective. We covered the Azure file shares and we covered how to install and configure the Azure file share sync service. We also looked at backup and restore of our files shared in Azure.

In the next chapter, we will introduce the *Deploying and Managing Virtual Machines* objective by covering how to create and configure VMs for Windows and Linux.

Questions

Answer the following questions to test your knowledge of the information in this chapter. You can find the answers in the *Assessments* section at the end of this book:

1. Can you use Azure Backup to back up Azure file shares?
   - Yes
   - No

2. Can you use Azure Backup in conjunction with MABS?
   - Yes
   - No

3. Can you use the Azure file share sync service to mount an Azure file share to your local computer?
   - Yes
   - No

Further reading

You can check out the following links for more information about the topics that were covered in this chapter:

- *What is Azure Files?*: https://docs.microsoft.com/en-us/azure/storage/files/storage-files-introduction
- *Planning for an Azure File Sync deployment*: https://docs.microsoft.com/en-us/azure/storage/files/storage-sync-files-planning
- *Deploy Azure File Sync*: https://docs.microsoft.com/en-us/azure/storage/files/storage-sync-files-deployment-guide?tabs=azure-portal
- *What is Azure Backup?*: https://docs.microsoft.com/en-us/azure/backup/backup-overview
- *Overview of the features in Azure Backup*: https://docs.microsoft.com/en-us/azure/backup/backup-introduction-to-azure-backup#which-azure-backup-components-should-i-use
- *About Site Recovery*: https://docs.microsoft.com/en-us/azure/site-recovery/site-recovery-overview

3
Section 3: Deploying and Managing Virtual Machines

In this section, you will learn how to deploy and manage virtual machines in Azure.

The following chapters will be covered in this section:

- Chapter 7, *Creating and Configuring VMs for Windows and Linux*
- Chapter 8, *Managing Azure VMs and VM Backups*

Creating and Configuring VMs for Windows and Linux

7

In the previous chapter, we covered Azure file shares and how to sync your on-premises file shares with Azure using the Azure File Sync service. You also learned how to back up and restore file shares in Azure.

This chapter introduces the *Deploying and Managing Virtual Machines* objective. In this chapter, we are going to cover **Virtual Machines** (**VMs**) in Azure, and the different VM sizes that are available for both Azure and Linux. You will learn how you can create and configure VMs for Windows and Linux. We will also cover high availability and what actions you can take to configure your VMs for high availability. You will also learn how to deploy your VMs using templates by using **Azure Resource Manager** (**ARM**) templates, and how to automate your deployment using scale sets.

The following topics will be covered in this chapter:

- VMs
- Deploying Windows and Linux VMs
- Configuring high availability
- Deploying and configuring scale sets
- Modifying and deploying ARM templates

Technical requirements

This chapter uses the following tools for our examples:

- Azure PowerShell: https://docs.microsoft.com/en-us/powershell/azure/install-az-ps?view=azps-1.8.0
- Visual Studio Code: https://code.visualstudio.com/download

The source code for this chapter can be downloaded from `https://github.com/PacktPublishing/Microsoft-Azure-Administrator-Exam-Guide-AZ-103/tree/master/Chapter07`.

VMs

You can run both Windows VMs as well as Linux VMs in Azure. VMs come in all sorts of sizes and a variety of prices, ranging from VMs with a small amount of memory and processing power for general purposes to large VMs that can be used for **Graphics Processing Unit** (**GPU**)-intensive and high-performance computing workloads.

To create a VM, you can choose from a number of predefined images. There are images available for operating systems such as Windows Server or Linux, as well as predefined applications, such as SQL Server images and complete farms, which consist of multiple VMs that can be deployed at once. An example of a farm is a three-tier SharePoint farm.

VMs can be created and managed either from the Azure portal, PowerShell, or CLI, and they come in the following series and sizes.

VM series and sizes

At the time of writing this book, the following VM series and sizes are available:

Series	Type	Description
B, Dsv3, Dv3, DSv2, Dv2, Av2, DC	General purpose	These VMs have a balanced CPU-to-memory ratio and are ideal for testing and development scenarios. They are also suitable for small and medium databases, and web servers with low-to-medium traffic.
Fsv2, Fs, F	Compute optimized	These VMs have a high CPU-to-memory ratio and are suitable for web servers with medium traffic, application servers, and network appliances for nodes in batch processing.

Esv3, Ev3, M, GS, G, DSv2, Dv2	Memory optimized	These VMs have a high memory-to-CPU ratio and are suitable for relational database servers, medium-to-large caches, and in-memory analytics.
Lsv2, Ls	Storage optimized	These VMs have high disk throughput and IO and are suitable for big data, SQL, and NoSQL databases.
NV, NVv2, NC, NCv2, NCv3, ND, NDv2 (Preview)	GPU	These VMs are targeted for heavy graphic rendering and video editing, deep learning applications, and machine learning model training. These VMs are available with single or multiple GPUs.
H	High-performance compute	These are the fastest VMs available. They offer the most powerful CPU with optional high-throughput network interfaces (**Remote Direct Memory Access (RDMA)**).

VM series are updated constantly. New series, types, and sizes are added and removed frequently. To stay up to date with these changes, you can refer to the following site for Windows VM sizes: `https://docs.microsoft.com/en-us/azure/virtual-machines/windows/sizes`. For Linux VM sizes, you can refer to `https://docs.microsoft.com/en-us/azure/virtual-machines/linux/sizes?toc=%2fazure%2fvirtualmachines%2flinux%2ftoc.json`.

Managed disks

Azure managed disks are the default disks selected when you create a VM in the Azure portal. They handle storage for your VMs completely. Previously, you would have had to manually create storage accounts to store VM hard disks, and when your VM needed to scale up, you had to add additional storage accounts to make sure you didn't exceed the limit of 20,000 **Input/Output Operations Per Second (IOPS)** per account.

With managed disks, this burden is now handled for you by Azure. You can now create 10,000 VM disks inside a subscription, which can result in thousands of VMs inside a subscription, without the need to copy disks between storage accounts.

Availability sets

To create a reliable infrastructure, adding your VMs to an availability set is key. There are several scenarios that can have an impact on the availability of your Azure VMs. These are as follows:

- **Unplanned hardware maintenance event**: When hardware is about to fail, Azure fires an unplanned hardware maintenance event. Live migration technology is used, which predicts the failure and then moves the VM, the network connections, memory, and storage to different physical machines, without disconnecting the client. When your VM is moved, the performance is reduced for a short time because the VM is paused for 30 seconds. Network connections, memory, and open files are still preserved.
- **Unexpected downtime**: The VM is down when this event occurs because Azure needs to heal your VM inside the same data center. A hardware or physical infrastructure failure often causes this event to happen.
- **Planned hardware maintenance event**: This type of event is a periodic update from Microsoft in Azure to improve the platform. Most of these updates don't have a significant impact on the uptime of VMs, but some of them may require a reboot or restart.

To provide redundancy during these types of events, you can group two or more VMs in an availability set. By leveraging availability sets, VMs are distributed across multiple isolated hardware nodes in a cluster. This way, Azure can ensure that during an event or failure, only a subset of your VMs is impacted and your overall solution will remain operational and available. This way, the 99.95% Azure **Service Level Agreement (SLA)** can still be met during outages and other failures.

VMs can only be assigned to an availability set during initial deployment.

Fault domains and update domains

When you place your VMs in an availability set, Azure guarantees to spread them across fault and update domains. By default, Azure will assign three fault domains and five update domains (which can be increased to a maximum of 20) to the availability set.

When spreading your VMs over fault domains, your VMs sit over three different racks in the Azure Datacenter. So, in the case of an event or failure of the underlying platform, only one rack gets affected and the other VMs remain accessible as depicted in the following diagram:

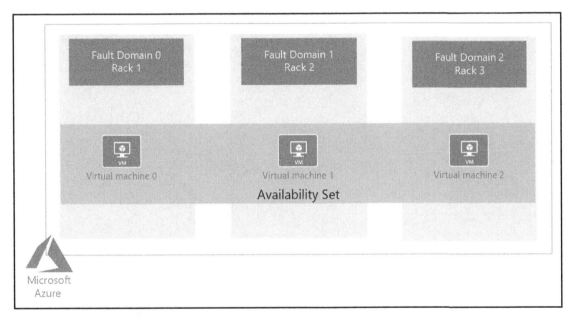

VMs spread over three fault domains

Update domains are useful in the case of an OS or host update. When you spread your VMs across multiple update domains, one domain will be updated and rebooted while the others remain accessible as depicted in the following diagram:

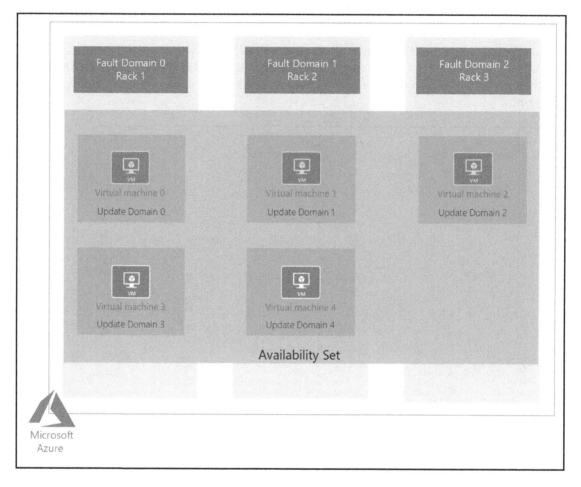

VMs spread over five update domains and three fault domains

In the next demonstration, we are going to create a new Windows VM in the Azure portal.

Deploying Windows and Linux VMs

In the upcoming demonstrations, we are going to deploy a Windows Server VM from both the Azure portal and PowerShell.

Deploying Linux machines is quite similar to deploying Windows machines. We are not going to cover how to deploy Linux machines. For more information about how to deploy Linux machines in Azure, you can refer to the *Further reading* section at the end of this chapter.

Deploying a Windows VM from the Azure portal

In this demonstration, we are going to deploy a Windows VM from the Azure portal. We are going to set up networking and storage, and select a VM size for this VM. We are also going to configure high availability for this VM, by placing it in an *availability set*. To do so, perform the following steps:

1. Navigate to the Azure portal by opening `https://portal.azure.com`.
2. In the left menu, click **Virtual machines**, and then, in the top menu, click **+ Add** as follows:

Creating a new VM

3. We are going to create a Windows VM, so in the **Basics** blade, add the following values:
   - **Subscription**: Choose a subscription.
   - **Resource group**: `PacktVMGroup`.
   - **Virtual machine name**: `PacktWindowsVM`.
   - **Region**: Choose a region.
   - **Availability options**: Here, select **Availability set**.
   - **Availability set**: Create new, and call it `PacktWindowsAS`. Keep the default fault domains and update the domains for this VM.
   - **Image**: **Windows Server Datacenter 2016**.

- **Size**: Here, you can choose between the different sizes. Click **Change size**, and select **Standard DS1 v2**.
- **Administrator account**: Provide a username and a password.
- **Inbound port rules**: Select **Allow selected ports** and enable **Remote Desktop Protocol (RDP)**. You will need this to log in to the server after creation.
- **Save money**: If you already have a valid Windows Server Datacenter license, you get a discount on this VM.

4. Click **Next: Disks**.

5. Here, you can select the disk type. Keep the default as follows, which is **Premium SSD**:

Create a virtual machine

Basics   Disks   Networking   Management   Advanced   Tags   Review + create

Azure VMs have one operating system disk and a temporary disk for short-term storage. You can attach additional data disks. The size of the VM determines the type of storage you can use and the number of data disks allowed.   Learn more

DISK OPTIONS

| * OS disk type ⓘ | Premium SSD ⌄ |

Enable Ultra SSD compatibility (Preview) ⓘ   ◯ Yes   ⦿ No

Ultra SSD compatibility is not available for this VM size and location.

DATA DISKS

You can add and configure additional data disks for your virtual machine or attach existing disks. This VM also comes with a temporary disk.

LUN	NAME	SIZE (GiB)	DISK TYPE	HOST CACHING

Create and attach a new disk   Attach an existing disk

⌄ ADVANCED

Select disk type

6. Click **Next: Networking**.

---

7. In the **Networking** blade, you can configure the virtual network. You can keep the default values for this machine as follows:

Create a virtual machine

Basics   Disks   Networking   Management   Advanced   Tags   Review + create

Define network connectivity for your virtual machine by configuring network interface card (NIC) settings. You can control ports, inbound and outbound connectivity with security group rules, or place behind an existing load balancing solution. Learn more

NETWORK INTERFACE

When creating a virtual machine, a network interface will be created for you.

CONFIGURE VIRTUAL NETWORKS

* Virtual network ⓘ	(new) PacktVMGroup-vnet ⌄
	Create new
* Subnet ⓘ	(new) default (10.0.2.0/24) ⌄
Public IP ⓘ	(new) PacktWindowsVM-ip ⌄
	Create new
NIC network security group ⓘ	◯ None ⦿ Basic ◯ Advanced
* Public inbound ports ⓘ	◯ None ⦿ Allow selected ports
* Select inbound ports	RDP ⌄

> ⚠ These ports will be exposed to the internet. Use the Advanced controls to limit inbound traffic to known IP addresses. You can also update inbound traffic rules later.

Accelerated networking ⓘ	◯ On ⦿ Off
	The selected VM size does not support accelerated networking.

LOAD BALANCING

You can place this virtual machine in the backend pool of an existing Azure load balancing solution. Learn more

Place this virtual machine behind an existing load balancing solution?	◯ Yes ⦿ No

---

Set networking for VM

8. Click **Next: Management**.

9. In the **Management** blade, you can configure monitoring, and create and select a storage account for monitoring. You can also assign a system-assigned managed identity, which can be used to authenticate to various Azure resources, such as Azure Key Vault, without storing any credentials in code. You can also enable auto shutdown in here as follows:

Create a virtual machine

Basics   Disks   Networking   **Management**   Advanced   Tags   Review + create

Configure monitoring and management options for your VM.

AZURE SECURITY CENTER

Azure Security Center provides unified security management and advanced threat protection across hybrid cloud workloads.

Learn more

✅ Your subscription is protected by Azure Security Center standard plan.

MONITORING

Boot diagnostics ⓘ	⦿ On ◯ Off
OS guest diagnostics ⓘ	◯ On ⦿ Off
* Diagnostics storage account ⓘ	(new) packtvmgroupdiag
	Create new

IDENTITY

System assigned managed identity ⓘ	◯ On ⦿ Off

AUTO-SHUTDOWN

Enable auto-shutdown ⓘ	⦿ On ◯ Off
Shutdown time ⓘ	7:00:00 PM
Time zone ⓘ	(UTC) Coordinated Universal Time
Notification before shutdown ⓘ	◯ On ⦿ Off

BACKUP

Enable backup ⓘ	◯ On ⦿ Off

Set management features

10. We can now create the VM. Click **Review + create** and the settings will be validated. After that, click **Create** to actually deploy the VM.

The steps for deploying Linux VMs are similar to creating Windows VMs, so we are going to skip this in this demonstration. For more information on how to deploy Linux VMs from the Azure portal, you can refer to, `https://docs.microsoft.com/en-us/azure/virtual-machines/linux/quick-create-portal`.

We have now deployed a Windows VM, placed it in an Availability Set, and looked at the networking, storage, and monitoring features, and capabilities for this VM. In the next section, we are going to deploy a Windows Server VM from PowerShell.

Deploying a Windows VM from PowerShell

In the next demonstration, we are going to create two Windows Server VMs from PowerShell and place them in an Availability Set. To do so you have to perform the following steps:

1. First, we need to log in to the Azure account as follows:

```
Login-AzureRmAccount
```

2. If necessary, select the right subscription as follows:

```
Select-AzureRmSubscription -SubscriptionId "********-****-****-
****-************"
```

3. Create a resource group for the Availability Set as follows:

```
New-AzResourceGroup -Name PacktVMResourceGroup -Location EastUS
```

4. Then, we can create an availability set for the VMs as follows:

```
New-AzAvailabilitySet `
    -Location "EastUS" `
    -Name "PacktVMAvailabilitySet" `
    -ResourceGroupName PacktVMResourceGroup `
    -Sku aligned `
    -PlatformFaultDomainCount 2 `
    -PlatformUpdateDomainCount 2
```

5. We have to set the administrator credentials for the VMs as follows:

```
$cred = Get-Credential
```

6. We can now create the two VMs inside the Availability Set as follows:

```
for ($i=1; $i -le 2; $i++)
{
    New-AzVm `
        -ResourceGroupName PacktVMResourceGroup `
        -Name "PacktVM$i" `
        -Location "East US" `
        -VirtualNetworkName "PacktVnet" `
        -SubnetName "PacktSubnet" `
        -SecurityGroupName "PacktNetworkSecurityGroup" `
        -PublicIpAddressName "PacktPublicIpAddress$i" `
        -AvailabilitySetName "PacktVMAvailabilitySet" `
        -Credential $cred
}
```

In the last two demonstrations, we created VMs inside an Availability Set from the Azure portal and PowerShell. In the next section, we are going to cover scale sets.

VM scale sets

VM scale sets are used for deploying multiple VMs at once without the need for manual actions or using scripts. You can then manage them all at once from a single place. VM scale sets are typically used to build large-scale infrastructures, where keeping all of your VMs in sync is key. The maintenance of VMs, including keeping them in sync, is handled by Azure. VM scale sets use Availability Sets under the hood. VMs inside a scale set are automatically spread over the fault and update domains by the underlying platform. VM scale sets use Azure Autoscale by default. You can, however, add or remove instances yourself instead of using Autoscale.

When creating a scale set, a couple of artefacts are created for you automatically. As well as the number of VMs you have specified are added to the set, an Azure Load Balancer and Azure Autoscale are added, along with a virtual network and a public IP address, as shown in the following screenshot:

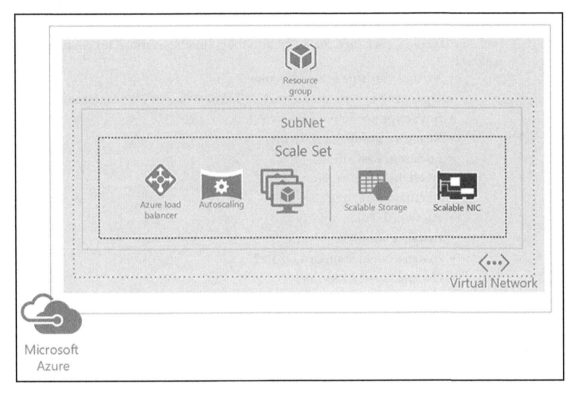

Azure VM scale set

In the next section, we are going to deploy and configure scale sets.

Deploying and configuring scale sets

To create a VM scale set from the Azure portal, take the following steps:

1. Navigate to the Azure portal by opening `https://portal.azure.com`.
2. Click on **Create a resource** and type in `Scale Set` in the search bar. Select **Virtual machine scale set**.
3. In the next screen, click on **Create** and add the following settings for creating the scale set:
   - **Virtual machine scale set name**: `PacktScaleSet`
   - **Operating system disk image**: **Windows Server 2016 Datacenter**
   - **Subscription**: Select a subscription
   - **Resource group**: `PacktVMGroup`
   - **Location**: **East US**
   - **Availability zone**: **None**
   - **Username**: `SCPacktUser`
   - **Password**: Fill in a password
   - **Instance count**: 2
   - **Instance size**: **Standard DS1 v2**
   - **Use managed disks**: **Yes**

- **Enable scaling beyond 100 instances**: No:

Create virtual machine scale set

BASICS

* Virtual machine scale set name	PacktScaleSet
* Operating system disk image ❶	Windows Server 2016 Datacenter
	Browse all images
* Subscription	SZ 1
* Resource group	PacktVMGroup
	Create new
* Location	(US) East US
Availability zone ❶	None
* Username ❶	SCPacktUser
* Password	••••••••••••
* Confirm password	••••••••••••

INSTANCES

* Instance count ❶	2
* Instance size ❶	**Standard DS1 v2** 1 vcpu, 3.5 GB memory Change size
Deploy as low priority ❶	◉ No ○ Yes

❶ Low priority is not available for the selected instance size

Use managed disks ❶	○ No ◉ Yes
- Hide advanced settings	
Enable scaling beyond 100 instances ❶	◉ No ○ Yes

Scale set

4. If you scroll down, you can configure the autoscale settings, you can choose between the different load balancing settings, and you can configure networking and monitoring capabilities as follows:

AUTOSCALE

Autoscale	◯ Disabled ◉ Enabled
* Minimum number of VMs	1
* Maximum number of VMs	10

Scale out

* CPU threshold (%)	75
* Number of VMs to increase by	1

Scale in

* CPU threshold (%)	25
* Number of VMs to decrease by	1

NETWORKING

Microsoft Azure Application Gateway is a dedicated virtual appliance providing application delivery controller (ADC) as a service.
Azure Load Balancer allows you to scale your applications and create high availability for your services.
Learn more about load balancer differences

RESOURCES	OPTIMAL FOR	SUPPORTED PROTOCOLS	SSL OFFLOADING	RDP TO INSTANCE
Application Gateway	Web-based traffic	HTTP/HTTPS/WebSoc...	Supported	Not supported
Load balancer	Stream-based traffic	Any	Not supported	Supported

Choose Load balancing options	◯ Application Gateway ◯ Load balancer ◉ None

CONFIGURE VIRTUAL NETWORKS

* Virtual network	PacktVMGroup-vnet
	Create new
* Subnet	default (10.0.2.0/24)
	Manage subnet configuration
Public IP address per instance	◯ On ◉ Off
Accelerated networking	◯ On ◉ Off

ⓘ The selected VM size does not support accelerated networking.

Scale set configuration settings

5. Click **Create**. The scale set with the number of provided VMs in it is now deployed.

In the next and last sections of this chapter, we are going to cover how to automate the deployment of VMs using ARM templates.

Modifying and deploying ARM templates

ARM templates define the infrastructure and configuration of your Azure solution. Azure is managed by an API, which is called the Resource Manager or ARM API. You can use this API to deploy infrastructure as code and configure your Azure environment. This API can be called from various tooling and resources; you can do it using the Azure portal, PowerShell, CLI, by calling the API directly, and by creating ARM templates.

You can create an ARM template in JSON format and use this to repeatedly deploy your solution across your Azure environment in a consistent state. The template is processed by Resource Manager like any other request, and it will parse the template and convert the syntax into REST API operations for the appropriate resource providers. The REST API uses the resources section inside the template to call the resource-specific APIs. An example of a resource provider is `Microsoft.Storage/storageAccounts`.

Microsoft offers various predefined ARM templates that can be downloaded and deployed. You can download the quick start templates from GitHub, and deploy them directly from GitHub, or download them and make the necessary adjustments: `https://github.com/Azure/azure-quickstart-templates`.

In the next section, we are going to modify an ARM template in the Azure portal.

Modifying an ARM template

In the demonstration, we are going to create an ARM template of a storage account it in the Azure portal. We are going to modify this template, so that it will generate a storage account name automatically. We will then deploy this template again and use it to create a new storage account from the Azure portal. Therefore, you have to take the following steps:

1. Navigate to the Azure portal by opening `https://portal.azure.com`.
2. In the left menu, select + **Create a resource**, then **Storage** and then **Storage account**.

3. Add the following values:
   - **Subscription**: Pick a subscription
   - **Resource group**: Create a new one and call it `PacktARMResourceGroup`
   - **Storage account name**: `packtarm`
   - **Location: (US) East US**
   - **Performance: Standard**
   - **Account kind: StorageV2 (general purpose v2)**
   - **Replication: Read-access geo-redundant storage (RA-GRS)**
   - **Access tier: Hot**:

Create a new storage account

4. Click **Review + create**. Do not select **Create**.
5. In the next step, but select **Download a template for automation**:

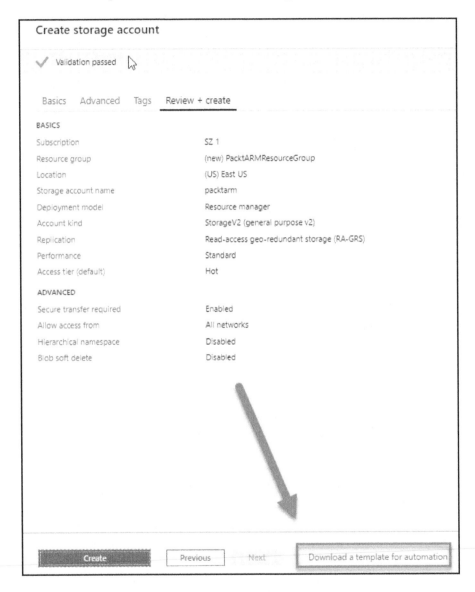

BASICS

Subscription	SZ 1
Resource group	(new) PacktARMResourceGroup
Location	(US) East US
Storage account name	packtarm
Deployment model	Resource manager
Account kind	StorageV2 (general purpose v2)
Replication	Read-access geo-redundant storage (RA-GRS)
Performance	Standard
Access tier (default)	Hot

ADVANCED

Secure transfer required	Enabled
Allow access from	All networks
Hierarchical namespace	Disabled
Blob soft delete	Disabled

Download template for automation

6. The editor will be opened and the generated template will be displayed. The main pane shows the template. It has six top-level elements: `schema`, `contentVersion`, `parameters`, `variables`, `resources`, and `output`. There are also six parameters. The `storageAccountName` is highlighted in the following screenshot. In the template, one Azure resource is defined. The type is `Microsoft.Storage/storageAccounts`. Select **Download** from the top menu:

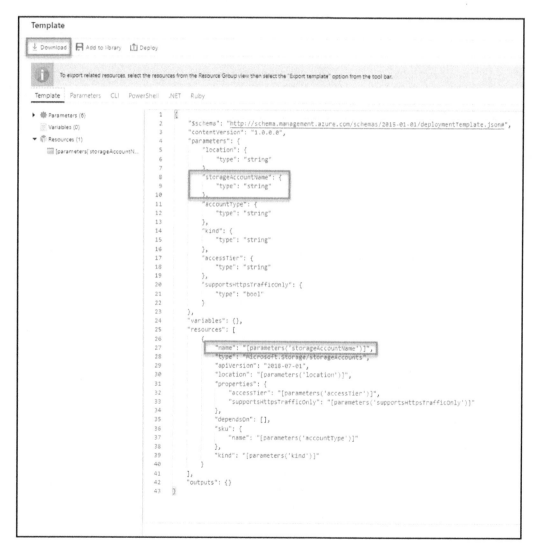

Main ARM template

7. Open the downloaded ZIP file, and then save `template.json` to your computer. In the next section, you use a template deployment tool to edit the template.

8. Select **Parameters** in the top menu, and look at the values. We will need this later during the deployment:

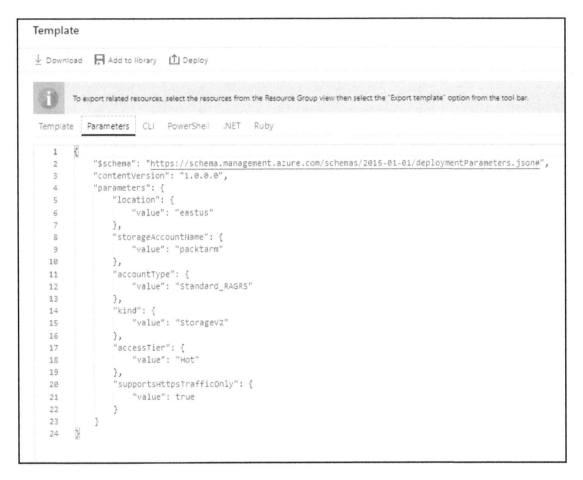

ARM template parameters

9. The Azure portal can be used for basic editing of ARM templates. More complex ARM templates can be edited using Visual Studio Code, for instance. We are going to use the Azure portal for this demonstration. Therefore, select **+ Create a resource**, then in the search box type `Template Deployment`. Then select **Create**.

10. In the next blade, you have different options for loading templates. For this demonstration, select **Build your own template in the editor**:

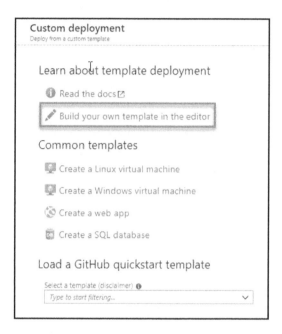

Template options

11. Select **Load file**, and then follow the instructions to load the `template.json` that we have downloaded in the last section. Make the following changes:

    1. Remove the `storageAccountName` parameter.

    2. Add a new variable:

    ```
    "storageAccountName":
    "[concat(uniqueString(subscription().subscriptionId),
    'storage')]"
    ```

3. Replace `"name": "[parameters('storageAccountName')]"`,
with `"name": "[variables('storageAccountName')]"`:

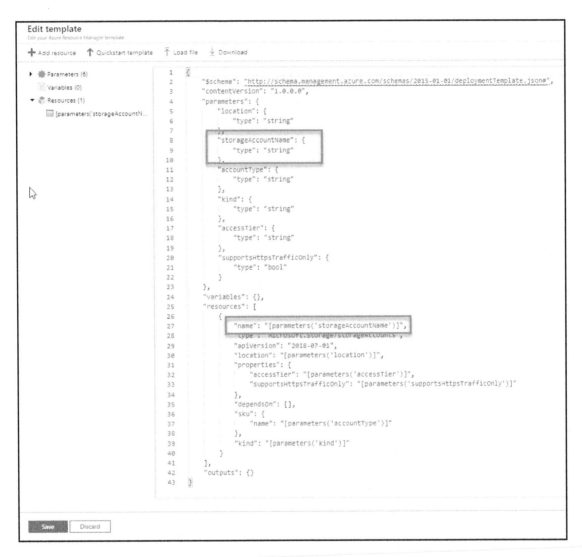

Make changes to the highlighted sections

4. The code of the template will look as follows:

The `schema` and `parameters` sections:

```
{
    "$schema":
"http://schema.management.azure.com/schemas/2015-01-01/depl
oymentTemplate.json#",
    "contentVersion": "1.0.0.0",
    "parameters": {
        "location": {
            "type": "string"
        },
        "accountType": {
            "type": "string"
        },
        "kind": {
            "type": "string"
        },
        "accessTier": {
            "type": "string"
        },
        "supportsHttpsTrafficOnly": {
            "type": "bool"
        }
    },
```

And the `variable` and `resources` section:

```
"variables": {
    "storageAccountName":
"[concat(uniqueString(subscription().subscriptionId),
'storage')]"
    },
    "resources": [
        {
            "name": "[variables('storageAccountName')]",
            "type": "Microsoft.Storage/storageAccounts",
            "apiVersion": "2018-07-01",
            "location": "[parameters('location')]",
            "properties": {
                "accessTier": "[parameters('accessTier')]",
                "supportsHttpsTrafficOnly":
"[parameters('supportsHttpsTrafficOnly')]"
            },
            "dependsOn": [],
            "sku": {
                "name": "[parameters('accountType')]"
            },
            "kind": "[parameters('kind')]"
        }
    ],
    "outputs": {}
}
```

5. Then select **Save.**

12. In the next screen, fill in the values for creating the storage account. You will see that the parameter for filling in the storage account name is removed. This will be generated automatically. Fill in the following values:

- **Resource group**: Select the resource group name you created in the previous section.
- **Location: Central US**
- **Account type: Standard_LRS**
- **Kind: StorageV2**
- **Access Tier: Hot**
- **Https Traffic Only Enabled: true**

- **I agree to the terms and conditions stated above**: Select this option:

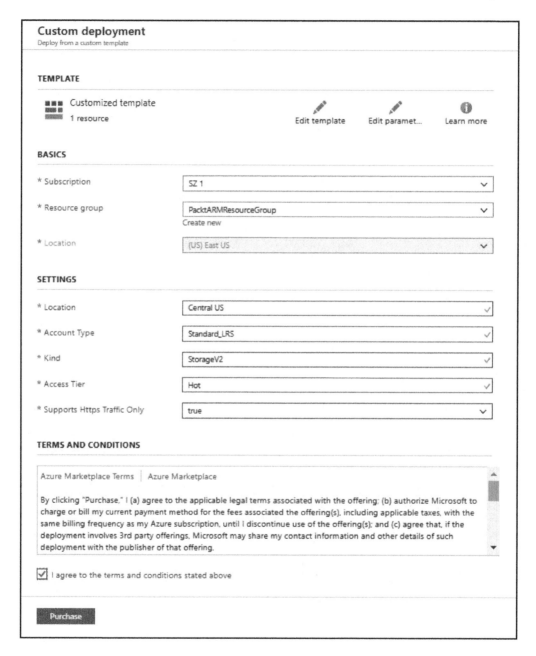

Fill in values

13. Select **Purchase**.
14. The ARM template will now be deployed. After deployment, go to the **Overview** blade of the resource group. You will see that the storage account name is automatically generated for you:

Storage account name

For more information about the syntax and structure of ARM templates, you can refer to the following website: `https://docs.microsoft.com/en-us/azure/azure-resource-manager/resource-group-authoring-templates`.

We have now modified an ARM template in the Azure portal and created a new storage account using the modified ARM templates. In the next demonstration, we are going to save a deployment as an ARM template.

Save a deployment as an ARM template

For this demonstration, we are going to save a deployment as an ARM template from the Azure portal. We are going to export the template of the two VMs that we created in an Availability Set using PowerShell.

Once downloaded, you can then make changes to it, and redeploy it in Azure using PowerShell or code. The generated ARM template consists of a large amount of code, which makes it very difficult to make changes to it. For saving a deployment as an ARM template, take the following steps:

1. Navigate to the Azure portal by opening `https://portal.azure.com`.
2. Open the resource group that we created in the previous demonstration and under **Settings**, select the **Export template** as follows:

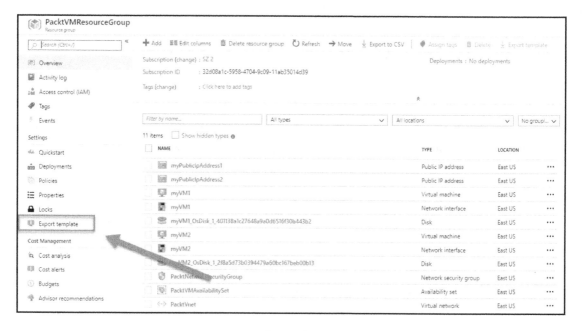

Export template

3. The template is generated for you based on the settings that we made during the creation of the different resources. You can download the template and redeploy it from here. You can also download the scripts for CLI, PowerShell, .NET, and Ruby, and create the different resources using these programming languages. Select **Download** from the top menu as follows:

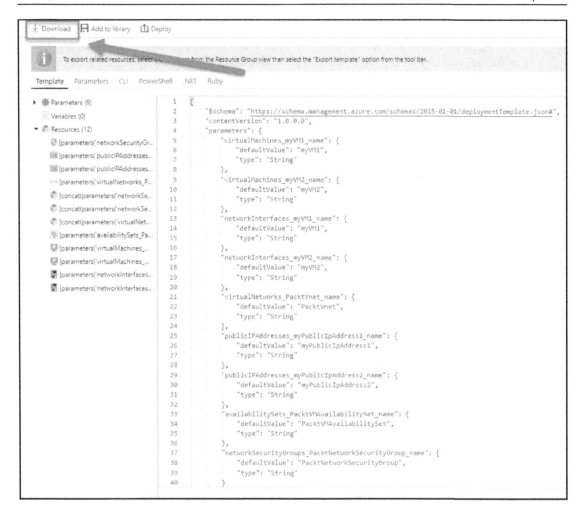

Download template

The template is downloaded as a ZIP file to your local filesystem.

4. You can now extract the template files from the ZIP file and open them in Visual Studio Code. If you don't have this installed, you can use the download link provided at the beginning of this chapter or use Notepad, or some other text editing tool. The ZIP file contains three different deployment files, created in different languages. There is one each for PowerShell, CLI, and Ruby. It also consists of a `DeploymentHelper.cs` file, a `parameters.json` file, and a `template.json` file.

5. In Visual Studio Code, you can make all the modifications to the parameters and template file that are needed. If you then want to deploy the template again to Azure, use one of the deployment files inside the container. In the case of PowerShell, right-click on `deploy.ps1` and select **Run with PowerShell**. Fill in the subscription ID, provide the resource group name and deployment name, and log in using your Azure credentials. This will start the deployment.

 Creating ARM templates can be part of the exam questions, so I strongly advise you to take the time to familiarize yourself with the syntax and the code blocks that are part of the templates.

Summary

In this chapter, we covered the first part of the *Deploying and Managing Virtual Machines* objective by covering how to create and configure VMs for Windows and Linux. You learned about the various aspects and parts that are created when you deploy a VM in Azure. We also covered how to automate the deployment of VMs using scale sets and ARM templates.

In the next chapter, we will continue with the second part of the *Deploying and Managing Virtual Machines* objective by covering how to manage Azure VMs and VM backups.

Questions

Answer the following questions to test your knowledge of the information in this chapter. You can find the answers in the *Assessments* section at the end of this book:

1. Can you use VM scale sets to automate the deployment of multiple VMs?
   - Yes
   - No

2. Can you use availability sets for spreading VMs across update and fault domains?
   - Yes
   - No

3. Do you have to define resource providers in your ARM templates to deploy the various resources in Azure?
    - Yes
    - No

Further reading

You can check out the following links for more information about the topics that were covered in this chapter:

- *Linux Virtual Machines*: https://docs.microsoft.com/en-us/azure/virtual-machines/linux/
- *Quickstart: Create a Linux virtual machine in the Azure portal*: https://docs.microsoft.com/en-us/azure/virtual-machines/linux/quick-create-portal
- *Virtual Machine Scale Sets Documentation*: https://docs.microsoft.com/en-us/azure/virtual-machine-scale-sets/
- *Manage the availability of Windows virtual machines in Azure*: https://docs.microsoft.com/en-us/azure/virtual-machines/windows/manage-availability
- *Azure Resource Manager overview*: https://docs.microsoft.com/en-us/azure/azure-resource-manager/resource-group-overview
- *Understand the structure and syntax of Azure Resource Manager templates*: https://docs.microsoft.com/en-us/azure/azure-resource-manager/resource-group-authoring-templates
- *Quickstart: Create and deploy Azure Resource Manager templates by using the Azure portal*: https://docs.microsoft.com/en-us/azure/azure-resource-manager/resource-manager-quickstart-create-templates-use-the-portal?toc=%2Fazure%2Ftemplates%2Ftoc.jsonbc=%2Fazure%2Ftemplates%2Fbreadcrumb%2Ftoc.json
- *Deploy resources with Resource Manager templates and Azure PowerShell*: https://docs.microsoft.com/en-us/azure/azure-resource-manager/resource-group-template-deploy
- *Azure Quickstart Templates*: https://azure.microsoft.com/en-us/resources/templates/
- *Define resources in Azure Resource Manager templates*: https://docs.microsoft.com/en-us/azure/templates/

Managing Azure VMs and VM Backups

8

In the previous chapter, we covered **Virtual Machines** (**VMs**) in Azure and how to create and configure them from the Azure portal and PowerShell. We also looked at how to automate these steps using ARM templates.

This chapter continues with the second part of *Deploying and Managing Virtual Machines* objective. In this chapter, we are going to focus on the different ways you can manage your VMs after creation. You will learn how to resize and deploy your VMs using the Azure portal, PowerShell, and CLI. You will also learn how to add additional data disks and network interfaces to your VMs. We are going to cover how you can automate the configuration management of your virtual machines, and you will learn how to configure backup and restore operations for your VMs.

The following topics will be covered in this chapter:

- Managing VM sizes
- Redeploying VMs
- Moving VMs
- Adding data disks and network interfaces
- Automating configuration management
- Configuring VM backup and restore operations

Technical requirements

This chapter uses Azure PowerShell (`https://docs.microsoft.com/en-us/powershell/azure/install-az-ps?view=azps-1.8.0`) for examples.

Managing VM sizes

In the first part of this chapter, we are going to look at some management capabilities for virtual machines. After creation, you can manage and change (vertical scale) the sizes of Windows and Linux VMs from the Azure portal, PowerShell, and CLI. **Vertical scaling,** also known as **scale up** and **scale down**, means increasing or decreasing VM sizes in response to different workloads.

In the upcoming demonstrations, we are going to resize VMs using the Azure portal and CLI.

Resizing a VM in the Azure portal

To manage and change the sizes of the VMs to scale up and down from the Azure portal, you have to take the following steps:

1. Navigate to the Azure portal by opening `https://portal.azure.com`.
2. Go to the overview blade of one of the VMs that we created earlier or create a new one.
3. Under **Settings**, select **Size**.
4. In the **Size** overview blade, you can easily select another VM size. In the top menu, there are different filters. You can filter on the different sizes, the VM generation type, the different VM types, the disk type, and you can add your own filter to it as well. Once you have selected the VM size, click the **Resize** button to actually resize it:

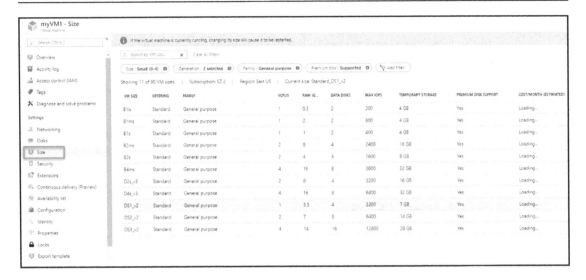

Resizing the VM

5. If the VM is currently running, then the changing its size will be implemented when the VM is restarted.

In the next section, we are going to resize the same VM using the CLI.

Resizing a VM using the CLI

You can also resize your VM using the CLI. You can run CLI scripts from the Azure Cloud Shell or from your local file system. You can use the Azure Cloud Shell for PowerShell scripts and commands as well. We are going to resize the VM from Azure Cloud Shell using the CLI in this demonstration.

To resize a VM using the CLI, you have to perform the following steps:

1. Navigate to the Azure portal by opening `https://portal.azure.com`.
2. Open Azure Cloud Shell by clicking the following menu item in the top-right menu in the Azure portal:

Opening Azure Cloud Shell

3. Make sure that the Bash shell is selected.

4. Add the following line of code to list the different available machine sizes for your region:

```
az vm list-vm-resize-options --resource-group PacktVMResourceGroup
--name myVM1 --output table
```

5. To resize your VM to a different size, add the following line of code. If the size is not available, you can replace the required VM size with one that is available for your subscription or region:

```
az vm resize --resource-group PacktVMResourceGroup --name myVM1 --
size Standard_DS3_v2
```

We have now resized our VM using the Azure portal and CLI. In the next section, we are going to move VMs across different regions and redeploy them.

Redeploying VMs

You can also redeploy the VMs after their creation. This can be helpful when you are facing difficulties troubleshooting **Remote Desktop Protocol (RDP)** connections or application access to Windows and Linux VMs. When you redeploy a VM, Azure will shut down the VM, move the VM to a new node within the Azure infrastructure, and then power it back on. All your configuration options and associated resources will remain during redeployment. After you redeploy a VM, the temporary disk is lost and any dynamic IP addresses associated with the virtual network interface are updated.

Redeploying Windows VMs can easily be done from the Azure portal, using PowerShell and the CLI as well. In the next demonstration, we are going to redeploy a VM from the Azure portal and PowerShell.

Redeploying a VM from the Azure portal

To redeploy a VM from the Azure portal, you have to take the following steps:

1. Navigate to the Azure portal by opening https://portal.azure.com.

2. Again, go to the overview blade of one of the VMs that we created earlier or create a new one.

3. Under **Support + troubleshooting**, select **Redeploy**. This will open the **Redeploy** blade, where you can select the **Redeploy** button to redeploy the VM:

Redeploying the VM

4. The VM will be unavailable during redeployment.

In the next demonstration, we are going to redeploy the same VM using PowerShell.

Redeploying a VM from PowerShell

To redeploy a VM from PowerShell, you have to take the following steps:

1. Navigate to the Azure portal by opening `https://portal.azure.com`.
2. Open the Azure Cloud Shell again by clicking the following menu item in the top-right menu in the Azure portal.
3. Make sure that this time **PowerShell** is selected.
4. Add the following line of code to redeploy the VM:

```
Set-AzVM -Redeploy -ResourceGroupName "PacktVMResourceGroup" -Name
"myVM1"
```

We have now covered most of the different ways to redeploy your VMs. In the next section, we are going to add extra data disks and network interfaces to a VM.

Moving VMs

You can also move VMs and other resources across different subscriptions and resource groups. You can move resources using the Azure portal, Azure PowerShell, Azure CLI, or the REST API to move resources.

When you move a VM to another resource group, both the source and the target are locked during the operation. Also, write and delete operations are blocked on the resource group until it has completely finished moving the VM. By locking these two operations, you can't add, update, or delete any resource in the resource group. However, applications that use these resources, for instance when you move an Azure SQL database to another resource group, will not experience any downtime.

Moving a resource only moves it to a new resource group. The actual location will remain the same, and this cannot be changed. Even when the new resource group is deployed in another location, the moved resource will still remain in the original location.

There are limitations for moving resources across different subscriptions and resource groups. This can be part of the exam questions. For more information, you can refer to the documentation at: `https://docs.microsoft.com/en-us/azure/azure-resource-manager/resource-group-move-resources`.

Adding data disks and network interfaces

You can add a new managed data disk and extra network interfaces to a Windows VM by using the Azure portal, PowerShell, and CLI. The size of the VM determines how many data disks you can attach to one single VM.

Adding a data disk

To add a data disk from the Azure portal, you have to perform the following steps:

1. Navigate to the Azure portal by opening `https://portal.azure.com`.
2. Go to the overview blade of one of the VMs that we created earlier.
3. Under **Settings**, select **Disks**. Click the **Add data disk** button:

Adding a data disk

4. You can now add an existing disk or create a new disk. We don't have an extra disk in place, so select **Create disk**:

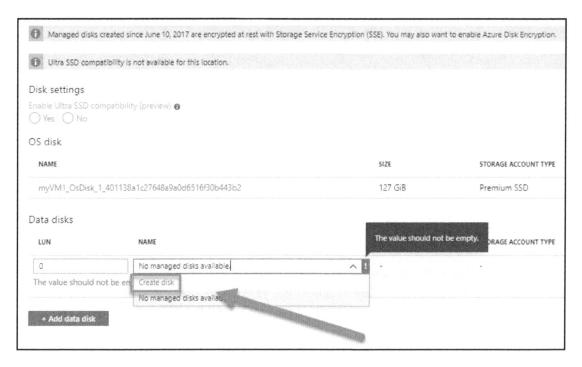

Creating a new disk

5. In the **Create managed disk** blade, add the following values:
    - **Disk name**: PacktDisk2.
    - **Resource group**: Keep the default selected group here.
    - **Account type**: Here, you can select three different options: **Standard HHD**, **Standard SSD**, and **Premium SSD**. Select any one.
    - **Size**: Keep the default size here.
    - **Source type**: Here, you can select three different options as well: **None**, **Snapshot**, **Storage Blob**. Select **None**:

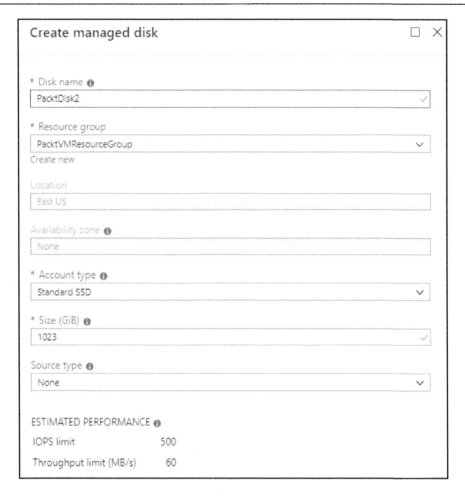

* Disk name ⓘ

PacktDisk2

* Resource group

PacktVMResourceGroup

Create new

Location

East US

Availability zone ⓘ

None

* Account type ⓘ

Standard SSD

* Size (GiB) ⓘ

1023

Source type ⓘ

None

ESTIMATED PERFORMANCE ⓘ

IOPS limit   500

Throughput limit (MB/s)   60

Disk settings

6. Click **Create** to create the disk.

The disk is now added to the VM. To initialize the new data disk, you can log into your server and create a new volume inside **Disk management**. After this, you can format the disk to complete the initialization of it.

Adding a network interface

To add an extra network interface to the VM from the Azure portal, you have to perform
the following steps:

1. From the **Overview** blade of the virtual machine, under **Settings**,
   select **Networking**. In there, click **Attach network interface**:

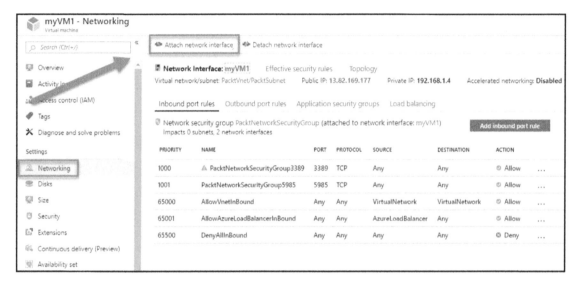

Adding a network interface

2. A popup will be displayed where you have to click the **Create network interface** to create a new network interface. You can also add existing network interfaces here:

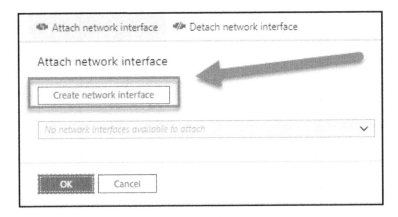

Creating a new network interface

3. In the **Create network interface** blade, add the following values:
    *   **Name**: PacktNIC.
    *   **Subnet**: Select the default subnet here.
    *   **Private IP address assignment**: Choose either **Dynamic** or **Static**.

- **Resource group**: Keep the default selected here:

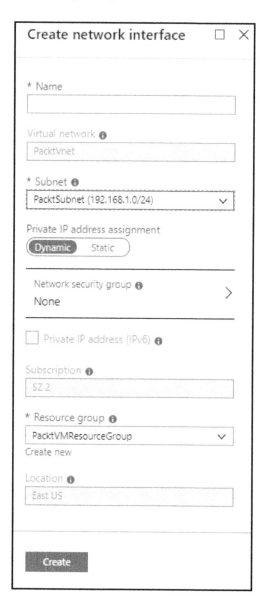

Network interface settings

4. Click **Create**.

The network interface is now added to the VM and can be configured by logging into the VM and by configuring the network adapter.

In the preceding sections, we managed our VMs using manual actions or single scripts. In the next part of this chapter, we are going to look at automating configuration management for our VMs.

Automating configuration management

There are various ways in Azure to automate the creation and the configuration of your infrastructure. You can use ARM templates to deploy your infrastructure as a code, or use Azure Automation, PowerShell scripts and more.

When the different Azure resources are deployed, there are some tools that you can use to manage the configuration of the resources. For example, when you want to automate the configuration of your VMs, Azure provides the following tools:

- **Chef**: Chef is a third-party solution that offers a DevOps automation platform for Linux, Windows, and macOS devices. It can be used for virtual and physical server configurations. It requires an agent to be installed on the virtual machines or servers, which connects to the Chef server to check whether there are available updates and other configurations for the machines. You can use the **Chef Automate** platform to package and deploy applications as well.
- **Puppet**: Puppet is a third-party solution as well, and it has similar capabilities to Chef. You can enable support for Puppet when you create a virtual machine from the Azure portal automatically. You can add it as an extension when you create a new virtual machine. It will install the Puppet agent, which connects to the Puppet master server.
- **Desired State Configuration (DSC)**: DSC is the process of forcing a configuration on a system. It uses configuration files that consist of PowerShell scripts. These scripts are responsible for making the required configurations to the system and for ensuring that these systems stay in sync. So, for example, when you have created a DSC file to configure IIS on a Windows Server and this is removed by an administrator, the DSC file will reinstall and configure IIS again.

- **Custom Script Extensions**: You can configure software installation tasks and various post deployment, configuration, and management tasks using Custom Script Extensions. Scripts can be downloaded from Azure storage or GitHub, or provided to the Azure portal at extension runtime, and are executed on the VMs. You can integrate Custom Script Extensions with ARM templates, and you can run them using PowerShell, CLI, the VM REST API, and the Azure portal.

Configuring VM backup and restore operations

In this demonstration, we will be performing a backup and restore operation for a VM. We are going to backup the VM that we used throughout this chapter and restore it from a **Recovery Services vault**.

Creating a Recovery Services vault

The first step is to create a Recovery Services vault, which can be used to store backups.

We are going to create the Recovery Services vault in Azure. You can create this using the Azure portal, PowerShell, and CLI. We are going to create the vault from the Azure portal. To create this, perform the following steps:

1. Navigate to the Azure portal by opening `https://portal.azure.com`.
2. Create a new resource. Then, select **Management tools** and then **Backup and Site Recovery**.
3. Add the following values to create a new vault:
    - **Name**: `PacktVMVault`.
    - **Subscription**: Select a subscription here.
    - **Resource group**: Create a new one and call it `PacktVMVault`.

- **Location**: Pick a location:

Recovery Services vault

Recovery Services vault

* Name

PacktVMVault

* Subscription

Microsoft Azure Sponsorship

* Resource group

(New) PacktVMVault

Create new

* Location

East US 2

Create   Automation options

Creating a new Recovery Services vault

4. Click the **Create** button.

We have now created a **Recovery Services vault**, which we can use to restore backups. We will create and configure a backup policy in the next section.

Creating and configuring a backup policy

From the **Recovery Services vault** overview blade, you can configure a backup policy. In this demonstration, we are going to configure one. Therefore, perform the following steps:

1. Navigate to the Azure portal by opening `https://portal.azure.com`.
2. Open the Recovery Services vault that we created in the previous step.

3. In the top menu, click **+ Backup**:

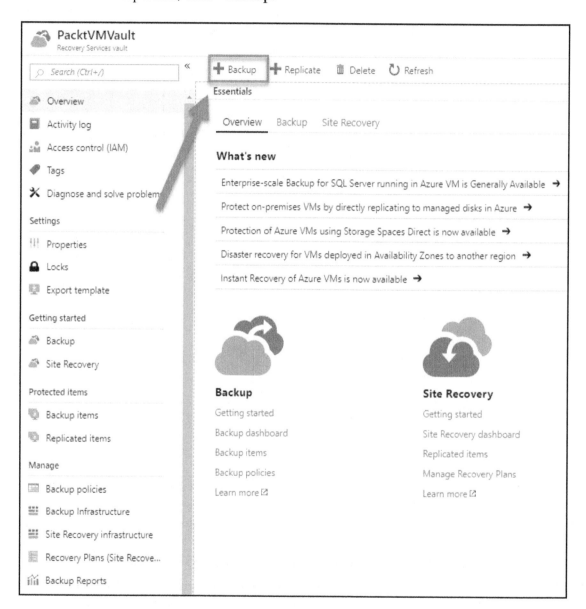

Creating a new backup

4. In the next screen, select the following and click **Backup**:

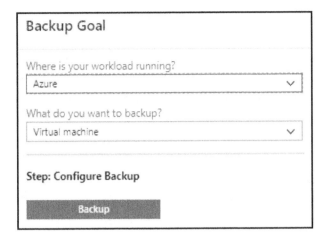

Setting a backup goal

5. Now we need to select a backup policy. We can use the default policy that is created for us by Azure, and which makes a daily backup, or we can create a custom policy in here. Under **Choose backup policy**, select **Create New**:

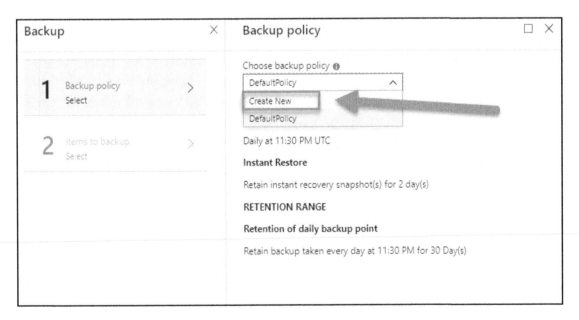

Creating a new backup policy

6. For the new policy, fill in the following values:

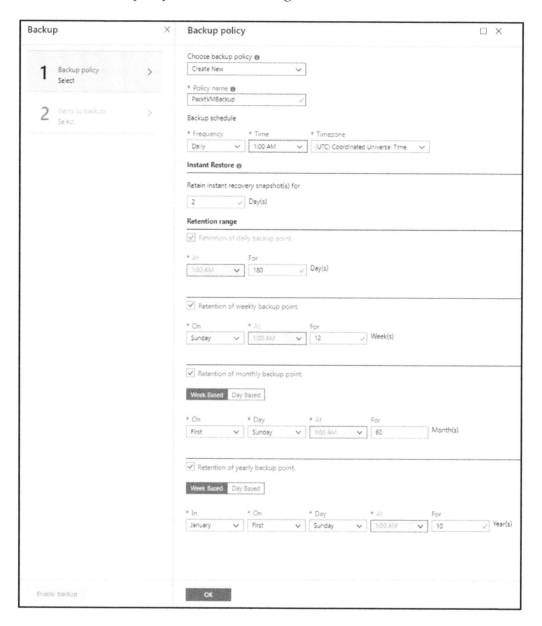

Creating a backup policy

7. Once you have filled in all the values, click **OK**.

8. Then we have to select the VMs that we want to backup. Select them and click **OK**:

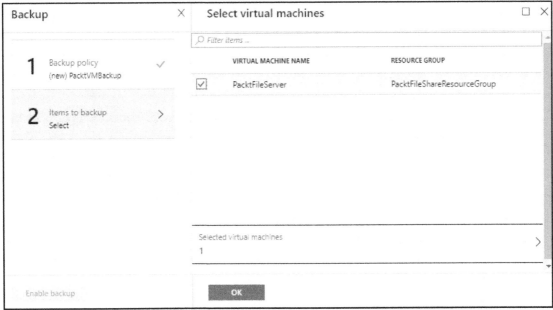

Selecting the VM to backup

9. Click **Enable backup**.

10. The VM will now be backed up every day at the same time.

11. If you open the VM overview blade, under **Operations**, select **Backup**. You will see that there is a backup policy applied and that the **Recovery Services vault** is displayed as well. Click **Backup now** in the top menu to perform a manual backup:

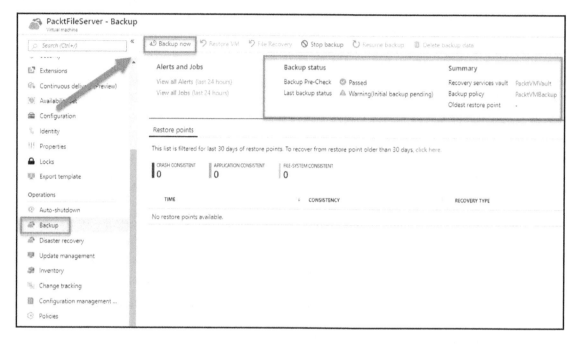

Backing up the VM

12. Keep the default retaining date and click **OK**.

13. Select **View all Jobs** to see the progress of the backup:

Backup jobs

14. All the jobs are displayed in the list:

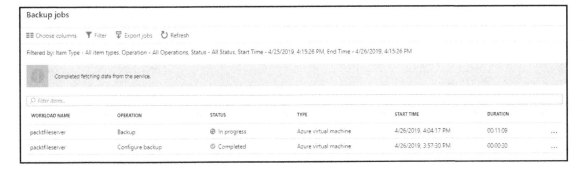

List of backups

When the backup is created, we can restore it. In the next and last section of this demonstration, we are going to restore the backup of the VM.

Restoring a backup

In this last demonstration, we are going to restore the backup of the VM that we created. Therefore, take the following steps:

1. In the **Overview** blade of the **Backup** section of the VM, select **Restore VM** in the top menu:

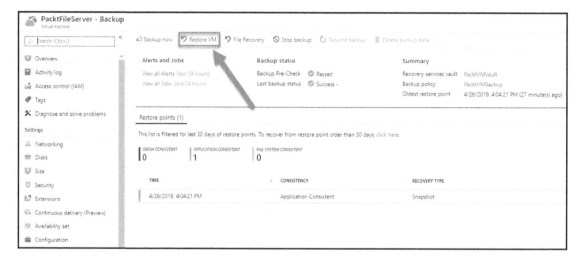

Restoring the backup

2. Select the restore point from the list and click **OK**:

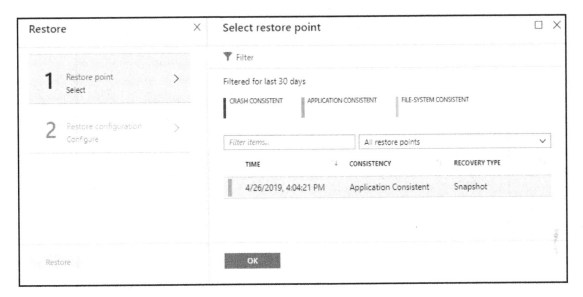

Selecting a restore point

3. In the next blade, you can set the restore configuration. You can choose between creating a new VM or replacing a VM. Select **Replace existing** and select the following values:

Setting the restore configuration

4. Make sure that the VM is turned off.
5. Click **OK** and **Restore**.

The backup will now be restored and the existing VM will be replaced by the backup.

 Azure Site Recovery is already covered in `Chapter 6`, *Configuring Azure Files and Implementing Azure Backup*. For more information about what features and capabilities it has to offer, you can refer to that chapter.

Summary

In this chapter, we covered how to manage your VMs and how to implement VM backups. We also covered how to manage your VMs from the Azure portal, and how to move and redeploy them using PowerShell and CLI. We looked into the automation of configuration management and we took a deep dive into Azure backup and restore operations for your VMs.

In the next chapter, we will begin with the first part of the *Deploying and Managing Virtual Networks* objective by covering how to implement and manage virtual networking.

Questions

Answer the following questions to test your knowledge of the information in this chapter. You can find the answers in the *Assessments* section at the end of this book:

1. Can you use both PowerShell and the CLI to move, redeploy, and resize your Windows and Linux VMs?
    - Yes
    - No

2. Can you only add extra data disks and network interfaces from the Azure portal?
    - Yes
    - No

3. Can you use Custom Script Extensions to configure macOS machines after deployment?
    - Yes
    - No

Further reading

You can check out the following links for more information about the topics that were covered in this chapter:

- *Resize a Windows VM*: `https://docs.microsoft.com/en-us/azure/virtual-machines/windows/resize-vm`.
- *Resize a Linux virtual machine using Azure CLI*: `https://docs.microsoft.com/en-us/azure/virtual-machines/linux/change-vm-size`.
- *Redeploy Windows virtual machine to new Azure node*: `https://docs.microsoft.com/en-us/azure/virtual-machines/troubleshooting/redeploy-to-new-node-windows`.
- *Redeploy Linux virtual machine to new Azure node*: `https://docs.microsoft.com/en-us/azure/virtual-machines/troubleshooting/redeploy-to-new-node-linux`.
- *Attach a data disk to a Windows VM with PowerShell*: `https://docs.microsoft.com/en-us/azure/virtual-machines/windows/attach-disk-ps`.
- *Move Azure VMs to another region*: `https://docs.microsoft.com/en-us/azure/site-recovery/azure-to-azure-tutorial-migrate?toc=%2fazure%2fvirtual-machines%2flinux%2ftoc.json`.
- *Custom Script Extension for Windows*: `https://docs.microsoft.com/en-us/azure/virtual-machines/extensions/custom-script-windows`.
- *Windows PowerShell Desired State Configuration Overview*: `https://docs.microsoft.com/en-us/powershell/dsc/overview/overview`.
- *What is Azure Backup?*: `https://docs.microsoft.com/en-us/azure/backup/backup-overview`.
- *About Site Recovery*: `https://docs.microsoft.com/en-us/azure/site-recovery/site-recovery-overview`.

Section 4: Deploying and Managing Virtual Networks

In this section, you will learn how to deploy and manage virtual networks in Azure.

The following chapters will be covered in this section:

9
Implementing and Managing Virtual Networking

In the previous chapter, we covered the last part of the *Deploying and Managing Virtual Machines* objective by covering how to manage Azure VMs and VM backups.

This chapter introduces the new objective, *Deploying and Managing Virtual Networks*. In this chapter, we are going to focus on virtual networking in Azure and how you can implement and manage this. You will learn about the basics of Azure virtual networking, including private and public IP addresses, and you will learn how to configure subnets, **Virtual Networks** (**VNets**), and public and private IP addresses. To finish this chapter, we are going to configure VNet peering.

The following topics will be covered in this chapter:

- Azure VNet
- IP addresses
- Configuring subnets and VNets
- Configuring private and public IP addresses
- Creating and configuring VNet peering

Technical requirements

This chapter uses Azure PowerShell for examples. For more details visit `https://docs.microsoft.com/en-us/powershell/azure/install-az-ps?view=azps-1.8.0`.

The source code for our sample application can be downloaded from `https://github.com/PacktPublishing/Microsoft-Azure-Administrator-Exam-Guide-AZ-103/tree/master/Chapter09`.

Azure VNet

An Azure VNet is a virtual representation of a traditional network, hosted in the cloud. It is totally software-based, whereas traditional networks use cables, routers, and more. VNets provide a secure and isolated environment, and they connect Azure resources with each other. By default, the different resources are not reachable from outside of the VNet. However, you can connect multiple VNets to each other or connect a VNet to your on-premises network as well. All the Azure resources that are connected to each other inside the same VNet must reside in the same region and subscription.

When you create a VNet, one subnet is automatically created for you. You can create multiple subnets inside the same VNet (with a maximum of 1,000 subnets per VNet). Connecting multiple VNets together is called VNet peering. A maximum of 10 peerings are allowed per Azure subscription.

The smallest subnet that can be used in Azure is the /29 subnet, which consists of eight addresses, and the largest is /8, which consists of 16 million addresses.

For more information on subnetting, you can refer to the *Subnet Mask Cheat Sheet*: https://www.aelius.com/njh/subnet_sheet.html.

IP addresses

A VNet in Azure can have private and public IP addresses. Private IP addresses are only accessible from within the VNet, and public IP addresses can be accessed from the internet as well. You can access private IP addresses from a VPN gateway or an ExpressRoute connection. Both private and public IP addresses can be static or dynamic, but when you create a new VNet, the IP address is static by default. You can change the IP address to *static* from the Azure portal, PowerShell, and CLI. The following are the two states of IP address:

- **Dynamic**: Dynamic IP addresses are assigned by Azure automatically and are selected from the configured subnet's address range from the virtual network where the Azure resource resides. The IP address is assigned to the Azure resource upon creation or start. The IP address will then be released when the resource is stopped and deallocated (when you stop the VM from the Azure portal, the VM is deallocated automatically), and added back to the pool of available addresses inside the subnet by Azure.

- **Static**: Static IP addresses (private and public) are preassigned and will remain the same until you delete the assignment. You can select a static private IP address manually. They can only be assigned to non-internet-facing connections, such as an internal load balancer. You can assign a private static IP address to a connection of your on-premises network or to an ExpressRoute circuit. Public static IP addresses are created by Azure automatically, and they can be assigned to internet-facing connections, such as an external load balancer.

Public IP address

Public IP addresses can be used for internal communication between Azure services and external communication over the internet. You can use IPv4 and IPv6 for public IP addresses, but support for IPv6 is limited. At the time of writing, you can only assign IPv6 addresses to external load balancers.

When the Azure resource is started or created, Azure will assign the public IP address to the network interface of the VNet. When an outbound connection is initiated, Azure will map the private IP address to the public IP addresses, that is, **source network address translation (SNAT)**.

Azure assigns the public IP address to the network interface when the Azure resource is started or created. When an outbound connection is initiated, Azure will map the private IP address to the public IP address (SNAT). Return traffic to the resource is allowed as well. Public IP addresses are typically used for VMs, internet-facing load balancers, VPN gateways, and application gateways. There is a maximum of 60 dynamic public IP addresses and 20 static public IP addresses per subscription. The first five static IP address are free to use.

Private IP addresses

Private IP addresses support IPv4 and IPv6 as well, but support for IPv6 is limited. They can only be assigned dynamically, and IPv6 addresses cannot communicate with each other inside a VNet. The only way to use IPv6 addresses is by assigning them to an internet-facing load balancer, where the frontend IP address is an IPv4 address and the backend is an IPV6 address. Private IP addresses are typically used for VMs, internal load balancers, and application gateways. Because of the fact that a VPN is always internet-facing, it cannot have a private IP address. There is a maximum amount of 4,096 private IP addresses per VNet. However, you can create multiple VNets (with a maximum amount of 50 VNets per subscription).

These limits are based on the default limits from the following page: `https://docs.microsoft.com/en-us/azure/azure-subscription-service-limits?toc=%2fazure%2fvirtual-network%2ftoc.json#networking-limits`. You can open a support request to raise the limits.

Now that we have some background information about the various networking aspects in Azure, we can configure a virtual network with a subnet.

Configuring virtual networks and subnets

In this demonstration, we are going to create and configure a virtual network and a subnet from the Azure portal. We already created both of these in earlier demonstrations, for instance, when we created VMs. We are now going to cover this topic in more detail.

In the next demonstration, we are going to configure a virtual network and a subnet using PowerShell. Therefore, we have to take the following steps:

1. First, we need to log in to the Azure account as follows:

    ```
    Connect-AzAccount
    ```

2. If necessary, select the right subscription as follows:

    ```
    Select-AzSubscription -SubscriptionId "********-****-****-****-************"
    ```

3. Create a resource group for the VNet as follows:

    ```
    New-AzResourceGroup -Name PacktVNetResourceGroup -Location EastUS
    ```

4. Next, we can create the VNet as follows:

    ```
    $virtualNetwork = New-AzVirtualNetwork `
      -ResourceGroupName PacktVNetResourceGroup `
      -Location EastUS `
      -Name PacktVirtualNetwork `
      -AddressPrefix 10.0.0.0/16
    ```

5. Then, create the subnet as follows:

    ```
    $subnetConfig = Add-AzVirtualNetworkSubnetConfig `
      -Name default `
      -AddressPrefix 10.0.0.0/24 `
      -VirtualNetwork $virtualNetwork
    ```

6. Last, associate the subnet to the virtual network as follows:

```
$virtualNetwork | Set-AzVirtualNetwork
```

We have now created a VNet and a subnet from PowerShell. We will use this for later demonstrations in this chapter. In the next section, we are going to configure a private and a public IP address in PowerShell, and associate them to this VNet.

Configuring private and public IP addresses

In this demonstration, we are going to configure a private and a public IP address. When we created the VNet, a private IP address was already created for us automatically by Azure. However, we are going to create another in this demonstration and associate it, together with the public IP address, to a **network interface card** (**NIC**). To configure a private and public IP address from PowerShell, you have to take the following steps:

1. In the same PowerShell window, add the following code to retrieve the VNet and subnet configuration:

```
$vnet = Get-AzVirtualNetwork -Name PacktVirtualNetwork -
ResourceGroupName PacktVNetResourceGroup
$subnet = Get-AzVirtualNetworkSubnetConfig -Name default -
VirtualNetwork $vnet
```

2. Next, create a private and public IP address and assign them to the configuration as follows:

```
$publicIP = New-AzPublicIpAddress `
    -Name PacktPublicIP `
    -ResourceGroupName PacktVNetResourceGroup `
    -AllocationMethod Dynamic `
    -Location EastUS

$IpConfig = New-AzNetworkInterfaceIpConfig `
  -Name PacktPrivateIP `
  -Subnet $subnet `
  -PrivateIpAddress 10.0.0.4 `
  -PublicIPAddress $publicIP `
  -Primary
```

3. Then, create a network interface and assign the configuration to it as follows:

```
$NIC = New-AzNetworkInterface `
  -Name PacktNIC `
  -ResourceGroupName PacktVNetResourceGroup `
  -Location EastUS `
  -IpConfiguration $IpConfig
```

We now have configured an NIC, a public, and a private IP address, and associated them with the VNet that we created in the earlier demonstration.

User-defined routes

When you create subnets, Azure creates system routes that enable all resources in a subnet to communicate with each other. Every subnet has the following default system route table that contains the following minimum routes:

- **Local VNet**: This is a route for resources that reside in the VNet. For these routes, there is no next hop address. If the destination IP address contains the local VNet prefix, traffic is routed there.
- **On-premises**: This is a route for defined on-premises address spaces. For this route, the next hop address will be the VNet gateway. If the destination IP address contains the on-premises address prefix, traffic is routed there.
- **Internet**: This route is for all traffic that goes over the public internet and the internet gateway is always the next hop address. If the destination IP address doesn't contain the VNet or on-premises prefixes, traffic is routed to the internet using **network address translation** (**NAT**).

You can override the system routes by creating **user-defined routes** (**UDRs**). This way, you can force traffic to follow a particular route. For instance, you have a network that consists of two subnets and you want to add a VM that is used as a **demilitarized zone** (**DMZ**) and has a firewall installed on it. You want traffic only to go through the firewall and not between the two subnets. To create UDRs and enable IP forwarding, you have to create a routing table in Azure. When this table is created and there are custom routes in there, Azure prefers the custom routes over the default system routes.

Creating user-defined routes

To create **UDRs**, follow these steps:

1. Navigate to the Azure portal by opening `https://portal.azure.com/`.
2. Click **Create a resource**, type `Route Table` in the search bar, and create a new one.
3. Add the following values, as shown in the following screenshot:
   - **Name**: `PacktRoutingTable`.
   - **Subscription**: Select a subscription.
   - **Resource Group**: Create a new one and call it `PacktRoutingTable`.
   - **Location**: **East US**:

Creating a new route table

4. Click **Create**.

5. A new and empty route table is created. After creation, open the **overview** blade of the route table. To add custom routes, click **Routes** in the left menu as follows:

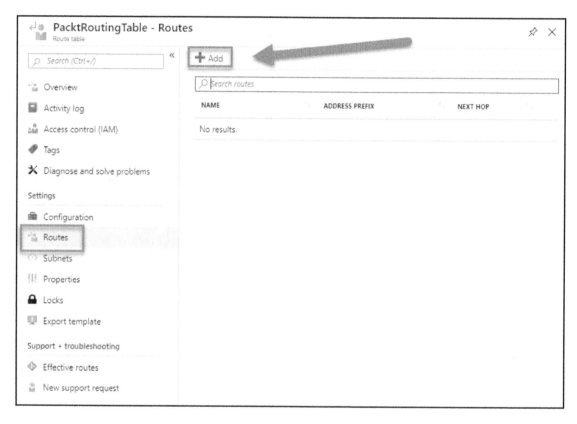

Adding a new route

6. In this example, we want all internet traffic to go through the firewall. So, add the following values, as shown in the following screenshot:
    - **Name**: DefaultRoute.
    - **Address prefix**: 0.0.0.0/0.
    - **Next hop type**: **Virtual appliance**; this is the firewall.

- **Next hop address**: `10.1.1.10`. This will be the internal IP address of the firewall:

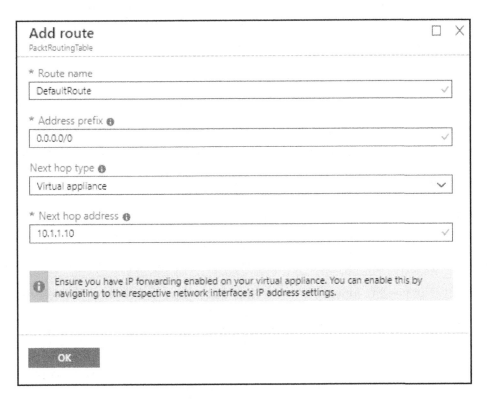

Adding route to table

7. Click **OK**. The route is created for you.

For more detailed instructions on how to create UDRs and a virtual appliance, you can refer to the following tutorial: `https://docs.` `microsoft.com/en-us/azure/virtual-network/tutorial-create-route-` `table-portal`.

We created a custom route table and added a route to it that routes all the traffic to a firewall. In the next section, we are going to look at VNet peering.

VNet peering

VNet peering is a mechanism that seamlessly connects two VNets in the same region through the Azure backbone infrastructure. Once peered, the VNets appear as one for connectivity purposes, just like routing traffic between VMs that are created in the same VNet. The VMs that reside in the peered VNets communicate with each other using private IP addresses.

Azure supports the following two different types of peering:

- **VNet peering**: This is used for connecting VNets in the same Azure region.
- **Global VNet peering**: This is used for connecting VNets across different Azure regions.

The network traffic between peered VNets is private. The traffic is kept on the Microsoft backbone network completely, so there is no need for using any additional gateways, or route traffic over the public internet. There is also no encryption required in the communication between the peered VNets. It uses a low-latency, high-bandwidth connection between the resources in the different virtual networks.

You can use VNet peering for connecting VNets that are created through the resource manager and the classic deployment model together, and it offers the ability to transfer data across Azure regions and Azure subscriptions.

VNet peering is different from using an Azure VPN gateway to connect two VNets together. When you use an Azure VPN Gateway to connect two VNets to each other, it is called a **VNet-to-VNet connection**. This is covered in Chapter 10, *Integrating On-Premise Networks with Azure Virtual Networks*.

Creating and configuring VNet peering

In the next demonstration, we are going to create and configure VNet peering from the Azure portal. We need two VNets for this. We are going to use the VNet that we created in the first demonstration, and we are going to create an additional VNet, which has a different address space than the first VNet. You can't use overlapping address spaces when you peer two VNets together.

To create the VNet and set up VNet peering from the Azure portal, take the following steps:

1. Navigate to the Azure portal by opening https://portal.azure.com/.
2. Click **Create a resource** | **Networking** | **Virtual network**. Create a new VNet.

3. Add the following values:
   - **Name**: `PacktVNetPeering`
   - **Address space**: `10.1.0.0/16`
   - **Subscription**: Pick a subscription
   - **Resource group**: `PacktVNetResourceGroup`
   - **Location**: **East US**
   - **Subnet**: `default`
   - **Address range**: `10.1.0.0/24`

These values are shown in the following screenshot:

Creating an additional VNet

4. Click **Create**.

5. The VNet is created for you. After creation, open the VNet overview blade of the VNet that we created in the first demonstration of this chapter, which is called `PacktVirtualNetwork`, as follows:

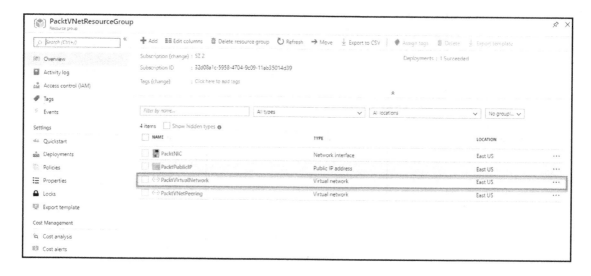

6. Then, under **Settings**, select **Peerings**. Click **Add** in the top menu as follows:

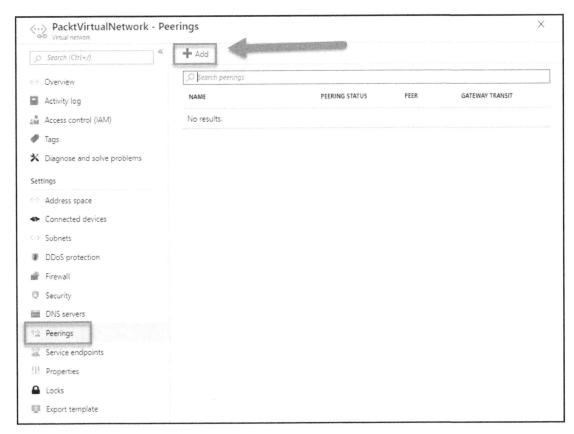

Adding new peering

7. In the **Add peering** blade, add the following values:
   - **Name of the peering from PacktVirtualNetwork to PacktVNetPeering**: `PacktPeering`.
   - **Virtual network deployment model: Resource manager**.
   - **Subscription**: Keep the default selected.
   - **Virtual network:** Select `PacktVNetPeering`.

These values are shown in the following screenshot:

Add peering

8. There are a couple of other settings that you can set here as well. The first one is **Allow forwarded traffic from PacktVirtualNetwork to PacktVNetPeering**: this means that you allow traffic from outside the peered VNet. The second one is **Configure gateway transit settings**: this means that the peered network uses the gateway of this VNet to connect to resources outside the peered VNet, for instance, an on-premises environment. The last one is **Configure Remote Gateway Settings:** for this setting, you have to enable the previous one as well, but by enabling this one, you are using the other VNet gateway to connect resources outside the VNet.

9. Click **OK,** and the peering is created.

We have now configured VNet peering from the Azure portal. This concludes this chapter.

 There are various ways to verify the network connectivity. In Chapter 11, *Monitoring and Troubleshooting Virtual Networking,* this is covered in more detail.

Summary

In this chapter, we covered the first part of the *Deploying and Managing Virtual Networks* objective by covering virtual networking in Azure. We have configured VNets and created private and public IP addresses. We also configured VNet peering from the Azure portal.

In the next chapter, we will continue with this objective, by covering how to integrate an on-premise network with an Azure VNet.

Questions

Answer the following questions to test your knowledge of the information in this chapter. You can find the answers in the *Assessments* section at the end of this book.

1. When you use VNet peering, do you have to create an Azure VPN Gateway to connect both the VNets to each other?
    - Yes
    - No

2. Can you create custom route tables to adjust the routing between the different resources inside your VNets?
   - Yes
   - No

3. Can you assign IPv6 addresses for all Azure resources?
   - Yes
   - No

Further reading

You can check out the following links for more information about the topics that were covered in this chapter:

- *IP address types and allocation methods in Azure*: https://docs.microsoft.com/en-us/azure/virtual-network/virtual-network-ip-addresses-overview-arm
- *Azure Networking Limits*: https://docs.microsoft.com/en-us/azure/azure-subscription-service-limits?toc=%2fazure%2fvirtual-network%2ftoc.json#networking-limits
- *Quickstart: Create a virtual network using the Azure portal*: https://docs.microsoft.com/en-us/azure/virtual-network/quick-create-portal
- *Quickstart: Create a virtual network using PowerShell*: https://docs.microsoft.com/en-us/azure/virtual-network/quick-create-powershell
- *Quickstart: Create a virtual network using the Azure CLI*: https://docs.microsoft.com/en-us/azure/virtual-network/quick-create-cli
- *Add, change, or remove IP addresses for an Azure network interface*: https://docs.microsoft.com/en-us/azure/virtual-network/virtual-network-network-interface-addresses
- *Create, change, or delete a public IP address*: https://docs.microsoft.com/en-us/azure/virtual-network/virtual-network-public-ip-address
- *Tutorial: Route network traffic with a route table using the Azure portal*: https://docs.microsoft.com/en-us/azure/virtual-network/tutorial-create-route-table-portal
- *Virtual network peering*: https://docs.microsoft.com/en-us/azure/virtual-network/virtual-network-peering-overview

10
Integrating On-Premise Networks with Azure Virtual Networks

In the previous chapter, we covered the first part of the *Deploying and Managing Virtual Networks* objective. We covered virtual networking in Azure, and we covered the basics of virtual networking and configured private and public IP addresses. We also covered VNet peering.

This chapter continues with this objective by covering how to integrate your on-premises network with an Azure virtual network. In this chapter, we are going to focus on VPN connections from your on-premises environment to Azure and from Azure to Azure as well. You will learn how to create an Azure VPN gateway, and you will learn how to configure a **Site-to-Site** (**S2S**) VPN using an on-premises server and the Azure VPN gateway. At the end of this chapter, we are going to look at a VNet-to-VNet connection and how this is similar to a S2S VPN.

The following topics will be covered in this chapter:

- Azure VPN gateway
- Creating and configuring an Azure VPN gateway
- Creating and configuring a S2S VPN
- Verifying on-premises connectivity
- VNet-to-VNet

Technical requirements

This chapter uses Azure PowerShell for the examples: `https://docs.microsoft.com/en-us/powershell/azure/install-az-ps?view=azps-1.8.0`.

The source code for this chapter can be downloaded from the following GitHub link `https://github.com/PacktPublishing/Microsoft-Azure-Administrator-Exam-Guide-AZ-103/tree/master/Chapter10`.

Azure VPN gateway

Azure VPN provides a secure gateway that can be used for sending encrypted traffic over the internet, between an Azure virtual network and an on-premises location. This gateway can be used for sending encrypted traffic between different Azure virtual networks and the Microsoft networks as well.

For each virtual network, you can only have one VPN gateway. You can, however, create multiple connections to the same VPN gateway. When creating multiple connections, all of the VPN tunnels will share the available gateway bandwidth.

A **virtual network gateway** is created with two or more virtual machines that are deployed in a **gateway subnet**. This is a specific subnet that is created for the VPN connection. The VMs that are deployed in the gateway subnet are created at the same time the virtual network gateway is created. The VMs are then configured to contain specific gateway services and routing tables to connect to the gateway in Azure. It is not possible to configure the gateway services and routing tables manually.

Azure VPN gateway offers the following pricing tiers:

- **Basic**: This tier provides a maximum of 10 S2S/VNet-to-VNet tunnels and a maximum of 128 **Point-to-Site (P2S)** connections. The average bandwidth is 100 Mbps.
- **VpnGw1**: This tier provides a maximum of 30 S2S/VNet-to-VNet tunnels and a maximum of 128 P2S connections. The average bandwidth is 650 Mbps.
- **VpnGw2**: This tier provides a maximum of 30 S2S/VNet-to-VNet tunnels and a maximum of 128 P2S connections. The average bandwidth is 1 Gbps.
- **VpnGw3**: This tier provides a maximum of 30 S2S/VNet-to-VNet tunnels and a maximum of 128 P2S connections. The average bandwidth is 1.25 Gbps.

S2S VPNs

An S2S VPN gateway connection is a connection over an IPsec/IKE (IKEv1 or IKEv2) VPN tunnel. These connections can be used for hybrid configurations and cross-premises configurations. It is designed to create a secure connection between a location and your virtual network over the internet. The location can be an office, for instance. Once the S2S VPN connection is configured, you can connect from every device from that location to Azure using the same VPN location.

An S2S connection requires a compatible VPN device located on-premises that has a public IP address assigned to it. It should not be located behind a NAT.

For more information about the compatible VPN devices, you can refer to the following documentation: `https://docs.microsoft.com/en-us/azure/vpn-gateway/vpn-gateway-vpn-faq#s2s`.

The following diagram shows a S2S VPN connection from an on-premises environment to Azure:

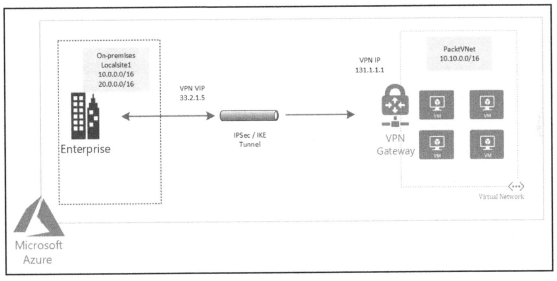

S2S VPN

In the next section, we are going to look at **multi-site VPNs**.

Multi-site VPNs

A multi-site VPN is a variation of the S2S connection. You use this type of connection for connecting to multiple on-premises sites from your virtual network gateway. It is required that multi-site connections use a route-based VPN type gateway. All connections through the gateway will share the available bandwidth. This is because each virtual network can only have one VPN gateway.

The following diagram shows a multi-site VPN connection from an on-premises environment to Azure:

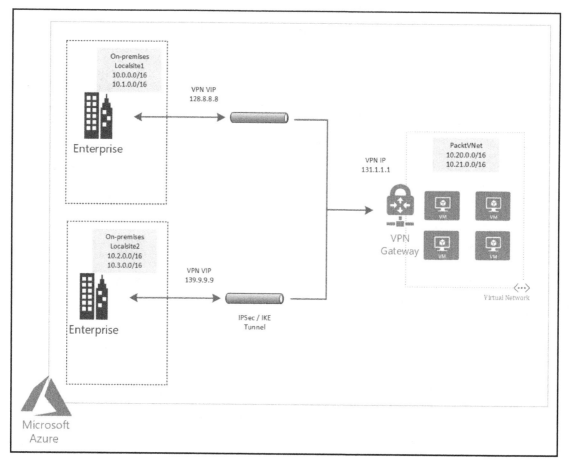

Multi-site VPN

In the next section, we are going to look at the **Point-to-Site (P2S)** VPN.

P2S VPNs

A P2S VPN gateway connection is designed to create a secure connection between an individual client and your virtual network over the internet. It is established from the client computer and is useful for people who are working from different locations, such as from their home or from a hotel. PS2 VPN is also the best solution if you only have a few clients to connect to a virtual network.

A P2S connection does not require an on-premises, public-facing IP address such as S2S VPN connections do. You can use P2S connections together with S2S connections over the same VPN gateway. You need to make sure that the configuration requirements for both connections are compatible so that you can use both connection types over the same gateway.

The following diagram shows a P2S VPN connection from an on-premises environment to Azure:

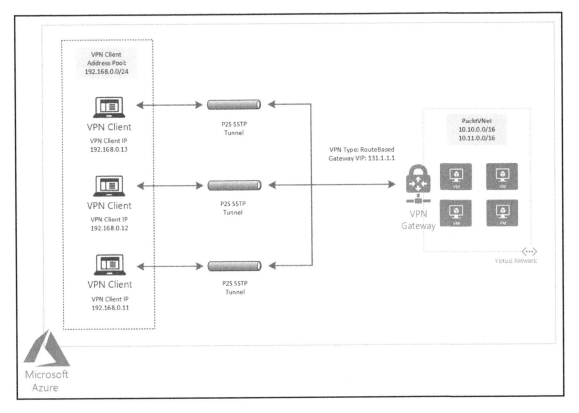

P2S VPN

In the next section, we are going to look at **ExpressRoute**.

ExpressRoute

ExpressRoute offers a private connection that is facilitated by a connectivity provider. ExpressRoute connections don't go over the public internet, but they use a more reliable connection. These types of connections offer lower latencies, higher security, and faster speeds than connections that go over the internet. You can use it to extend your on-premises networks to Azure and Office 365. Connections can be made from an any-to-any (IP VPN) network, a virtual cross-connection at a co-location facility, and a point-to-point Ethernet network connection.

ExpressRoute uses a virtual network gateway, which is configured with a gateway type of ExpressRoute instead of VPN. By default, the traffic is not encrypted, but you can create a solution that encrypts the traffic that goes over the ExpressRoute circuit.

The following diagram shows an ExpressRoute connection from an on-premises environment to Azure:

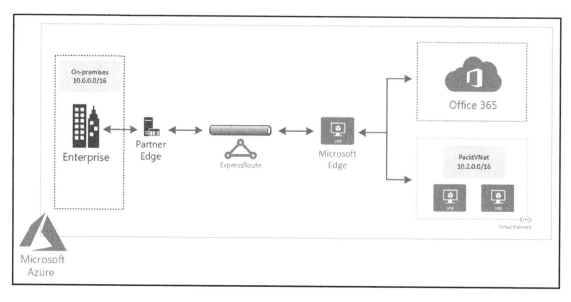

ExpressRoute

Now that we have looked at the different types of VPN connections you can configure, we are now going to create and configure an Azure VPN gateway.

Creating and configuring an Azure VPN gateway

In the upcoming sections, we are going to configure an Azure VPN gateway, configure a S2S VPN, and verify the connectivity between Azure and the on-premises environment.

We are going to use Windows Server 2012 with **Routing and Remote Access Service (RRAS)** enabled on it to serve as the compatible VPN device that is installed on the on-premises environment.

Creating and configuring the on-premises VPN device

First, we are going to set up Windows Server 2012 and activate RRAS on it to set up the VPN. For this demonstration, I've created a virtual machine on my laptop with Windows Server 2012 R2 installed on it. To enable RRAS, perform the following steps:

> Make sure that the network adapter is set to bridged mode. The VPN gateway in Azure can't connect to a VPN that is behind a NAT.

1. Go to **Server Manager** | **Manage** | **Add Roles and Features** to enable RRAS:

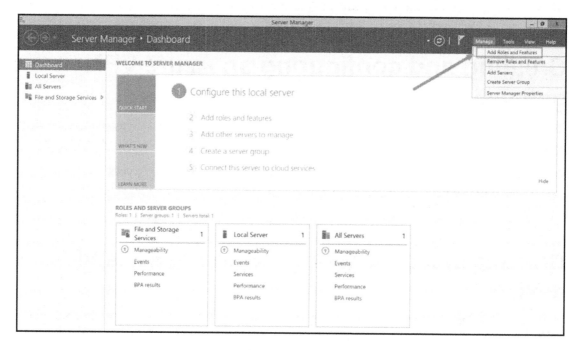

Enabling RRAS on Windows Server 2012

2. Click **Next** on the first screen of the **Add Roles and Features Wizard**. On the next
   screen, select **Role-based or feature-based installation** and click **Next**. Select the
   server and click **Next**. On the **Server Roles** screen, select **Remote Access** and
   click **Next**:

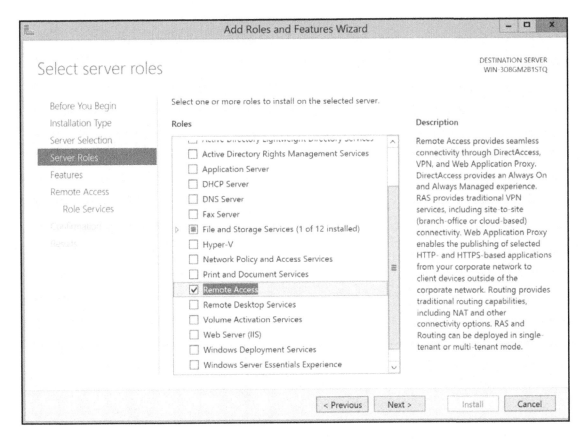

Enabling Remote Access

3. On the **Features** screen, we can click **Next** immediately. On the **Remote Access** screen, click **Next**:

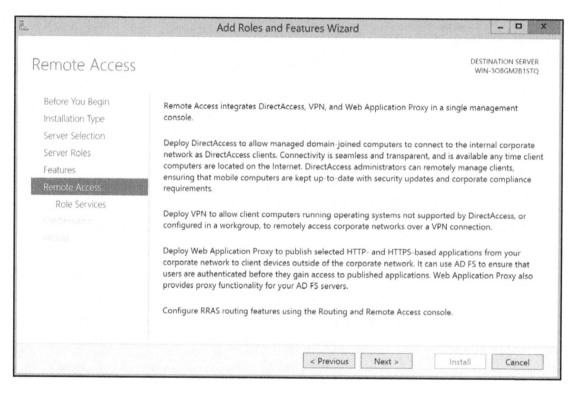

Remote Access

4. On the **Role Services** screen, select **DirectAccess and VPN (RAS)**. A window will pop up asking you to add the required features. Click **Add features** and then click **Next**:

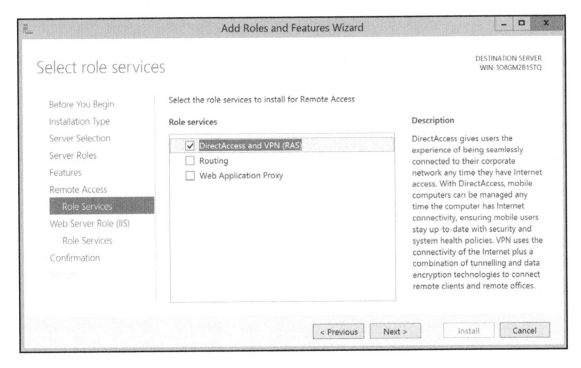

Role Services

5. On the **Web Server Role (IIS)** screen, click **Next**. On the IIS role services screen, keep all of the default settings as they are and click **Next** again. In the last screen, verify the settings and click the **Install** button:

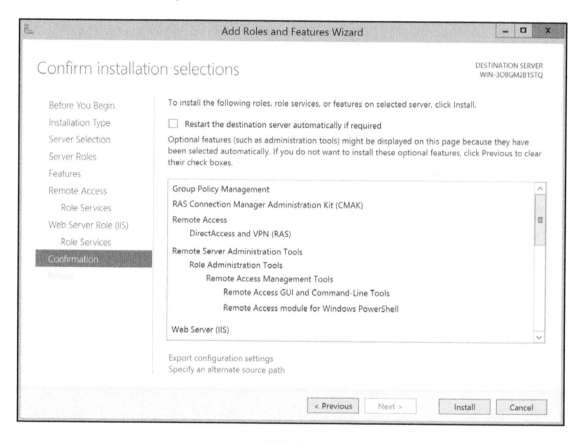

Confirmation

The next step is to configure a VNet.

Creating a virtual network

Now that we've gone through the configuration of the on-premises VPN device, we are going to create a VNet. Therefore, perform the following steps:

1. Navigate to the Azure portal by opening `https://portal.azure.com/`.
2. `Select` **Create a resource** `and then select` **Networking** `and the next` **Virtual network**.
3. In the **Create virtual network** blade, add the following values:
   - **Name:** `PacktVPNVNet`.
   - **Address space:** `172.17.0.0/16`.
   - **Resource group:** Create a new resource group and name it `PacktVPNResourceGroup`.
   - **Location:** **East US**.
   - **Subnet:** **Frontend**.

- **Address range**: `172.17.0.0/24`:

Creating the VNet

4. Click **Create** to create the VNet.

5. Now we need to create a **Gateway subnet** that contains the reserved IP addresses that are used by the virtual network gateway services. Open the VNet resource and under **Settings**, click **Subnets** and then click **+ Gateway subnet** in the top menu:

Adding a gateway subnet

6. In the **Add subnet** blade, adjust the address range to `172.17.255.0/27`:

Adjusting the address range

7. Click **OK**.

Creating an Azure VPN gateway

Now we are going to configure the Azure VPN gateway. Perform the following steps:

1. Navigate to the Azure portal by opening `https://portal.azure.com/`.
2. In the left menu, click **Create a resource** and type `Virtual network gateway` in the search box.
3. In the **Create virtual network gateway**, add the following values:
    - **Name**: `PacktVnetGateway`.
    - **Gateway type**: **VPN**.
    - **VPN type**: **Route-based**.
    - **SKU**: `VpnGw1`.
    - **Location**: **East US**.
    - **Virtual network**: Click **Virtual network/Choose a virtual network**. Select `PacktVPNVNet`.
    - **Public IP address**: In here, you set the public IP address that is associated with the VPN gateway. The Azure VPN gateway only supports dynamically assigned IP addresses.

However, once the IP address is associated with the VPN gateway, it will not change. The IP address will only change when the VPN gateway is recreated or deleted. Leave **Create new** selected. Name the IP address `PacktVNetGWIP`:

Create virtual network gateway	□ ×

Azure has provided a planning and design guide to help you configure the various VPN gateway options. Learn more.

* Name

| PAcktVhetGateway | ✓ |

Gateway type ❶
◉ VPN ○ ExpressRoute

VPN type ❶
◉ Route-based ○ Policy-based

* SKU ❶

| VpnGw1 | ∨ |

☐ Enable active-active mode ❶

* Virtual network ❶

| PacktVPNVNet | › |

* Public IP address ❶
◉ Create new ○ Use existing

| PacktVNetGWIP | ✓ |

∧ Configure public IP address
    SKU
    Basic

    * Assignment
    ◉ Dynamic ○ Static

☐ Configure BGP ASN ❶

* Subscription

| Microsoft Azure Sponsorship | ∨ |

Resource group ❶
PacktVPNResourceGroup

* Location ❶

| East US | ∨ |

Azure recommends using a validated VPN device with your virtual network gateway. To view a list of validated devices and instructions for configuration, refer to Azure's documentation regarding validated VPN devices.

| Create | Automation options |

Gateway settings

4. Click **Create** to create the Azure VPN gateway.

5. We need the public IP address for the VPN gateway later in this demonstration, so go to the overview of the Azure VPN gateway when it has been created. In there, copy the public IP address to Notepad:

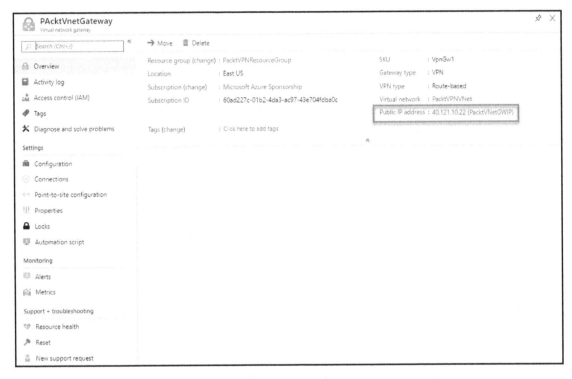

Obtaining the public IP address

6. After the creation of the gateway, open the **Overview** page of the VNet resource that we created earlier. The VPN gateway is displayed on the **Overview** page:

VPN gateway in VNet

The Azure VPN gateway has been created, so we can now set up the S2S VPN connection with the on-premises environment.

Creating and configuring S2S VPN

To create the S2S VPN, we are going to connect the VPN gateway with the on-premises environment we created earlier with RRAS enabled on it. This will serve as a compatible VPN device.

To be able to complete this step, we need the public IP address of the on-premises environment. I've used VMware for this demonstration and set it up in bridged mode. This way, the public IP address of your provider is used. You can check the public IP address using multiple tools, such as https://www.whatsmyip.org/.

Creating the local network gateway

First, we need to create the local network gateway. This refers to the on-premises location where we have Windows Server 2012 R2 installed with RRAS enabled.

To create the local network gateway, perform the following steps:

1. Navigate to the Azure portal by opening `https://portal.azure.com/`.
2. In the left menu, click **Create a resource** and type `Local network gateway` in the search box. Select **Local network gateway** from the list and create a new one.
3. In the **Create local network gateway** screen, add the following values:
   - **Name**: `PacktOnPremisesGateway`.
   - **IP address**: Here, you need to fill in the public IP address from the on-premises VPN device where Azure needs to connect to.
   - **Address space**: `82.173.0.0/16`. This represents the address ranges for the on-premises network. You can add multiple address ranges.
   - **Configure BGP settings**: Don't select this.
   - **Subscription**: Select the same subscription that was used for the previous examples.
   - **Resource group**: Select the resource group that we already created, that is, `PacktVPNResourceGroup`.

- **Location:** Select the same location where the VNet resides, that is, **East US**:

Local network gateway settings

4. Click **Create**.

Configuring the on-premises VPN device

As we described in the previous section, S2S connections require a compatible VPN device. We already configured this in the first step. Now we need to configure this to connect to the Azure VPN gateway.

To configure RRAS so that they can connect to Azure, we need the following artifacts:

- **Shared key**: We are going to create a shared key that is used for connecting to the on-premises device.
- **The public IP address of the Azure VPN gateway**: This is the public IP address that we copied to Notepad in one of the previous steps.

To create a new connection, perform the following steps:

1. Open the local gateway that we created previously and under **Settings**, select **Connections**. Click the **Add** button at the top of the screen:

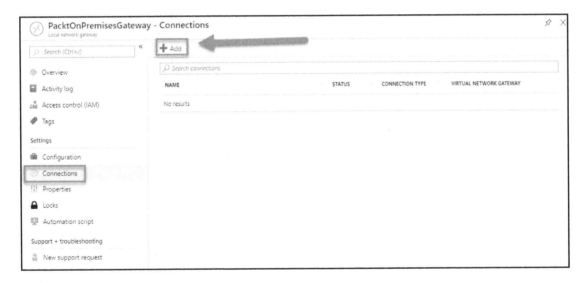

Connections

2. In the **Add connection** blade, add the following values:
   - **Name**: `PacktVNetToSite`.
   - **Connection type**: **Site-to-site (IPSec)**.
   - **Virtual network gateway**: Click **Choose a local network gateway** and select `PacktVNetGateway`.

- **Local network gateway**: This is a fixed value.
- **Shared Key**: This value must be the same as for your local on-premises device. Fill this in with `Packt123`:

Add a connection

3. Click **OK** to create the connection.

4. After creation, you can select the connection from the **Connections** page. From there, you can download the configuration package that can be used to configure the on-premises VPN device. Click **Download configuration** from the top menu:

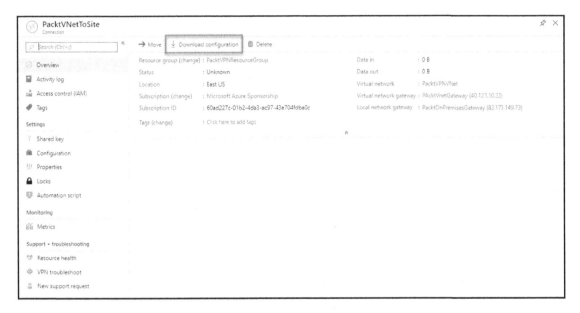

Downloading the configuration package

5. Since we are using RRAS, which is part of Windows Server, we need to select the following values:

- **Device vendor**: Generic Samples.
- **Device family**: Device Parameters.

- **Firmware version**: 1.0:

Downloading configuration

6. Click **Download configuration**.
7. The configuration package consists of a text file with all the necessary configuration values in it.

Switch over to the on-premises VM with Windows Server 2012 R2 on it and RRAS enabled. Perform the following steps on the VPN device with the Azure VPN gateway:

1. Download the script from GitHub. This link is provided under the *Technical requirements* section at the beginning of this chapter. We are going to use this script to configure RRAS. We need to make some adjustments to the script so that we can add the Azure VPN gateway and local network addresses. You can use the IP address and the subnet address from the downloaded configuration file as input.

2. The first part of the script gives some additional information about the script and creates the `Invoke-WindowsApi` function:

```
# Windows Azure Virtual Network

# This configuration template applies to Microsoft RRAS running
on Windows Server 2012 R2.
# It configures an IPSec VPN tunnel connecting your on-premise
VPN device with the Azure gateway.

# !!! Please notice that we have the following restrictions in
our support for RRAS:
# !!! 1. Only IKEv2 is currently supported
# !!! 2. Only route-based VPN configuration is supported.
# !!! 3. Admin privileges are required in order to run this
script

Function Invoke-WindowsApi(
    [string] $dllName,
    [Type] $returnType,
    [string] $methodName,
    [Type[]] $parameterTypes,
    [Object[]] $parameters
    )
```

3. In the next part, we are going to build the dynamic assembly and define the method:

```
{
  ## Begin to build the dynamic assembly
  $domain = [AppDomain]::CurrentDomain
  $name = New-Object Reflection.AssemblyName 'PInvokeAssembly'
  $assembly = $domain.DefineDynamicAssembly($name, 'Run')
  $module = $assembly.DefineDynamicModule('PInvokeModule')
  $type = $module.DefineType('PInvokeType',
"Public,BeforeFieldInit")

  $inputParameters = @()

  for($counter = 1; $counter -le $parameterTypes.Length;
$counter++)
  {
      $inputParameters += $parameters[$counter - 1]
  }

  $method = $type.DefineMethod($methodName,
'Public,HideBySig,Static,PinvokeImpl',$returnType,
$parameterTypes)
```

4. Next, we need to apply the `P/Invoke` constructor, thus creating the temporary type and invoking the method:

```
## Apply the P/Invoke constructor
$ctor =
[Runtime.InteropServices.DllImportAttribute].GetConstructor([st
ring])
    $attr = New-Object Reflection.Emit.CustomAttributeBuilder
$ctor, $dllName
    $method.SetCustomAttribute($attr)

    ## Create the temporary type, and invoke the method.
    $realType = $type.CreateType()

    $ret = $realType.InvokeMember($methodName,
'Public,Static,InvokeMethod', $null, $null, $inputParameters)

    return $ret
}
```

5. Then, we are going to prepare the parameter values and invoke the API:

```
Function Set-PrivateProfileString(
    $file,
    $category,
    $key,
    $value)
{
    ## Prepare the parameter types and parameter values for the
Invoke-WindowsApi script
    $parameterTypes = [string], [string], [string], [string]
    $parameters = [string] $category, [string] $key, [string]
$value, [string] $file

    ## Invoke the API
    [void] (Invoke-WindowsApi "kernel32.dll" ([UInt32])
"WritePrivateProfileString" $parameterTypes $parameters)
}
```

6. Now we are going to install the RRAS role on the server:

```
# Install RRAS role
Import-Module ServerManager
Install-WindowsFeature RemoteAccess -IncludeManagementTools
Add-WindowsFeature -name Routing -IncludeManagementTools

# !!! NOTE: A reboot of the machine might be required here
after which the script can be executed again.
```

7. As we can see, the S2S VPN is installed from here:

```
# Install S2S VPN
Import-Module RemoteAccess
if ((Get-RemoteAccess).VpnS2SStatus -ne "Installed")
{
   Install-RemoteAccess -VpnType VpnS2S
}
```

8. Next, we need to add and configure it:

```
# Add and configure S2S VPN interface

Add-VpnS2SInterface `
 -Protocol IKEv2 `
 -AuthenticationMethod PSKOnly `
 -NumberOfTries 3 `
 -ResponderAuthenticationMethod PSKOnly `
 -Name <IP address of your Azure gateway> `
 -Destination <IP address of your Azure gateway> `
 -IPv4Subnet @("<IP range of your subnet in Azure>:100") `
 -SharedSecret <shared key>

Set-VpnServerIPsecConfiguration `
 -EncryptionType MaximumEncryption

Set-VpnS2Sinterface `
 -Name <IP address of your Azure gateway> `
 -InitiateConfigPayload $false `
 -Force
```

9. In the last part of the script, we are going to set the connection to be persistent, restart the RRAS server, and dial-in to the Azure gateway:

```
# Set S2S VPN connection to be persistent by editing the
router.pbk file (required admin privileges)
Set-PrivateProfileString $env:windir\System32\RRAS\router.pbk
"<IP address of your Azure gateway>" "IdleDisconnectSeconds"
"0"
Set-PrivateProfileString $env:windir\System32\RRAS\router.pbk
"<IP address of your Azure gateway>" "RedialOnLinkFailure" "1"

# Restart the RRAS service
Restart-Service RemoteAccess

# Dial-in to Azure gateway
Connect-VpnS2SInterface `
 -Name <IP address of your Azure gateway>
```

This script will also enable RRAS on your server. We did this manually in one of the first sections, so we have skipped this part.

We have finished configuring the on-premises VPN device. In the next section, we are going to verify on-premises connectivity.

Verifying on-premises connectivity

There are two different ways to verify on-premises connectivity. You can do this using the RRAS console on-premises and in the Azure portal.

To verify the connection using the RRAS console, open Windows search and type `Remote Access Management`. Then, open the node that is displayed in the following screenshot. As you can see, RRAS is connected with the Azure VPN gateway:

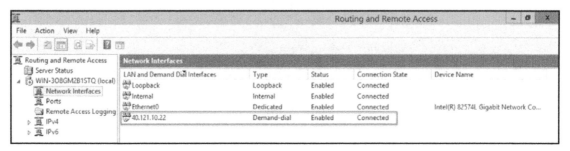

Verifying the connection in the RRAS console

To verify the connection from the Azure portal, perform the following steps:

1. Navigate to the Azure portal by opening `https://portal.azure.com/`.
2. Open the `PAcktVnetGateway` resource and under **Settings**, select **Connections**:

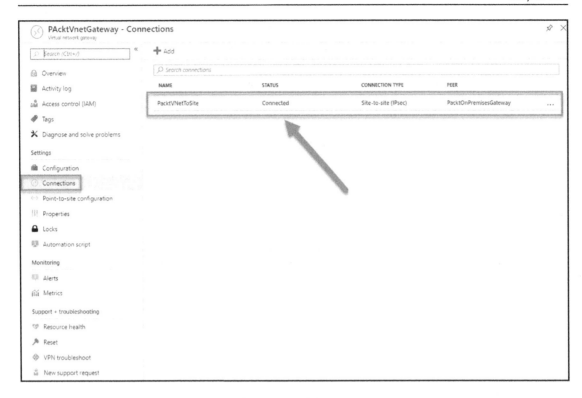

Verifying the connection in the Azure portal

When you select **Connections**, you will be able to see that the
PacktVNetToSite connection is connected, as shown in the preceding screenshot.

VNet-to-VNet

Configuring a VNet-to-VNet connection is a simple way to connect VNets. Connecting a
virtual network to another virtual network is similar to creating a S2S IPSec connection to
an on-premises environment. Both the connection types use the Azure VPN gateway. The
VPN gateway provides a secure tunnel IPsec/IKE and they communicate in the same way.
The difference is in the way the local network gateway is configured.

When you create a VNet-to-VNet connection, the local network gateway address space is automatically created and populated. If you update the address space for one VNet, the other VNet automatically routes to the updated address space. This makes it faster and easier to create a VNet-to-VNet connection than a S2S connection.

To create a VNet-to-VNet connection from the Azure portal, you can refer to the following tutorial: `https://docs.microsoft.com/en-us/azure/ vpn-gateway/vpn-gateway-howto-vnet-vnet-resource-manager-portal`.

Summary

In this chapter, we covered the second part of the *Deploying and Managing Virtual Networks* objective, by covering how to create and configure an Azure VPN gateway, how to create and configure S2S VPNs, and how to verify on-premises connectivity with Azure.

In the next chapter, we will continue with the third part of of the *Deploying and Managing Virtual Networks* objective by covering how to monitor and manage networking.

Questions

Answer the following questions to test your knowledge of the information in this chapter. You can find the answers in the *Assessments* section at the end of this book:

1. ExpressRoute traffic is encrypted by default:
    - Yes
    - No

2. Your organization has a requirement for employees to connect from locations other than the office. Do you need to set up a P2S VPN connection for this?
    - Yes
    - No

3. When you set up the on-premises VPN device for a S2S connection, your server isn't allowed to be behind a NAT:
    - Yes
    - No

Further reading

You can check out the following links for more information about the topics that were covered in this chapter:

- *Azure VPN Gateway Documentation*: `https://docs.microsoft.com/en-us/azure/vpn-gateway/`
- *About Point-to-Site VPN*: `https://docs.microsoft.com/en-us/azure/vpn-gateway/P2S-about`
- *Create a Site-to-Site connection in the Azure portal*: `https://docs.microsoft.com/en-us/azure/vpn-gateway/vpn-gateway-howto-S2S-resource-manager-portal`
- *Create a VNet with a Site-to-Site VPN connection using PowerShell*: `https://docs.microsoft.com/en-us/azure/vpn-gateway/vpn-gateway-create-S2S-rm-powershell`
- *Create a virtual network with a Site-to-Site VPN connection using CLI*: `https://docs.microsoft.com/en-us/azure/vpn-gateway/vpn-gateway-howto-S2S-resource-manager-cli`
- *ExpressRoute overview*: `https://docs.microsoft.com/en-us/azure/expressroute/expressroute-introduction`
- *Create and modify an ExpressRoute circuit*: `https://docs.microsoft.com/en-us/azure/expressroute/expressroute-howto-circuit-portal-resource-manager`
- *Configure a VNet-to-VNet VPN gateway connection by using the Azure portal*: `https://docs.microsoft.com/en-us/azure/vpn-gateway/vpn-gateway-howto-vnet-vnet-resource-manager-portal`

11
Monitoring and Troubleshooting Virtual Networking

In the previous chapter, we covered the second part of the *Deploying and Managing Virtual Networks* objective. We've covered how to integrate your on-premises network with an Azure virtual network.

This chapter covers the third part of the *Deploying and Managing Virtual Networks* objective by covering how to monitor and troubleshoot virtual networking. In this chapter, we are going to focus on how you can monitor your virtual networks using **Network Watcher**. You will learn how to manage your virtual network connectivity and how you can monitor and troubleshoot on-premises connectivity as well use Network Watcher. We will end this chapter by covering how to manage external networking.

We will look at the following topics in this chapter:

- Network Watcher
- Network resource monitoring
- Managing virtual network connectivity
- Monitoring and troubleshooting on-premises connectivity
- Managing external networking

Network Watcher

Azure Network Watcher is a network monitoring solution that provides tools to diagnose, monitor, and view metrics and logging for resources in an Azure Virtual Network. This includes application gateway traffic, Load Balancers, ExpressRoute circuits, and more.

Azure Network Watcher offers the following capabilities:

- **Monitoring**: Connection monitor is a cloud-based hybrid network monitoring solution that can monitor the communication between virtual machines and endpoints. An endpoint can be another **Virtual Machine (VM)**, a URL, an IPv4 address, or a **Fully Qualified Domain Name (FQDN)**. The network communication is monitored at regular intervals and information about latency, network topology changes, and the reachability between a VM and the endpoint is collected. If an endpoint becomes unreachable, Network Watcher will inform the user about the error. The reason for this can be a problem with the memory or CPU of a VM, a security rule for the VM, or the hop type of a custom route. Latency problems are also monitored. The connection monitor will provide the average, minimum, and maximum latency observed over time. The monitoring solution is capable of monitoring network performance between various points in the network infrastructure and it can generate alerts and notifications.
- **Diagnostics**: You can diagnose network traffic filtering for VMs. The VM can, for instance, become unable to communicate with other resources because of a security rule.

An IP flow can verify and test the communication and informs you as to whether the connection has succeeded or failed. An IP flow can tell you which security rule allowed or denied the connection and communication. Network Watcher can also diagnose network routing problems from a VM. When a virtual network is created, there are several default outbound routes created for that VNet as well. Outbound traffic from all resources that are deployed in a virtual network are routed based on Azure's default routes.

In cases where you want to override the default routing rules, or create additional rules, **next hop** can be used to test the communication between the different routes. When the communication fails, you can then change, add, or remove a route to resolve the problem.

Using Azure Network Watcher, you can diagnose outbound connection from a VM. You can also diagnose problems with an Azure Virtual Network gateway and connections, capture packets to and from a VM, view security rules for a network interface, and determine relative latencies between Azure regions and internet service providers:

- **Metrics**: The network subscription limit feature can provide a summary of how many network resources there are deployed in a subscription or region. If the limitations of the maximum amount of network resources are met, a summary is provided.
- **Logs**: **Network Security Groups** (**NSGs**) are responsible for allowing or denying the inbound and outbound traffic to a network interface in the virtual machine. The NSG flow log feature can log the port, protocol, whether traffic is allowed or denied, and can log the source and IP address. These logs can be analyzed using several tools, such as the traffic analytics feature and Power BI. Traffic analytics can provide rich visualization of the data that is written to the NSG flow logs.
- **Automatic enablement**: Network Watcher will be automatically enabled when a new virtual network is created or updated. There is no extra charge for enabling Network Watcher inside a subscription.

In the following sections, we are going to see Network Watcher in action.

Network resource monitoring

In this demonstration, we are going to monitor the network on VMs. For this demonstration, create three Windows Server 2016 datacenter VMs inside one virtual network. We can use these VMs for monitoring.

Before we are able to monitor the network using network resource monitoring, we need to install the Network Watcher agent on the three VMs. After that, we are going to inspect the network traffic.

Installing the Network Watcher agent

To install the Network Watcher agent on a VM in Azure, take the following steps:

1. Navigate to the Azure portal by opening `https://portal.azure.com/`.
2. Open the VM settings, and under **Settings**, select **Extensions**, and then click the **Add** button:

Adding a VM extension

3. Add the **Network Watcher Agent for Windows** extension to the VM (extensions can be installed on the VM during creation as well), and click **Create**:

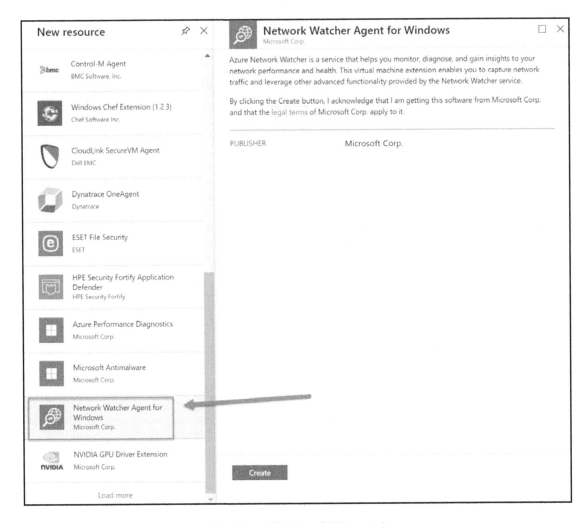

Adding the Network Watcher Agent for Windows extension

4. Repeat these steps for the other two VMs as well, and install the agent on it.

Now that the **Network Watcher Agent for Windows** is installed on all the VMs, we can enable it for a specific region.

Enabling Network Watcher

To enable Network Watcher in a specific region, take the following steps:

1. Navigate to the Azure portal by opening `https://portal.azure.com/`.
2. Select **All services**, and in the top menu, type `network watcher`:

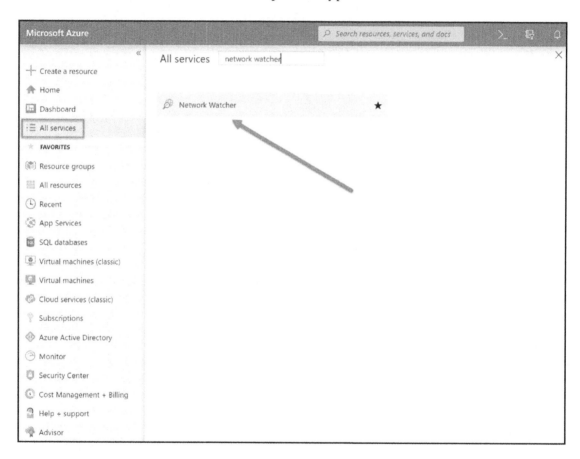

Opening Network Watcher

3. In the **Network Watcher** overview page, select the subscription and the region where the VMs are created. In my case, this is **East US**. Then click the three dots and enable Network Watcher for that region, as follows:

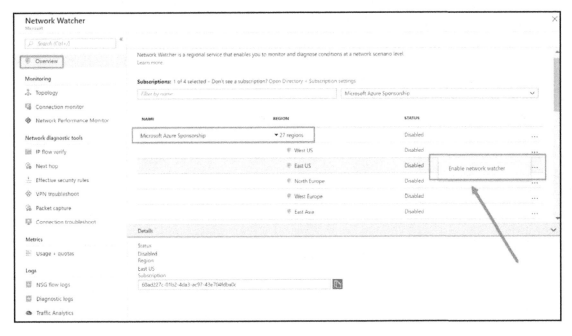

Enabling Network Watcher

Now that Network Watcher is enabled, we can actually start monitoring the network resources.

Monitoring the network connectivity

Network monitoring can be used for monitoring connection reachability, latency, and network topology changes. To do this you need to set up a connection monitor instance. Take the following steps to set this up:

1. With the Network Watcher resource still open, under **Monitoring**, select **Connection monitor**:

Connection monitor

2. We are going to use the monitor resource for testing the connectivity between VM1 and VM2. Therefore, add the following values:
   - **Name**: VM1-VM2-Test.
   - **Subscription**: Select the subscription where the VMs are deployed.
   - **Source virtual machine**: VM1.
   - **Destination virtual machine**: VM2.

- **Port:** 22:

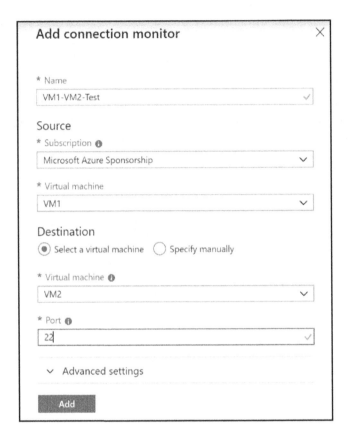

Connection monitor settings

3. Click **Add**.

We are now able to monitor the network connectivity. In the next section, we are going to look at how to manage the connectivity.

Managing virtual network connectivity

You can manage your virtual network connectivity from the Azure portal. In the upcoming section, we are going to look at the possibilities that the Azure portal has to offer to manage the virtual network connectivity.

Network topology

The network topology section in the Azure portal displays an overview of the virtual networks inside an Azure subscription and a resource group. To go to the network topology section, you have to take the following steps:

1. Navigate to the Azure portal by opening `https://portal.azure.com/`.

2. Select **All services**, and, in the top menu, type `network watcher` again.

3. Under **Monitoring**, select **Topology**. In there, you need to select the subscription, resource group, and, if relevant, the virtual network, as shown in the following screenshot:

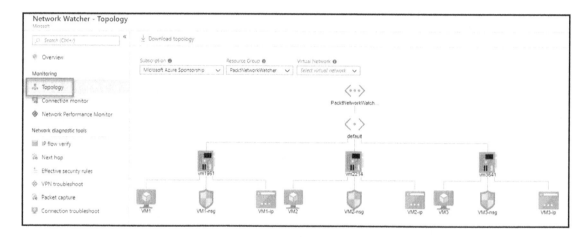

Network topology

4. You can now drill down into all the components of the network, such as the VNet, NIC, VMs, IP address, and more, by clicking on the items in the topology. This will take you to the settings of the different resources.

5. You can download the topology as well, by clicking the **Download topology** button in the top menu, as follows:

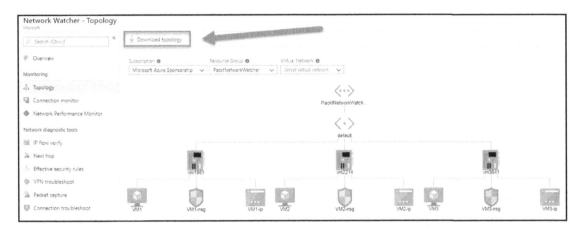

Downloading the network topology

Besides monitoring the networks in Azure, you can also monitor the on-premises connectivity. We are going to look at this in the next section.

Monitoring and troubleshooting on-premises connectivity

You can monitor your on-premises connectivity using Network Watcher as well. It offers two different features for this, **Network Performance Monitor** and **VPN Troubleshoot**, which, just like the other features, are accessible from the Azure portal.

Network Performance Monitor

Network Performance Monitor is a hybrid network monitoring solution. It can monitor network connectivity for on-premises and cloud networks, and between various points in your network infrastructure. It can detect issues such as routing errors and **blackholing**. The monitoring solution is stored inside Azure Log Analytics.

Network Performance Monitor can create alerts and notifications when network performance errors appear and it can localize the source of the problem to a specific network device or segment.

It offers the following capabilities:

- **Performance monitor**: A performance monitor can monitor the network connectivity across cloud deployments and on-premises locations. It can also monitor connectivity between multiple data centers, branch offices, multi-tier applications, and microservices.
- **Service connectivity monitor**: You can identify the network bottlenecks inside the network infrastructure and detect the exact locations of the issues in the network. You can also monitor connectivity between users and services.
- **ExpressRoute monitor**: You can monitor the ExpressRoute connection between the on-premises locations and Azure.

Next hop

You can use the **next hop** feature to specify a source and destination IPv4 address. The communication between these addresses is then tested, and you will get informed about what type of next hop is used to route the traffic. When you experience a routing error or problem, you can add, change, or remove a route to resolve this.

To see this in action, you need to take the following steps:

1. Navigate to the Azure portal by opening `https://portal.azure.com/`.
2. Select **All services**, and in the top menu, type `network watcher`.
3. Under **Network diagnostic tools**, select **Next hop**.
4. In the settings blade, add the following values:
    - **Resource group**: `PacktNetworkWatcher`.
    - **Virtual machine**: `VM2`.
    - **Network interface**: This is selected automatically.
    - **Source IP address**: This is selected automatically as well.
    - **Destination IP address**: `13.107.21.200` (the Bing server again).
5. Select **Next hop**.

6. You will see the following result. In this case, there is no next hop, because the connection is going straight to the internet:

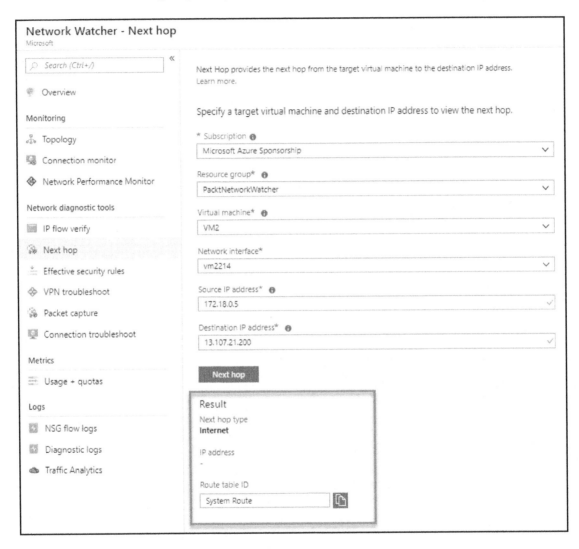

Next hop to internet

7. If you change the destination IP address to one of the IP addresses of the other VMs, which in my case is `172.18.0.6`, you will see the following result:

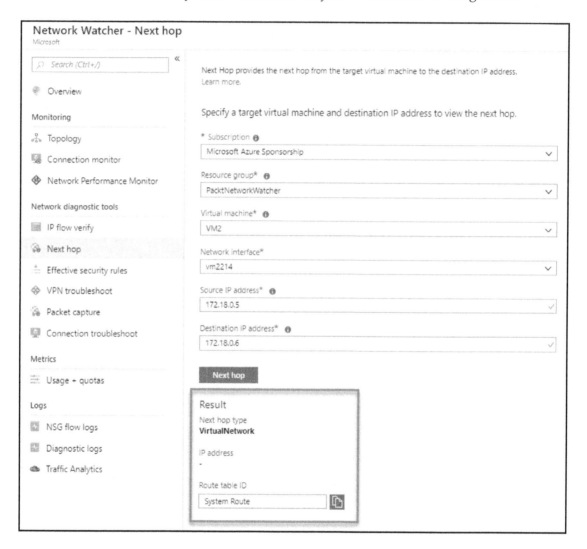

Next hop to another VM

In the next section, we are going to look at how to troubleshoot a VPN connection.

VPN troubleshoot

For the VPN troubleshoot demonstration, we are going to use the VPN connection that we created in the previous chapter.

You can diagnose the VPN connection by taking the following steps:

1. From the **Network Watcher** blade, select **VPN troubleshoot**.
2. In the **Network Watcher - VPN troubleshoot** blade, you can diagnose the gateway by selecting the subscription, resource group, location, and the following checkbox. You also need to select or create a storage account for storing the diagnostic information. After selecting the checkbox, you can start the troubleshooting process by clicking **Start troubleshooting** in the top menu, as shown in the following screenshot:

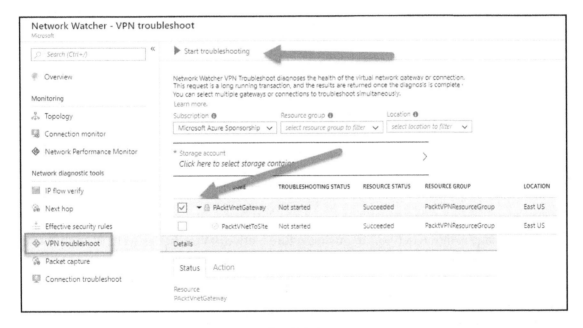

VPN troubleshooting

3. This will start the troubleshooting process, and, in my case, the VPN connections seem unhealthy. You can click on the **Action** tab to see the recommendations:

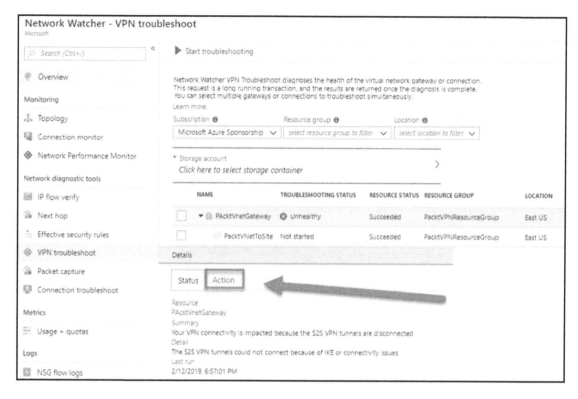

Unhealthy VPN connection

You can manage external networking using Azure Network Watcher as well. We will cover this in the upcoming section.

Managing external networking

Azure Network Watcher offers three features to monitor and troubleshoot external networking. Their features are **IP flow verify**, **Effective security rules**, and **Connection troubleshoot**, which are going to be covered in the next sections.

IP flow verify

With **IP flow verify**, you can detect whether a package is allowed or denied to or from a network interface of a virtual machine. Included in the information are the protocol, the local and remote IP addresses, the direction, and the local and remote ports. When a packet is denied, the name of the routing rule that denies the packet is returned. You can use this to diagnose connectivity issues from or in the on-premises environment and to and from the internet. You can basically choose any source or IP address to verify the connectivity.

To run IP flow verify, you need to enable an instance of Network Watcher in the region where you plan to run the tool. This is similar to the demonstration covered in the *Enabling Network Watcher* section that appeared earlier in this chapter, where we enabled Network Watcher for a particular region.

Using IP flow verify

In this demonstration, we are going to use IP flow verify to test the connection between two of the VMs that we created in the first demonstration. To use IP flow verify, take the following steps:

1. Inside the Network Watcher resource blade, under **Network diagnostic tools**, select **IP flow verify**.
2. In the settings page, add the following settings:
   - **Resource group**: `PacktNetworkWatcher`.
   - **Virtual machine**: `VM1`.
   - **Network interface**: This will be filled in automatically after selecting the VM.
   - **Protocol**: TCP.
   - **Direction**: Outbound.
   - **Local IP address**: This is filled in automatically as well.
   - **Local port**: `60000`.
   - **Remote IP address**: `13.107.21.200` (address of Bing).
   - **Remote port**: `80`.

3. Click the **Check** button:

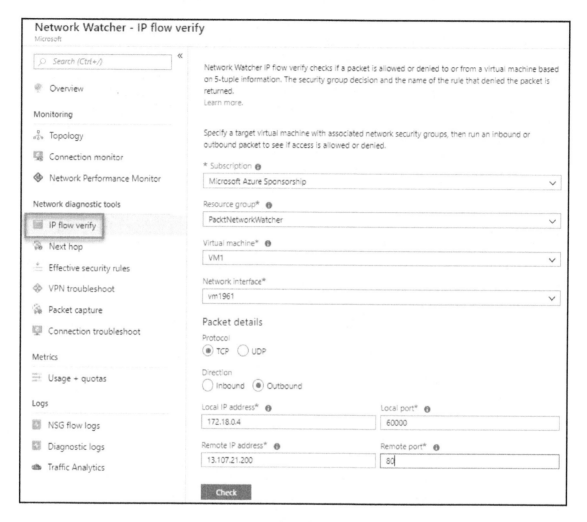

IP flow verify

4. The request is executed and the result it will return will be that access is allowed, because of the `AllowInternetOutBound` security rule, as shown in the following screenshot:

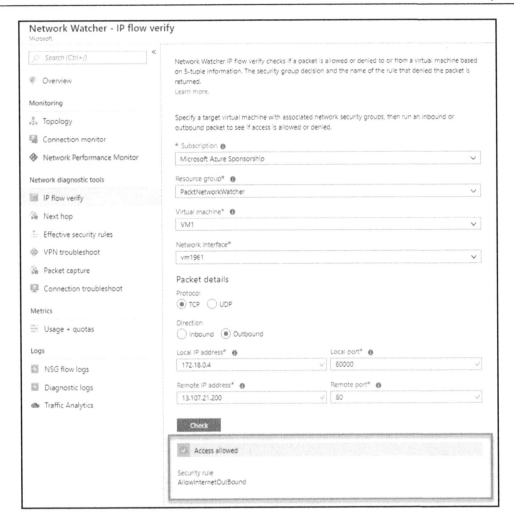

IP flow verify access allowed

5. Repeat the previous steps, but change the **Remote IP address** to 172.31.0.100. This will result in access being denied because of the DefaultOutboundDenyAll security rule:

IP flow verify access denied

6. Lastly, repeat the step again, and this time make the following changes:
    - **Direction**: **Inbound**
    - **Local port**: 80
    - **Remote port**: 60000

7. This will result in the following:

Access denied

We've looked at how to use IP flow verify to test the connection between two of the VMs. In the next part, we are going to look at effective security rules.

Effective security rules

The **Effective security rules** feature displays all the security rules that are applied to the network interface and the subnet where the network interface is. It then aggregates both. This will give you a complete overview of all the rules that are applied to a network interface, and it will give you the ability to change, add, or remove rules.

You need to select the right subscription, the resource group, and the VM to get the overview of the applied security rules, as shown in the following screenshot:

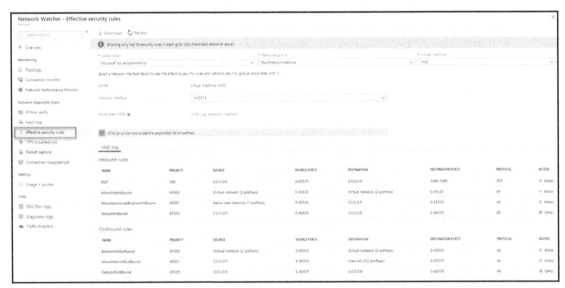

Effective security rules

We've now seen an overview of the security rules that are applied to the network interface. In the next section, we are going to cover connection troubleshoot.

Connection troubleshoot

Azure Network Watcher Connection troubleshoot enables you to troubleshoot network performance and connectivity issues in Azure. It provides visualization of the hop-by-hop path from source to destination, identifying issues that can potentially impact your network performance and connectivity.

Azure Network Watcher connection troubleshoot provides the following features and insights:

- A graphical topology view from your source to destination.
- It checks the connectivity between the source (VM) and the destination (VM, URI, FQDN, IP) address.
- It offers hop-by-hop latency.
- It can identify configuration issues that are impacting reachability.
- It provides all possible hop-by-hop paths from the source to the destination.
- It checks latency, such as minimum, maximum, and average latency, between the source and destination.
- The number of packets dropped during the connection troubleshoot check.

Connection troubleshoot requires that the source VM has the **AzureNetworkWatcherExtension** VM extension installed. For installing the extension on a Windows VM, you can refer to `https://docs.microsoft.com/en-us/azure/virtual-machines/extensions/network-watcher-windows?toc=%2Fazure%2Fnetwork-watcher%2Ftoc.json`, and for a Linux VM, you can refer to `https://docs.microsoft.com/en-us/azure/virtual-machines/extensions/network-watcher-linux?toc=%2Fazure%2Fnetwork-watcher%2Ftoc.json`.

To check network connectivity using **Connection troubleshoot**, you have to take the following steps:

1. From the Network Watcher overview blade in the Azure portal, under **Network diagnostic tools**, select **Connection troubleshoot**.
2. Select a virtual machine and provide an outbound connection, such as the following:

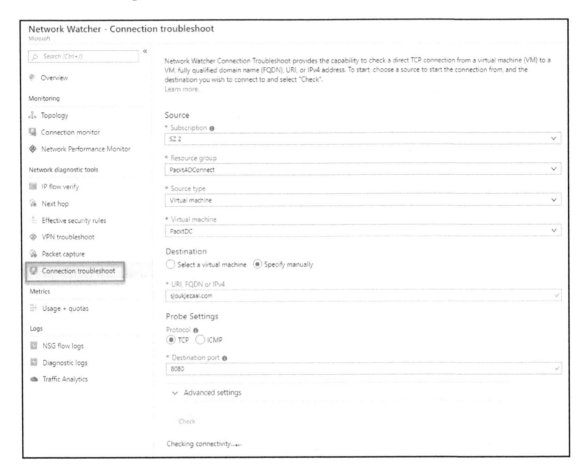

Selecting source and destination

3. Click **Check**.
4. The agent will automatically be installed on the source machine when you click the check button.

5. After checking, the results will be displayed:

Status		Agent extension version		Source virtual machine	
⚠ Unreachable		1.4		PacktDC	

Grid view   Topology view

Hops

NAME	IP ADDRESS	STATUS	NEXT HOP IP ADDRESS	RTT FROM SOURCE (MS)
🖥 PacktDC	10.3.0.4	⊘	10.3.0.4	-

Probes Sent
30

Probes Failed
30

Unreachable endpoint

We have now checked an outbound connection from a VM using **Connection troubleshoot**.

Summary

In this chapter, we covered the third part of the *Deploying and Managing Virtual Networks* objective, by covering how to monitor and troubleshoot your network traffic in Azure Network Watcher. We also covered how to monitor and troubleshoot on-premises and external network connectivity using Network Watcher.

In the next chapter, we are going to continue with the fourth part of this objective, by covering how to create and configure Azure security groups and Azure DNS.

Questions

Answer the following questions to test your knowledge of the information in this chapter. You can find the answers in the *Assessments* section at the end of this book:

1. Azure Network Watcher is only for monitoring and diagnosing network connectivity in Azure:
    - True
    - False

2. Can you use IP flow verify to verify outbound connections from a VNet in Azure?
   - Yes
   - No

3. Can you use IP flow verify to verify connections between two different VMs inside a VNet?
   - Yes
   - No

Further reading

You can check the following links for more information about the topics that are covered in this chapter:

- *What is Azure Network Watcher?*: https://docs.microsoft.com/en-us/azure/network-watcher/network-watcher-monitoring-overview
- *Quickstart: Diagnose a virtual machine network traffic filter problem using the Azure portal*: https://docs.microsoft.com/en-us/azure/network-watcher/diagnose-vm-network-traffic-filtering-problem
- *Network Performance Monitor solution in Azure*: https://docs.microsoft.com/en-us/azure/azure-monitor/insights/network-performance-monitor?toc=%2Fazure%2Fnetwork-watcher%2Ftoc.json
- *Introduction to IP flow verify in Azure Network Watcher*: https://docs.microsoft.com/en-us/azure/network-watcher/network-watcher-ip-flow-verify-overview
- *Tutorial: Diagnose a communication problem between networks using the Azure portal*: https://docs.microsoft.com/en-us/azure/network-watcher/diagnose-communication-problem-between-networks

12
Azure Security Groups and Azure DNS

In the previous chapter, we covered the third part of the *Deploying and Managing Virtual Networks* objective by covering how to monitor and troubleshoot your network traffic in Azure Network Watcher. We've covered how to use Azure Network Watcher for network traffic inside Azure, as well as for on-premises and external networks.

In this chapter, we are first going to focus on **Network Security Groups (NSGs)** in Azure. We will cover the basics of NSGs, and how you can use them to filter network traffic, and you will also learn how to create and configure them. We are also going to associate an NSG with a subnet or **Network Interfaces (NICs)**, and we are going to create and evaluate security rules for NSGs. In the second part of this chapter, we are going to cover Azure DNS. You will learn how to set up Azure DNS and how to add DNS zones and DNS records.

The following topics will be covered in this chapter:

- NSGs
- Creating and configuring an NSG
- Associating an NSG with a subnet or NIC
- Creating and evaluating security rules
- Azure DNS
- Configuring private and public DNS zones

Technical requirements

The source code for our sample application can be downloaded from `https://github.com/ PacktPublishing/Microsoft-Azure-Administrator-Exam-Guide-AZ-103/tree/master/ Chapter12`.

NSGs

You can use an NSG to filter network traffic to and from Azure resources that reside in an Azure virtual network. An NSG is an access control list inside Azure where you can add inbound and outbound security rules that allow or deny traffic from several types of resources.

When a connection is established between VMS, VNets, or other cloud services, this list is checked to see whether the connection is allowed or denied. NSGs can be applied to one or more subnets or individual NICs. This means that all resources that are associated with this subnet or NIC will automatically have all the rules applied. NSG rules are processed in priority order using the five-tuple information (source, source port, destination, destination port, and protocol) to allow or deny traffic. They are evaluated by priority, with lower numbers before higher numbers, and they can be applied to inbound or outbound traffic.

 There is a limit to how many rules per NSG can create per Azure location and subscription. For details, see the documentation on Azure limits at : `https://docs.microsoft.com/en-us/azure/azure-subscription-service-limits?toc=%2fazure%2fvirtual-network%2ftoc.json#azure-resource-manager-virtual-networking-limits`.

Service tags

To help minimize the complexity of security rule creation, Azure offers service tags. They represent a group of IP address prefixes and you can use service tags in place of specific IP addresses when creating security rules. These service tags can't be created manually; they are created and managed by Azure.

Azure offers an exhaustive list of service tags, such as the following:

- **VirtualNetwork**: This tag includes the virtual network address space, all connected on-premises address spaces, peered virtual networks, and all virtual networks connected to a virtual network gateway.
- **AzureLoadBalancer**: This tag covers the Azure Load Balancer. It translates to the virtual IP address of the host from where the health probes originate.

- **Internet**: This tag is for the IP address space that is outside the virtual network and reachable from the public internet.
- **AzureKeyVault**: This tag is for the address prefixes of the Azure Key Vault service. If you specify `AzureKeyVault` for the value, traffic is allowed or denied to Azure Key Vault. You can also only access Azure Key Vault in a specific region.

 For a complete overview of all the service tags that Azure has to offer, you can refer to the documentation at: `https://docs.microsoft.com/en-us/azure/virtual-network/security-overview`.

In the next demonstration, we are going to create and configure an NSG in the Azure portal.

Creating and configuring an NSG

NSGs can be created from the Azure portal, PowerShell, and CLI. In this demonstration, we are going to create an NSG from the Azure portal and configure it. We are going to associate the NSG with a subnet and create and evaluate security rules.

To create an NSG from the Azure portal, take the following steps:

1. Navigate to the Azure portal by opening `https://portal.azure.com`.
2. Click **Create a resource** in the left menu and type `Network Security Group` into the search bar.
3. Create a new NSG.
4. Add the following settings:
    - **Name**: `PacktNSG`.
    - **Subscription**: Select the subscription that we used for creating the VNet in `Chapter 9`, *Implementing and Managing Virtual Networking*.
    - **Resource group**: Select the subscription that we used for creating the VNet in `Chapter 9`, *Implementing and Managing Virtual Networking*. In my case, this is `PacktVNetResourceGroup`.

- **Location: (US) East US**:

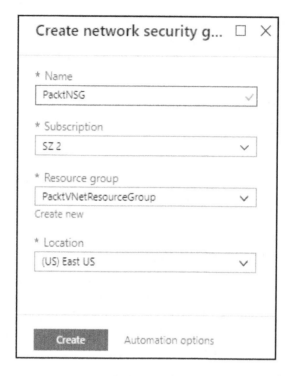

Creating a new NSG

5. Click **Create**.

We have now created a new NSG and added it to the `PacktVNetResourceGroup`. This is the same resource group as where the virtual networks reside. In the next part of this demonstration, we are going to associate the NSG with a subnet and NIC.

Associating an NSG with a subnet or NIC

To associate the NSG with a subnet, you have to take the following steps:

1. After creating the NSG, navigate to its overview page.
2. Under **Settings**, select **Subnets** to associate the NSG with a subnet. Click **Associate** in the top menu:

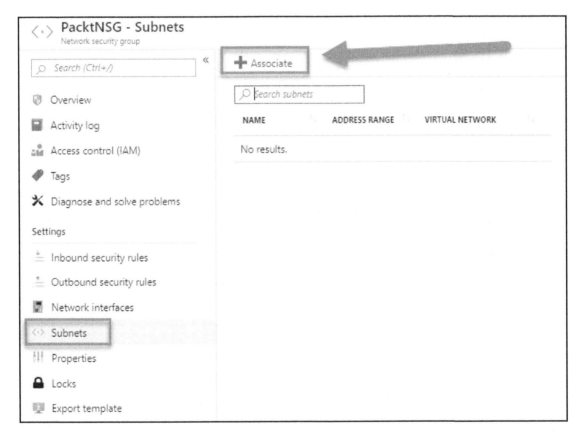

Associating an NSG with a subnet

3. First, we need to select a virtual network. Select `PacktVNet`:

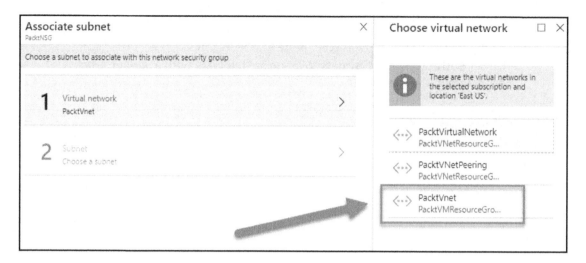

Selecting a virtual network

4. Next, we need to select **Subnet**:

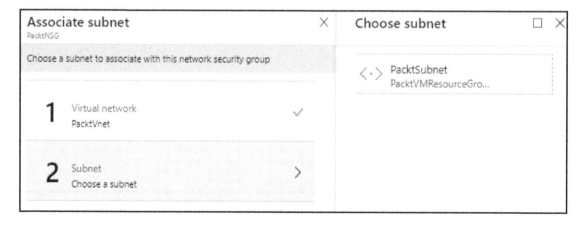

Selecting the subnet

5. Click **OK**. The NSG will now be associated with the subnet.

6. To associate the NSG with an NIC, under **Settings**, select **Network interfaces**. Select **Associate** in the top menu:

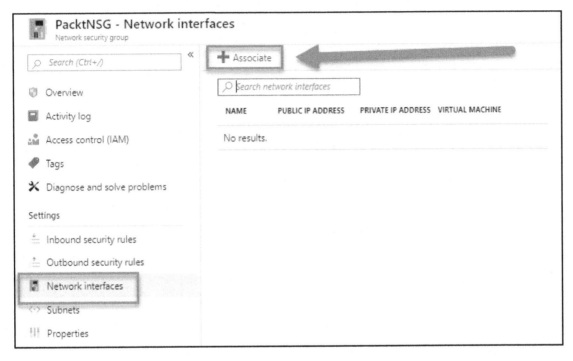

Associating NSG with a NIC

7. There, you can select an NIC that resides in the same region as where the NSG was created:

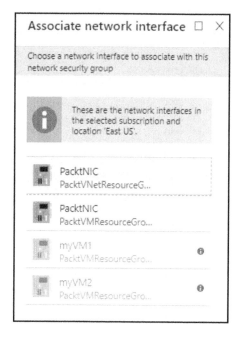

Selecting an NIC

8. After selecting the NIC, the NSG is associated with it.

In this demonstration, we've covered how to associate an NSG with a subnet and a NIC. In the next demonstration, we are going to cover how to create and evaluate security rules.

Creating and evaluating security rules

When you create an NSG, there are some default inbound and outbound security rules created for you automatically. The default rules are low-priority rules. You can also add custom rules to them. You can create inbound and outbound security rules. In this demonstration, we are going to create an inbound security rule that denies RDP traffic to the associated subnet. Therefore, you have to take the following steps:

1. First, go the overview page of the NSG. In there, you can see the default inbound and outbound security rules:

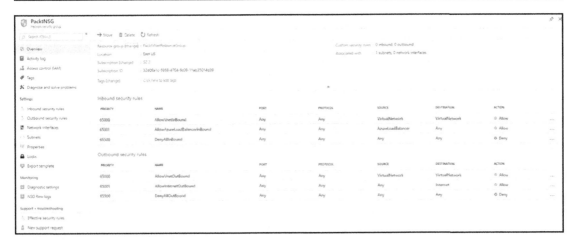

Default security rules

2. Then, under **Settings**, select **Inbound security rules** to add a custom rule. Then click **Add** in the top menu:

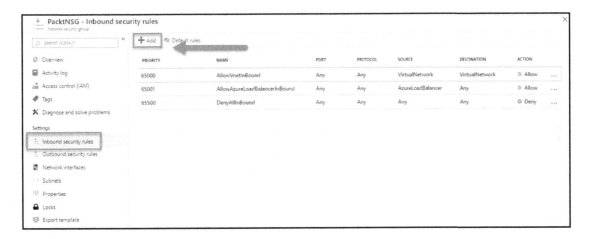

3. We are going to deny all traffic over port 3389, which is the RDP port. Therefore, we select the **Service Tag for Source** field and the **Internet for Source** service tag, set the destination to **VirtualNetwork** and the destination port ranges to 3389 over any protocol. The action will be set to **Deny**. We are going to set the priority to **100**, which is the highest priority:

Creating a security rule

4. Click **Add**.

5. We have now created an inbound security rule that denies all RDP traffic. This rule is bound to the subnet, because we associated this NSG with a subnet.

6. To evaluate this security rule, deploy a VM inside this resource group, virtual network, and subnet. Also, enable RDP for it. After deployment, try connecting to it. If the security rule got applied correctly, you should receive the following error message:

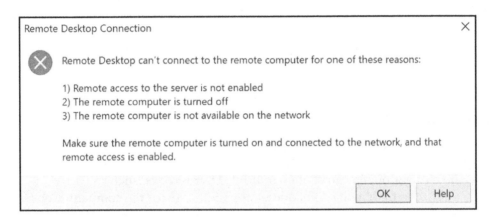

Error message

This concludes the Azure NSG section. In the last part of this chapter, we are going to cover **Azure DNS**.

Azure DNS

Azure DNS is a hosting service for DNS domains that can be used for name resolution. The process of name resolution involves converting a hostname (such as `www.packt.com`) into an IP address (such as `192.168.1.1`). DNS servers eliminate the need for humans to memorize difficult IP addresses. In Azure, you can manage your DNS records using the Microsoft Azure infrastructure and the same tools and billing as you use for your other Azure resources.

Azure DNS can't be used as a domain registrar, However, you can host your DNS names that are registered somewhere else, such as a third-party domain name registrar, for instance, in Azure DNS for record management. You then have to delegate the domain to Azure DNS in order for the DNS queries for a certain domain to reach Azure DNS.

Domain names

The DNS consists of a hierarchy of different domains. They are globally distributed over DNS servers around the world. The root domain is simply named .. Below the root domain comes the top-level domains, such as .com, .net., .org, and more. Below that comes the second-level domains, such as .org.uk.

You can buy your domain name from a domain registrar. This will give the right to control the DNS hierarchy under that name allowing you to do things, such as redirecting the domain to your own website. You can let the registrar host the domain at its nameservers on your behalf, or you can specify alternative nameservers for your domain. Azure DNS can be used as such an alternative name server where you can control the DNS hierarchy.

Public DNS zones

To start hosing your domain in Azure DNS, you first need to create a DNS zone for your domain. This is used to host all the different DNS records. For instance, the www.packt.com domain can contain multiple DNS records, such as mail.packt.com for a mail server and www.packt.com for the company website.

When you create a DNS zone in Azure DNS, you have to keep the following things in mind:

- The name of the zone must be unique within the resource group. The zone must also not already exist in the resource group.
- You can reuse the same zone across different resource groups or different subscriptions.
- When you have multiple zones with the same name across different resource groups or subscriptions, each instance must contain a different nameserver address. Only one set of addresses can be configured with the domain name registrar.

Private DNS zones

With **private DNS zones**, you can manage and resolve domain names in a virtual network without the need to add a custom DNS solution. You can use your own custom DNS names, rather than the Azure-provided names that are available. You can use these custom domain names to tailor your virtual network architecture to suit your organization's needs.

Private DNS zones provide name resolution for VMs within a VNet and between different VNets. You can also configure zone names that share private and public DNS zones to share the same name.

To publish a private DNS zone to a VNet, you first need to specify a list of virtual networks that are allowed to resolve records within the private DNS zone. These virtual networks are then called **resolution virtual networks**. You can also specify a registration virtual network, which is then used by Azure DNS for maintaining the hostname records when a VM is created. It is also used for IP changes of the VM, and when a VM is deleted.

 At the time of writing this book, the Azure DNS private zone feature is in public preview.

Record types

Each DNS record that you create inside the DNS zone has a name and a type. The different records are organized into various types according to the type of data that they contain. For instance, an A record maps the domain name to an IPv4 address. Another example is an MX record, which maps a name to a mail server.

 For more information about the different record types, you can go to https://docs.microsoft.com/en-in/azure/dns/dns-zones-records. SPF records are represented using TXT records in Azure DNS: https://docs.microsoft.com/en-in/azure/dns/dns-zones-records#spf-records.

You can also create record sets in Azure DNS. They can be used to map different records in a zone together that have the same name and are of the same type—for instance, when you have a company website that is hosted on two different IP addresses:

```
www.packt.com.  3600 IN A 134.170.185.46
www.packt.com.  3600 IN A 134.170.188.221
```

When you've created the A record in the packt.com zone pointing to the first IP address, you can then add the second record to the existing records set, instead of creating a new an additional record set.

In the upcoming section, we are going to configure private and public DNS zones in Azure DNS.

Configuring a public DNS zone

To configure private and public DNS zones from the Azure portal, you have to take the following steps:

1. Navigate to the Azure portal by opening `https://portal.azure.com`.
2. Click **Create a resource** in the left menu and type `DNS Zone` in the search bar. Create a new DNS zone.
3. Add the following values to create a new DNS zone:
    - **Subscription**: Select a subscription.
    - **Resource group**: Create a new one, and call it `PacktDNSResourceGroup`.
    - **Name**: `packtdns.com`.
    - **Resource group location: (US) East US**:

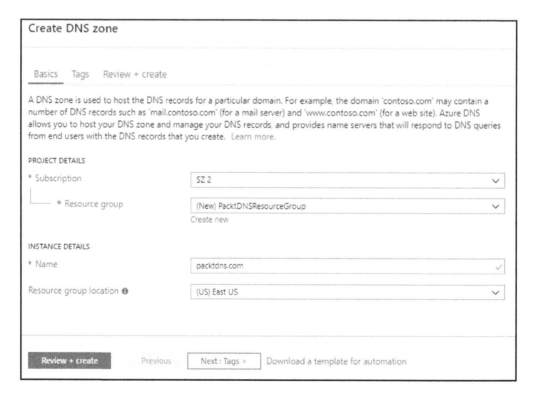

Creating a new DNS zone

4. Click **Review + create**.

5. When the resource is deployed, you can add DNS records to it. From the overview page, in the top menu, select **+ Record set**:

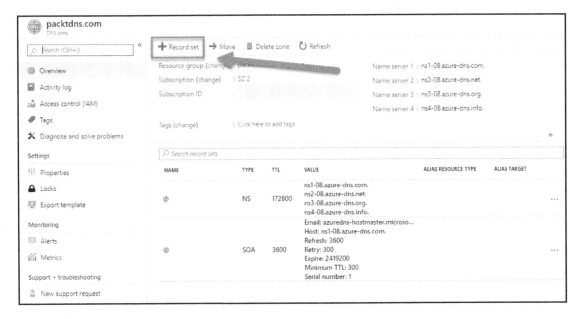

Adding a new record

6. To create an A record, add the following values:
   - **Name**: www.
   - **Type**: Select **A**.
   - **TTL**: Type 1. The **Time-to-live (TTL)** parameter of the DNS request specifies for how long DNS servers and clients can cache a response.
   - **TTL unit**: Select **Hours**. This is the time unit for the **TTL** value.

- **IP address**: 10.10.10.10:

Adding a new record

7. Click **OK**.

8. When the record is added, we can test it using the `nslookup` command. First, we need to copy one of the nameservers:

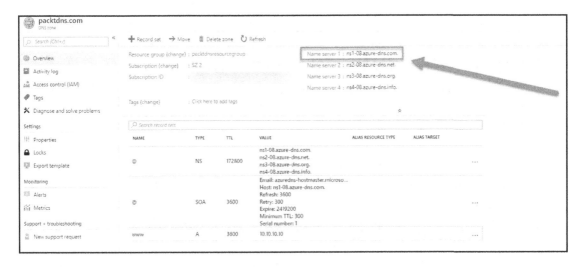

Copying the name server value

9. Then, open a command prompt and enter the following command:

nslookup www.packtdns.com ns1-08.azure-dns.com.

10. You will see something such as the following, which means that name resolution is working correctly:

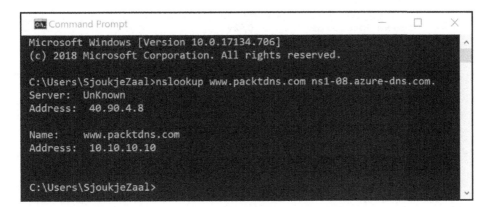

DNS name resolution

In this demonstration, we configured a public DNS zone. In the next demonstration, we are going to cover how you can configure a private DNS zone using the CLI and Azure Cloud Shell.

Configuring a private DNS zone

In this demonstration, we are going to create a private DNS zone in a new resource group.

To configure a private DNS zone using the CLI from Azure Cloud Shell, you have to take the following steps:

1. Navigate to the Azure portal by opening `https://portal.azure.com`.
2. In the top-right menu, select the Azure Cloud Shell icon. Make sure that **Bash** is selected.
3. First, we need to create a new resource group. Add the following command for this:

   ```
   az group create --name PacktPrivateDNSResourceGroup --location
   "East US"
   ```

4. Then, we are going to create a new VNet:

   ```
   az network vnet create \
     --name PacktPrivateDNSVNet \
     --resource-group PacktPrivateDNSResourceGroup \
     --location eastus \
     --address-prefix 10.2.0.0/16 \
     --subnet-name backendSubnet \
     --subnet-prefixes 10.2.0.0/24
   ```

5. Next, we need to create the private DNS zone:

   ```
   az network dns zone create -g PacktPrivateDNSResourceGroup \
     -n private.packtdns.com \
     --zone-type Private \
     --registration-vnets PacktPrivateDNSVNet
   ```

6. Now, create two virtual machines to test the private DNS zone. You need to provide an admin password when you run this command:

   ```
   az vm create \
     -n packtVM01 \
     --admin-username test-user \
     -g PacktPrivateDNSResourceGroup \
   ```

```
-l eastus \
--subnet backendSubnet \
--vnet-name PacktPrivateDNSVNet \
--image win2016datacenter

az vm create \
-n packtVM02 \
--admin-username test-user \
-g PacktPrivateDNSResourceGroup \
-l eastus \
--subnet backendSubnet \
--vnet-name PacktPrivateDNSVNet \
--image win2016datacenter
```

7. We are going to create an additional DNS in the `private.packtdns.com` DNS zone. We are going to create a record with the relative name of `db` in the `private.packt.com` DNS zone. The fully qualified name of the record set is `db.private.packtdns.com`. The record type is A, with an IP address of `10.2.0.4`:

```
az network dns record-set a add-record \
   -g PacktPrivateDNSResourceGroup \
   -z private.packtdns.com \
   -n db \
   -a 10.2.0.4
```

8. We can now test the name resolution for the private zone. We are going to ping both the VMs, and therefore we need to configure the firewall for both VMs to allow inbound ICMP packets. Connect to both VMs using RDP, and open a Windows PowerShell window with administrator privileges. Enter the following command:

```
New-NetFirewallRule -DisplayName "Allow ICMPv4-In" -Protocol ICMPv4
```

9. After configuring both the VMs, from `PacktVM02`, enter the following command in PowerShell to ping `PacktVM01`:

```
ping PacktVM01.private.packtdns.com
```

You will see an output similar to the following screenshot:

```
Administrator: Windows PowerShell

Windows PowerShell
Copyright (C) 2016 Microsoft Corporation. All rights reserved.

PS C:\Users\test-user> ping PacktVM01.private.packtdns.com

Pinging PacktVM01.private.packtdns.com [10.2.0.4] with 32 bytes of data:
Reply from 10.2.0.4: bytes=32 time=1ms TTL=128
Reply from 10.2.0.4: bytes=32 time=1ms TTL=128
Reply from 10.2.0.4: bytes=32 time=1ms TTL=128
Reply from 10.2.0.4: bytes=32 time=1ms TTL=128

Ping statistics for 10.2.0.4:
    Packets: Sent = 4, Received = 4, Lost = 0 (0% loss),
Approximate round trip times in milli-seconds:
    Minimum = 1ms, Maximum = 1ms, Average = 1ms
PS C:\Users\test-user> _
```

Private DNS output

In this demonstration, we configured a private DNS zone using the CLI.

Summary

In this chapter, we covered how to configure and manage NSGs and Azure DNS. We covered the basics for both NSGs and Azure DNS. You have also learned how to create and configure NSGs. We have also covered how to create public and private zones using Azure DNS, and how to add DNS records to it.

In the next chapter, we will cover the last part of the *Deploying and Managing Virtual Networks* objective, by covering how to implement **Azure Load Balancer**.

Questions

Answer the following questions to test your knowledge of the information in this chapter. You can find the answers in the *Assessments* section at the end of this book:

1. Can you assign an NSG to a subnet and a NIC?
    - Yes
    - No

2. Can you buy a domain name using Azure DNS and host it on there?
    - Yes
    - No

3. Private DNS zones cannot be configured from the Azure portal.
    - True
    - False

Further reading

You can check out the following links for more information about the topics that were covered in this chapter:

- *Security groups*: https://docs.microsoft.com/en-us/azure/virtual-network/security-overview
- *Create, change, or delete an NSG*: https://docs.microsoft.com/en-us/azure/virtual-network/manage-network-security-group
- *What is Azure DNS?*: https://docs.microsoft.com/en-in/azure/dns/dns-overview
- *Overview of DNS zones and records*: https://docs.microsoft.com/en-in/azure/dns/dns-zones-records
- *Quickstart: Create an Azure DNS zone and record using the Azure portal*: https://docs.microsoft.com/en-us/azure/dns/dns-getstarted-portal
- *Use Azure DNS for private domains*: https://docs.microsoft.com/en-us/azure/dns/private-dns-overview

Implementing Azure Load Balancer

13

In the previous chapter, we covered the fourth part of the *Deploying and Managing Virtual Networks* objective. We've covered **Network Security Groups (NSGs)** and Azure DNS. You also learned how to create and configure NSGs and how to set up and configure Azure DNS.

This chapter covers the fifth and final part of this objective, by covering how to configure internal and external load balancers using **Azure Load Balancer**. In this chapter, we are going to focus on the features and capabilities of Azure Load Balancer. You will learn how to configure an internal load balancer and how to create health probes and configure load balancing rules. This chapter will finish by covering how you can configure a public load balancer.

The following topics will be covered in this chapter:

- Azure Load Balancer
- Configuring an internal load balancer
- Creating health probes
- Creating load balancing rules
- Configuring a public load balancer

Technical requirements

The source code for this chapter can be downloaded from the GitHub repository at `https:/` `/github.com/PacktPublishing/Microsoft-Azure-Administrator-Exam-Guide-AZ-103/` `tree/master/Chapter13`.

Azure Load Balancer

Azure Load Balancer is a load balancer that operates at the transport layer (Layer 4 in the OSI network reference stack). Azure Load Balancer supports the **Transmission Control Protocol (TCP)** and **User Datagram Protocol (UDP)** and it can be used to load-balance traffic to your VMs. It provides high throughput and low latency, it can scale up to millions of flows, and it supports various inbound and outbound scenarios.

Azure Load Balancer can be used for the following:

- **Public Load Balancer**: Incoming internet traffic is load balanced to VMs.
- **Internal Load Balancer**: Traffic can be load balanced across VMs inside a virtual network. You can use it in a hybrid scenario as well, where it reaches a Load Balancer inside an on-premises network.
- **Port forwarding**: You can forward traffic to specific ports on specific VMs using inbound **Network Address Translation (NAT)** rules.
- **Outbound connectivity**: You can also provide outbound connectivity for VMs inside a virtual network using it on Azure Load Balancer as a public load balancer.

Azure Load Balancer offers the following features and capabilities:

- **Load balancing**: Traffic can be distributed from a frontend pool to a backend pool using rules. Azure Load Balancer uses a five-tuple hash by default, which is composed of the source IP address, source port, destination IP address, destination ports, and the IP protocol number to map flows to the available servers in the backend pool.
- **Port forwarding**: Inbound NAT rules can be created to forward traffic from a specific port of the frontend IP address of the load balancer to a specific port of a backend instance inside an Azure Virtual Network. Therefore, the same hash-based distribution is used as for load balancing. This can be used for the **Remote Desktop Protocol (RDP)** and **Secure Shell (SSH)** sessions to VMs inside the VNet. Multiple internal endpoints can be mapped to various ports on the same frontend IP address. The VMs can be remotely administered using the frontend IP address. This way, an additional jump box is not needed.
- **Automatic reconfiguration**: The load balancer will automatically reconfigure itself when instances are scaled up or down. There is no need for additional operations on the load balancer when VMs are added or removed from the backend pool.

- **Health probes**: Azure Load Balancer uses health probes to determine the health on the VMs in the backend pool. The load balancer will stop sending new connections to an instance when a probe fails to respond. There are different health probes provided for HTTP, HTTPS, and TCP endpoints.
- **Outbound connections (SNAT)**: Outbound connections are automatically translated to the public frontend IP address of the load balancer.

Azure Load Balancer comes in two different pricing tiers:

- **Basic**: The Basic Balancer is free to use. It has the following capabilities:
    - **Backend pool size**: The Basic tier supports up to 100 instances inside a backend pool.
    - **Health probes**: TCP and HTTP.
    - **Availability zones**: Not available.
    - **Outbound connections**: A single frontend is supported, which is selected at random when multiple frontends are configured. The default **Source Network Address Translation (SNAT)** is used when there is only an internal load balancer that is serving a VM, VM scale set, or availability set.
    - **Outbound rules**: Not available.
    - **Diagnostics**: Support for Azure Log Analytics for a public load balancer only, backend pool health count, and SNAT exhaustion alert.
    - **HA Ports**: Not available.
    - **Secure by default**: Open by default; NSGs are optional.
    - **TCP Reset on Idle**: Not available.
    - **Multiple frontends**: Not available.
    - **Management Operations**: 60-90+ seconds.
    - **SLA**: Not available.
- **Standard**: You are charged for using the Standard tier of the Azure Load Balancer. The charge is based on the number of rules and the data that is associated with the resource and are processed inbound and outbound:
    - **Backend pool size**: The standard tier supports up to 1,000 instances inside a backend pool.
    - **Health probes**: TCP, HTTP, and HTTPS.
    - **Availability Zones**: Support for zone-redundant and zonal frontends for inbound and outbound connections and cross-zone load balancing.

- **Outbound connections**: Multiple frontends can be used per load balancing rule opt-out. Pool-based outbound NAT can be explicitly defined using outbound rules. Outbound scenarios must be explicitly created to use outbound connectivity for the VM, VM scale set, or availability set. Virtual network service endpoints can be reached without defining outbound connectivity. Public IP addresses and **Platform as a Service (PaaS)**, that are not available using VNet service endpoints, must be reached with outbound connectivity.

- **Outbound rules**: Outbound NAT configuration needs to be defined using public IP addresses, public IP prefixes, or both. You can configure the outbound idle timeout as well as custom SNAT port allocation.

- **Diagnostics**: Azure Load Balancer has support for Azure Monitor, with features including health probe status, outbound connection health (SNAT successful and failed flows), multi-dimensional metrics, and active data plane measurements.

- **HA Ports**: Highly available ports for the internal load balancer only.

- **Secure by default**: Unless internal load balancers are whitelisted by an NSG, the endpoints are closed to inbound flows by default. Public IP addresses and load balancer endpoints are secured as well.

- **TCP Reset on Idle**: This can be enabled on the idle timeout on any rule.

- **Multiple frontends**: For inbound and outbound connections.

- **Management operations**: < 30 seconds for most operations.

- **SLA**: 99.99% for a data path with two healthy virtual machines.

Configuring an internal load balancer

In this demonstration, we are going to create and configure a load balancer from the Azure portal. We are going to route internal traffic with a basic load balancer to spread incoming requests to multiple virtual machines. For this demonstration, we are going to create a load balancer, backend servers, and network resources at the Basic pricing tier.

Creating the VNet

First, we are going to create the VNet, backend servers, and a test VM. To do this, take the following steps:

1. Navigate to the Azure portal by opening `https://portal.azure.com/`.
2. In the left menu, select **Create a resource** | **Networking,** and then select **Virtual Network.**
3. Add the following values:
   - **Name:** `PacktLBVnet`
   - **Address space:** `172.16.0.0/16`
   - **Subscription:** Select a subscription
   - **Resource group:** Create a new one and call it **PacktLoadBalancer**
   - **Location: East US**
   - **Subnet name:** `PacktLBBackendSubnet`
   - **Subnet address range:** `172.16.0.0/24`
   - **DDoS protection: Basic**
   - **Service endpoints: Disabled**

- **Firewall: Disabled**:

Create virtual network

* Name

PacktLBVnet

* Address space

172.16.0.0/16

172.16.0.0 - 172.16.255.255 (65536 addresses)

* Subscription

Microsoft Azure Sponsorship

* Resource group

(New) PacktLoadBalancer

Create new

* Location

East US

Subnet

* Name

PacktLBBackendSubnet

* Address range

172.16.0.0/24

172.16.0.0 - 172.16.0.255 (256 addresses)

DDoS protection

◉ Basic ◯ Standard

Service endpoints

Disabled | Enabled

Firewall

Disabled | Enabled

Create   Automation options

VNet settings

4. Click **Create**.

Creating the VMs

The next step is to create the VMs that are used inside the backend pool and for testing. To do this, take the following steps:

1. To create the VMs, select **Create a resource** in the left menu, and then select **Compute** and then **Windows Server 2016 Datacenter**.
2. In the **Create a virtual machine** blade on the **Basic** tab, fill in the following values:
   - **Subscription: Select a subscription**
     Resource group: `PacktLoadBalancer` (which is created in the previous step).
   - **Virtual machine name**: `PacktLBVM1`.
   - **Region: East US**.
   - **Availability options**: Select **Availability set** and create a new one named `PacktLBAvailabilitySet`. Leave the default domain and update the domain settings.
   - **Image: Windows Server 2016 Datacenter**.
   - **Size: Standard DS1 v2**.
   - **Credentials**: Specify a username and password for the VM.
   - **Public inbound ports: Allow selected ports** | select **RDP (3389)**.
3. Select the **Networking** tab and select the virtual network that we created in the previous step with the subnet, and fill in the following values:
   - **NIC network security group**: Select **Advanced** and create a new network security group. Keep the default name for the new network security group.
4. Select the **Management** tab. Under **Monitoring**, set **Boot diagnostics** to **Off**.
5. Click the **Review + create** button to create the VM.
6. Repeat the preceding steps to create a second VM called `PacktLBVM2` and a third VM called `PacktLBVMTest` using the same settings, and place them in the same subscription, resource group, Availability Set and the same network security group.

Creating the load balancer

Now we can create the load balancer as follows:

1. To create the basic load balancer, in the top menu, select **Create a resource** | **Networking** | **Load Balancer**.

2. Add the following values:
   - **Subscription:** Pick a subscription
   - **Resource group**: `PacktLoadBalancer`.
   - **Name**: `PacktLoadBalancer`.
   - **Region**: **East US**.
   - **Type**: **Internal**.
   - **SKU**: **Basic**.
   - **Virtual Network**: Select `PacktLBVNet`.
   - **Subnet**: Select `PacktLBBackendSubnet`.
   - **IP address assignment**: **Static**.
   - **Private IP address:** Provide an IP address that is in the address space of your virtual network and subnet, such as `172.16.0.7`.

3. Click **Review + Create. Then click Create**:

Create load balancer

Basics   Tags   Review + create

Azure load balancer is a layer 4 load balancer that distributes incoming traffic among healthy virtual machine instances. Load balancers uses a hash-based distribution algorithm. By default, it uses a 5-tuple (source IP, source port, destination IP, destination port, protocol type) hash to map traffic to available servers. Load balancers can either be internet-facing where it is accessible via public IP addresses, or internal where it is only accessible from a virtual network. Azure load balancers also support Network Address Translation (NAT) to route traffic between public and private IP addresses. Learn more.

PROJECT DETAILS

* Subscription	SZ 1
└── * Resource group	PacktLoadBalancer
	Create new

INSTANCE DETAILS

* Name	PacktLoadBalancer
* Region	(US) East US
* Type ❶	◉ Internal ○ Public
* SKU ❶	◉ Basic ○ Standard

CONFIGURE VIRTUAL NETWORK.

* Virtual network ❶	PacktLBVnet
* Subnet	PacktLBBackendSubnet (172.16.0.0/24)
	Manage subnet configuration
* IP address assignment	◉ Static ○ Dynamic
* Private IP address	172.16.0.7

Review + create	Previous	Next : Tags >	Download a template for automation

Creating the load balancer

Creating a backend address pool

Now, the VMs and the Azure Load Balancer instance have been created and the networking is configured, so it is time to create the backend pool, which is used by the load balancer to distribute the traffic to the VMs. The backend pool consists of the IP addresses of the **Network Interface Cards (NICs)**.

We are going to create a backend pool with `PacktLBVM1` and `PacktLBVM2` in it:

1. Open the load balancer resource that we created in the previous step inside the Azure portal.
2. Under **Settings**, select **Backend pools**, and then click the **Add** button:

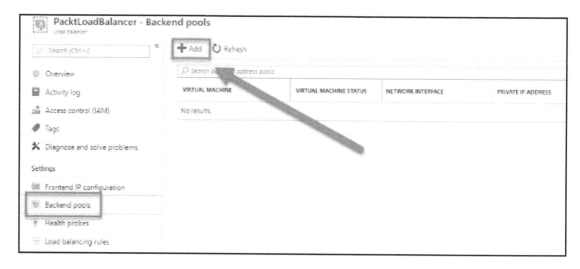

Creating the backend pool

3. Add the following values:
    - **Name**: `PacktLBBackendPool`.
    - **Associated to**: Select **Availability set**.
    - **Availability set**: Select `PacktLBAvailabilitySet`.
    - Select **Add a target network IP configuration** and add `PacktLBVM1` and `PacktLBVM2` to the backend pool.

4. Click **OK**:

Adding the VMs to the backend pool

Creating health probes

The next step is to create a health probe for the load balancer. The health probe is used for the load balancer to monitor the status of the VM. The probe will dynamically add or remove VMs from the load balancer rotation, based on the response to the health checks that are performed by the health probe.

To create a health probe, take the following steps:

1. Again, open the Load Balancer resource.
2. Under **Settings**, select **Health probes**, and then select **Add**:

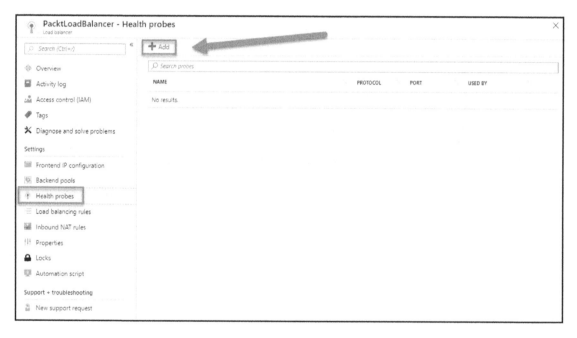

Creating a new health probe

3. Add the following values:
   - **Name**: PacktHealthProbe.
   - **Protocol**: HTTP.
   - **Port**: 80.
   - **Path**: /.

- **Interval**: 15—this is the number of seconds between probe attempts.
- **Unhealthy threshold**: 2—this value is the number of consecutive probe failures that occur before a VM is considered unhealthy.

4. Click **OK**:

Health probe settings

Creating load balancing rules

Load balancing rules define how the traffic is distributed to the VMs inside the backend pool. When you create a new rule, you define the frontend IP configuration for incoming traffic, the backend IP pool that receives the traffic, and the required source and destination ports.

The rule that we are going to create listens to port 80 at the frontend. The rule then sends the network traffic to the backend pool, also on port 80.

To create the rule, take the following steps:

1. Again, open the Load Balancer resource.
2. Under **Settings**, select **Load balancing rules**, and then select **Add**:

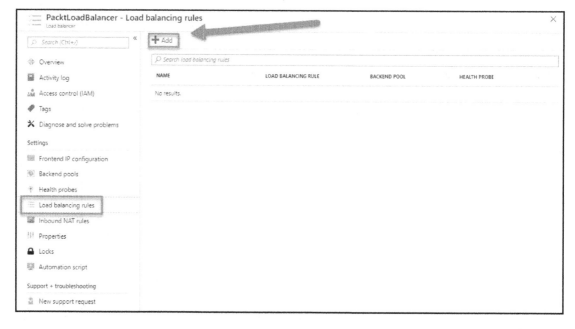

Creating a new rule

3. Add the following values:
   - **Name:** PacktLoadBalancerRule
   - **Frontend IP address:** LoadBalancerFrontEnd
   - **Protocol:** TCP
   - **Port:** 80

- **Backend port**: 80
- **Backend pool**: PacktLBBackendPool
- **Health probe**: PacktHealthProbe

4. Click **OK**:

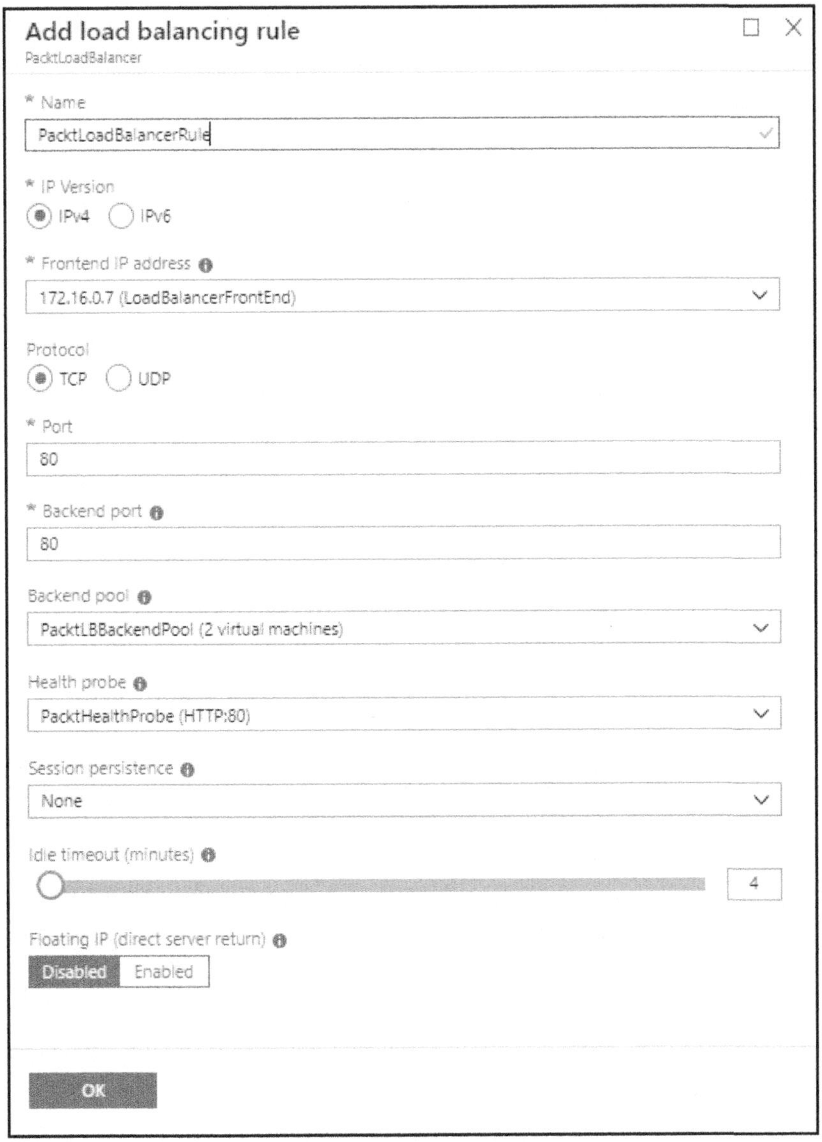

Add load balancing rule

PacktLoadBalancer

* Name

PacktLoadBalancerRule

* IP Version

( ) IPv4   ( ) IPv6

* Frontend IP address ●

172.16.0.7 (LoadBalancerFrontEnd)

Protocol

( ) TCP   ( ) UDP

* Port

80

* Backend port ●

80

Backend pool ●

PacktLBBackendPool (2 virtual machines)

Health probe ●

PacktHealthProbe (HTTP:80)

Session persistence ●

None

Idle timeout (minutes) ●

4

Floating IP (direct server return) ●

| Disabled | Enabled |

OK

Configuring the rule

Testing the load balancer

To test the VMs properly, we are going to install **Internet Information Services (IIS)** on the PacktLBVM1 and PacktLBVM2 VMs using PowerShell. Then, we can use the PacktLBVMTest VM to test the load balancer by calling its private IP address.

First, we need to obtain the private IP address of the load balancer. Take the following steps:

1. In the **Overview** page of the load balancer, copy the private IP address as follows:

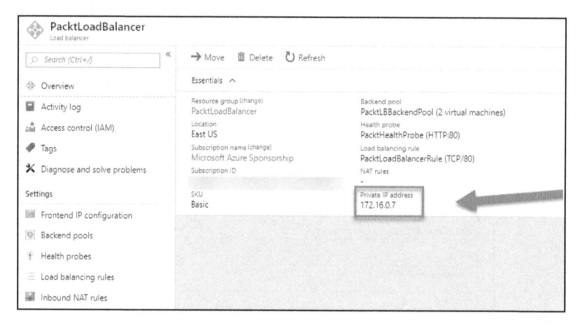

Obtaining the private IP address

2. Now, we need to connect to the PacktLBVM1 and PacktLBVM2 VM using an RDP session and install IIS and a testing web page on it. Connect to both the VMs, open the PowerShell console, and provide the following PowerShell script:

```
# Install IIS
Install-WindowsFeature -name Web-Server -IncludeManagementTools

# Remove default htm file
remove-item C:\inetpub\wwwroot\iisstart.htm
```

```
#Add custom htm file
 Add-Content -Path "C:\inetpub\wwwroot\iisstart.htm" -Value
 $("Hello World from " + $env:computername)
```

3. Next, connect to the `PacktLBVMTest` VM using RDP as well, open a browser session, and navigate to the private IP address of the load balancer. Refresh the browser a couple of times to see the load balancer distributing the requests over the two VMs, as the following screenshot shows:

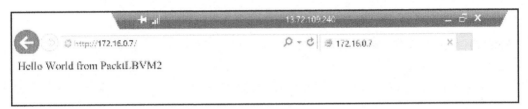

Testing the load balancer

Configuring a public load balancer

In this section, we are going to create a public load balancer using the Azure CLI. You can copy the code snippets in Azure Cloud Shell, which is accessible from the Azure portal.

The full script for creating the public load balancer can be downloaded from GitHub as well. Refer to the location specified under the *Technical requirements* section at the beginning of this chapter.

Creating the load balancer

To create the public load balancer, a series of steps need to be taken. In the upcoming sections, we will create the public load balancer with all the necessary components.

Creating a resource group

We start by creating a resource group for the load balancer and other resources as follows:

```
# Create a resource group
az group create \
 --name PacktResourceGroupSLB \
 --location eastus
```

Creating a public IP address

Next, we are going to configure a public IP address for the load balancer to access it from the internet. A standard load balancer only supports standard public IP addresses, as shown in the following code:

```
# Create a public IP address
az network public-ip create --resource-group PacktResourceGroupSLB --name
PacktPublicIP --sku standard
```

Creating the load balancer

In the following sections, we are going to create the load balancer and will create the components, including a frontend IP pool, backend IP pool, a health probe, and a load balancer rule.

To create the load balancer, add the following code:

```
# Create the Load Balancer
az network lb create \
  --resource-group PacktResourceGroupSLB \
  --name PacktLoadBalancer \
  --sku standard
  --public-ip-address PacktPublicIP \
  --frontend-ip-name PacktFrontEnd \
  --backend-pool-name PacktBackEndPool
```

Creating the health probe

All VM instances are checked by the health probe to define whether they are healthy enough to send network traffic to them. Virtual machine instances that are unhealthy are removed from the load balancer until the probe check determines that they are healthy again.

To create the health probe, add the following code:

```
#Create the health probe
az network lb probe create \
    --resource-group PacktResourceGroupSLB \
    --lb-name PacktLoadBalancer \
    --name PacktHealthProbe \
    --protocol tcp \
    --port 80
```

Creating the load balancer rule

The load balancer rule defines the frontend IP configuration for the incoming traffic and the backend IP pool to receive the traffic, together with the required source and destination ports, as follows:

```
#Create the Load Balancer rule
az network lb rule create \
  --resource-group PacktResourceGroupSLB \
  --lb-name PacktLoadBalancer \
  --name PacktHTTPRule \
  --protocol tcp \
  --frontend-port 80 \
  --backend-port 80 \
  --frontend-ip-name PacktFrontEnd \
  --backend-pool-name PacktBackEndPool \
  --probe-name PacktHealthProbe
```

Creating the virtual network

We now need to create the virtual network to deploy the VMs too, with the following code:

```
#Create a virtual network
az network vnet create \
    --resource-group PacktResourceGroupSLB \
    --location eastus \
    --name PacktVnet \
    --subnet-name PacktSubnet
```

Creating an NSG

Next, we will create an NSG. It is a requirement for a standard load balancer that the VMs in the backend have NICs that are placed in an NSG. We need to create the NSG to define the inbound connections to the virtual network as follows:

```
az network nsg create \
    --resource-group PacktResourceGroupSLB \
    --name PacktNetworkSecurityGroup
```

Creating an NSG rule

To allow inbound connections through port 80, create an NSG rule as follows:

```
#Create a Network Security Group rule
az network nsg rule create \
    --resource-group PacktResourceGroupSLB \
    --nsg-name PacktNetworkSecurityGroup \
    --name PacktNetworkSecurityGroupRuleHTTP \
    --protocol tcp \
    --direction inbound \
    --source-address-prefix '*' \
    --source-port-range '*' \
    --destination-address-prefix '*' \
    --destination-port-range 80 \
    --access allow \
    --priority 200
```

Creating NICs

We need to create two network interfaces and associate them with the NSG and the public IP address, as follows:

```
#Create NICs
for i in `seq 1 2`; do
 az network nic create \
 --resource-group PacktResourceGroupSLB \
 --name PacktNic$i \
 --vnet-name PacktVnet \
 --subnet PacktSubnet \
 --network-security-group PacktNetworkSecurityGroup \
 --lb-name PacktLoadBalancer \
 --lb-address-pools PacktBackEndPool
done
```

Creating backend servers

Next is creating the backend servers. We are going to create two VMs that are going to be used as backend servers for the load balancer. We are also going to install **NGINX** (which is an open source, high-performance HTTP server, and reverse proxy) on it to test the load balancer.

Creating an availability set

To create an availability set, add the following piece of code:

```
#Create an Availability set
az vm availability-set create \
 --resource-group PacktResourceGroupSLB \
 --name PacktAvailabilitySet
```

Creating two virtual machines

We are going to create two VMs with NGINX installed on it. We are also going to create a `Hello World` Node.js app on the Linux virtual machines. For this, we need to create a file called `cloud-init.txt` and paste the configuration in it. The following `cloud-init` configuration installs all the required packages, then creates the `Hello World` app, and then starts the app. To create the `cloud-init.txt` file, add the following line:

```
sensible-editor cloud-init.txt
```

Select an editor and paste in the following configuration. First, add the packages:

```
#cloud-config
package_upgrade: true
packages:
  - nginx
  - nodejs
  - npm
```

Then set up the server:

```
write_files:
  - owner: www-data:www-data
  - path: /etc/nginx/sites-available/default
    content: |
      server {
        listen 80;
        location / {
          proxy_pass http://localhost:3000;
          proxy_http_version 1.1;
          proxy_set_header Upgrade $http_upgrade;
          proxy_set_header Connection keep-alive;
          proxy_set_header Host $host;
          proxy_cache_bypass $http_upgrade;
        }
      }
```

Next, create the app:

```
 - owner: azureuser:azureuser
   - path: /home/azureuser/myapp/index.js
     content: |
       var express = require('express')
       var app = express()
       var os = require('os');
       app.get('/', function (req, res) {
         res.send('Hello World from host ' + os.hostname() + '!')
       })
       app.listen(3000, function () {
         console.log('Hello world app listening on port 3000!')
       })
```

And, finally, run the app:

```
runcmd:
  - service nginx restart
  - cd "/home/azureuser/myapp"
  - npm init
  - npm install express -y
  - nodejs index.js
```

With the above blocks of code, we now created the cloud-init.txt file for our VMs. save the file in the editor and exit it. Now, we can continue with creating the two virtual machines and apply the configuration on it, as follows:

```
#Create two virtual machines
for i in `seq 1 2`; do
 az vm create \
   --resource-group PacktResourceGroupSLB \
   --name myVM$i \
   --availability-set PacktAvailabilitySet \
   --nics PacktNic$i \
   --image UbuntuLTS \
   --generate-ssh-keys \
   --custom-data cloud-init.txt \
   --no-wait
 done
```

Testing the load balancer

To test the load balancer, we need to obtain the public IP address of it and paste this into a browser window. Wait for the VMs to be fully provisioned and running. You can check this in the Azure portal. Then, to obtain the public IP address, add the following line of code:

```
#Obtain public IP address
az network public-ip show \
    --resource-group PacktResourceGroupSLB \
    --name PacktPublicIP \
    --query [ipAddress] \
    --output tsv
```

Paste the output of this line of code into your browser window to see the Azure Load Balancer in action:

Testing the public load balancer

Summary

In this chapter, we covered how to configure internal and external load balancers. You also learned how to configure load balancing rules and health probes.

In the next chapter, we will continue with the fifth part of *Deploying and Managing Virtual Networks* objective by covering how to integrate an on-premises network with an Azure Virtual Network.

Questions

Answer the following questions to test your knowledge of the information in this chapter. You can find the answers in the *Assessments* section at the end of this book:

1. Can a basic load balancer only be created from the Azure portal?
   - Yes
   - No

2. Is it necessary for a standard load balancer that the VMs in the backend have NICs that are placed in an NSG?
   - Yes
   - No

3. Does a standard load balancer needs a standard public IP address to function properly?
   - Yes
   - No

Further reading

You can check the following links for more information about the topics that are covered in this chapter:

- *Load Balancer*: https://docs.microsoft.com/en-us/azure/load-balancer/
- *Quickstart: Create a load balancer to load balance VMs using Azure CLI*: https://docs.microsoft.com/en-us/azure/load-balancer/quickstart-create-basic-load-balancer-cli
- *Quickstart: Create a public load balancer using Azure PowerShell*: https://docs.microsoft.com/en-us/azure/load-balancer/quickstart-create-basic-load-balancer-powershell
- *Quickstart: Create a Standard Load Balancer to load balance VMs using the Azure portal*: https://docs.microsoft.com/en-us/azure/load-balancer/quickstart-load-balancer-standard-public-portal
- *Quickstart: Create a Standard Load Balancer using Azure PowerShell*: https://docs.microsoft.com/en-us/azure/load-balancer/quickstart-create-standard-load-balancer-powershell

Section 5: Managing Identities

In this section, you will learn how to manage identities in Azure.

The following chapters will be covered in this section:

- Chapter 14, *Managing Azure Active Directory*
- Chapter 15, *Implementing and Managing Hybrid Identities*
- Chapter 16, *Implementing Multi-Factor Authentication*

14
Managing Azure Active Directory

In the previous chapter, we covered how to configure an internal and external load balancer using Azure Load Balancer. The main focus was on the features and capabilities of Azure Load Balancer, and also on how to create health probes and configure load balancing rules.

This chapter introduces the final objective of this book: the *Managing Identities* objective. In this chapter, we are going to cover how to create and manage users and groups in **Azure Active Directory (Azure AD)**. You will learn how to manage this from the Azure portal and how to perform bulk updates inside your Azure AD tenant. You will learn how to configure self-service password reset for your users to reduce user management overhead. We are also going to cover Azure AD Join and how you can manage your devices that are registered or joined in Azure AD. To finish this chapter, we will add a custom domain to Azure AD.

The following topics will be covered in this chapter:

- Azure AD
- Creating and managing users and groups
- Adding and managing guest accounts
- Performing bulk user updates
- Configuring self-service password reset
- Azure AD Join
- Managing device settings
- Adding custom domains

Azure AD

Azure AD offers a directory and identity management solution from the cloud. It offers traditional username and password identity management, and roles and permissions management. On top of that, it offers more enterprise-grade solutions, such as **Multi-Factor Authentication** (**MFA**) and application monitoring, solution monitoring, and alerting. Azure AD can easily be integrated with your on-premises Active Directory to create a hybrid infrastructure.

Azure AD offers the following pricing plans:

- **Free**: This offers the most basic features, such as support for up to 500,000 objects, **single sign-on** (**SSO**), Azure B2B for external users, support for Azure AD Connect synchronization, self-service password change, groups, and standard security reports.
- **Basic**: This offers no object limit, a SLA of 99.9%, self-service password reset, company branding features, and support for the Application Proxy.
- **Premium P1**: This offers advanced reporting, MFA, conditional access, MDM auto-enrollment, cloud app discovery, and Azure AD Connect Health.
- **Premium P2**: This offers identity protection and Privileged Identity Management.

For a detailed overview of the different pricing plans and all the features that are offered for each plan, you can refer to the following pricing page: https://azure.microsoft.com/en-us/pricing/details/active-directory/.

Note that Azure AD Premium is part of the Enterprise Mobility and Security Suite.

In the next section, we are going to create and manage users and groups inside an Azure AD tenant.

Creating and managing users and groups

In this demonstration, we are going to create and manage users and groups in the Azure portal. You can also use PowerShell and CLI to create users.

We are not going to create an Azure AD tenant in this demonstration. I assume that you already have one. If you need to create an Azure AD tenant, you can refer to the following tutorial: `https://docs.microsoft.com/en-us/azure/active-directory/develop/quickstart-create-new-tenant`.

You can also create multiple Azure AD tenants in one subscription. These directories can be used for development and test purposes, for instance.

Creating users in Azure AD

We will begin by creating a couple of users in our Azure AD tenant from the Azure portal. Therefore, you have to take the following steps:

1. Navigate to the Azure portal by opening `https://portal.azure.com`.
2. In the left menu, select **Azure Active Directory**.
3. In the **Overview** blade of Azure AD, in the left menu, select **Users | All users**. Select **+ New user** from the top menu, as follows:

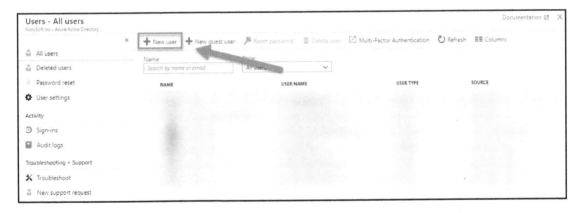

Creating a new user

4. We are going to create three users. Add the following values, which are shown in the following screenshot:
   - **Name:** `PacktUser1`.
   - **Username:** The username is the identifier that the user enters to sign in to Azure AD. Use your domain name that is configured and add this to the end of the username. In my case, this is `PacktUser1@sjoukjezaal.com`.

- **Profile**: Here, you can create a new profile for your user. Add the **First name**, **Last name**, **Job title**, and **Department**. After that, click **OK**, as follows:

Creating a profile for your user

- **Group**: You can also add your user to a group from here. We are going to do this in the following demonstration, so you can skip this part for now.

- **Directory role**: Here, you can assign the user to the **User, Global administrator**, or **Limited administrator** role. Select **User**, as follows:

Selecting directory role

5. Click **Create**.
6. Repeat these steps and create `PackUser2` and `PacktUser3`.

Now that we have created a couple of users in our Azure AD tenant, we can add them to a group in Azure AD.

Creating groups in Azure AD

To create and manage groups from the Azure AD tenant in the Azure portal, you have to perform the following steps:

1. Navigate to the Azure portal by opening `https://portal.azure.com`.
2. In the left menu, select **Azure Active Directory.**
3. In the **Overview** blade of Azure AD, in the left menu, select **Groups | All groups**. Select **+ New group** from the top menu, as follows:

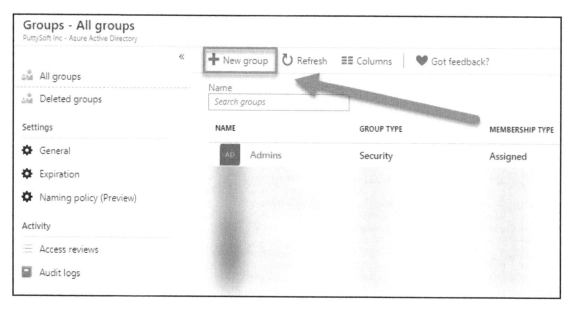

Creating a new group

4. Add the following values to create the new group:
   - **Group type**: **Security.**
   - **Group name**: `PacktGroup`.

- **Membership type**: Here, you can choose between three different values. The first is **Assigned**, where you assign the members manually to the group; then, there's **Dynamic user**, where the group membership is determined based on certain user properties. Dynamic group membership eliminates the management overhead of adding and removing users. The last option is **Dynamic device**, and here the group membership is determined based on certain device properties. Select the first option: **Assigned.**

5. Click the **Members** tab to add members to this group. Select the three user accounts that we created in the previous demonstration, as follows:

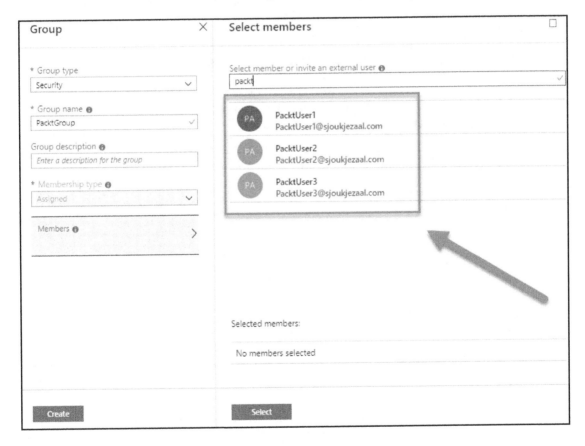

Adding users to a group

6. Click **Select** to add the members, and then **Create** to create the group.

We have now created a new group inside Azure AD and added the user accounts to it that we created in the previous demonstration. In the next section, we are going to cover how to add and manage guest accounts.

Adding and managing guest accounts

You can also add guest accounts in Azure AD using Azure AD **business-to-business (B2B)**. Azure AD B2B is a feature on top of Azure AD that allows organizations to work safely with external users. To be added to Azure B2B, external users don't need to have a Microsoft work or personal account that has been added to an existing Azure AD tenant. All sorts of accounts can be added to Azure B2B.

You don't have to configure anything in the Azure portal to use B2B; this feature is enabled by default for all Azure AD tenants. Perform the following steps:

1. Adding guest accounts to your Azure AD tenant is similar to adding internal users to your tenant. When you go to the users overview blade, you can choose **+ New guest user** in the top menu, as follows:

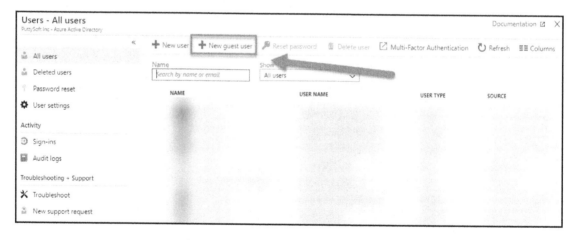

Adding a guest user

2. Then, you can provide an email address and a personal message, which is sent to the user's inbox. This personal message includes a link to log in to your tenant:

External user properties

3. Click **Invite** to add the user to your Azure AD tenant and send out the invitation to the user's inbox.

4. To manage external users after creation, you can select them from the user overview blade. They will have a **USER TYPE**, which is named **Guest**. Simply select the user in the list and you will be able to manage the settings that are displayed in the top menu for this user, as follows:

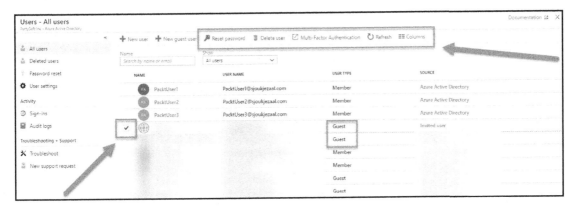

Managing external users

In the next section, we are going to cover how to perform bulk user updates from the Azure portal.

Performing bulk user updates

Performing bulk user updates is similar to managing single users (internal and guest). The only property that can't be set for multiple users is resetting the password. This has to be done for a single user.

To perform a bulk user update, you have to perform the following steps:

1. Go to the users overview blade again.
2. You can select multiple users in the overview blade. From the top menu, select the property that you want to configure, as follows:

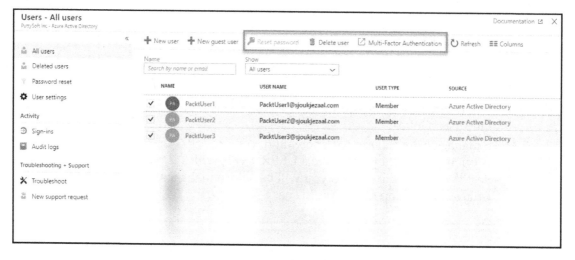

Performing a bulk user update

This concludes the demonstration for performing bulk user updates. In the next section, we are going to cover how you can configure self-service password reset for your users.

Configuring self-service password reset

By enabling self-service password for your users, they are able to change their passwords automatically, without calling the help desk. This eliminates management overhead significantly.

Self-service password reset can easily be enabled from the Azure portal. Therefore, you have to perform the following steps:

1. Navigate to the Azure portal by opening `https://portal.azure.com`.
2. In the left menu, select **Azure Active Directory**.
3. In the Azure AD overview blade, in the left menu, under **Manage**, select **Password reset**, as follows:

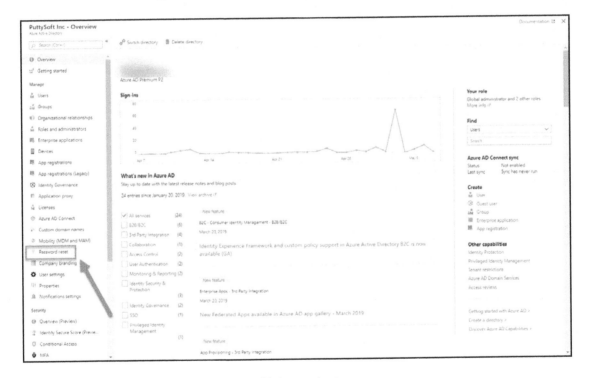

Selecting password reset

4. In the password reset overview blade, you can enable self-service password reset for all your users by selecting **All**, or for selected users and groups, by selecting **Selected**. For this demonstration, enable it for all users and click **Save** in the top menu, as follows:

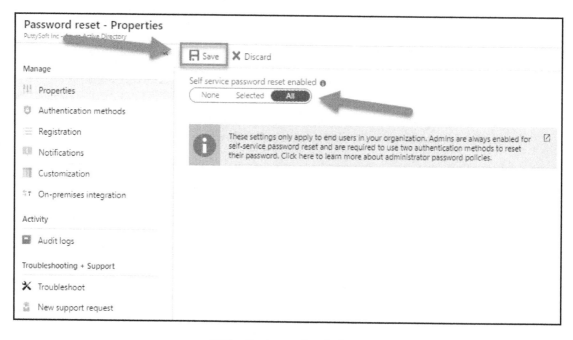

Enabling self-service password reset for all users

5. Next, we need to set the different required authentication methods for your users. For this, under **Manage**, select **Authentication methods**.

6. In the next blade, we can set the number of authentication methods that are required to reset a password and what methods there are available for your users, as follows:

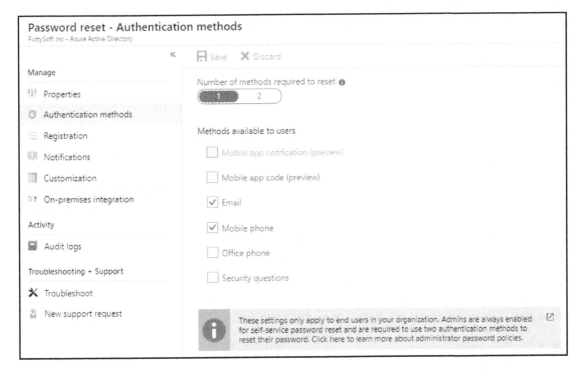

Password reset - Authentication methods
PuttySoft Inc - Azure Active Directory

»   💾 Save   ✕ Discard

Manage

⫿⫿ Properties

◎ Authentication methods

≡ Registration

🖺 Notifications

▦ Customization

⇅ On-premises integration

Activity

🖫 Audit logs

Troubleshooting + Support

✗ Troubleshoot

🖺 New support request

Number of methods required to reset ℹ

(1   2)

Methods available to users

☐ Mobile app notification (preview)

☐ Mobile app code (preview)

☑ Email

☑ Mobile phone

☐ Office phone

☐ Security questions

ℹ These settings only apply to end users in your organization. Admins are always enabled for self-service password reset and are required to use two authentication methods to reset their password. Click here to learn more about administrator password policies.

Different authentication methods

7. Make a selection and click **Save**.

If you want to test self-service password reset after configuration, make sure that you use a user account without administrator privileges.

We have now configured self-service password reset for all our users inside our Azure AD tenant. In the next section, we are going to manage device settings in Azure AD.

Azure AD Join

With Azure AD Join, you are able to join devices directly to Azure AD without the need to join your on-premises Active Directory in a hybrid environment. While hybrid Azure AD Join with an on-premises AD may still be preferred for some scenarios, Azure AD Join simplifies adding devices and modernizes device management for your organization. This can result in the reduction of device-related IT costs. Your users are getting access to the corporate assets through their devices. To protect these corporate assets, you want to control these devices. This allows your administrators to make sure that your users are accessing resources from devices that meet your standards for security and compliance.

Azure AD Join is a good solution when you want to manage devices with a cloud device management solution, modernize your application infrastructure, simplify device provisioning for geographically distributed users, and when your company is adopting Microsoft 365 as the productivity suite for your users.

Managing device settings

Azure AD offers the ability to ensure that users are accessing Azure resources from devices that meet corporate security and compliance standards. Device management is the foundation for device-based conditional access, where you can ensure that access to your resources in your environment is only possible from managed devices.

Device settings can be managed from the Azure portal. To manage your device settings, your device needs to be registered or joined to Azure AD.

To manage the device settings from the Azure portal, you have to perform the following steps:

1. Navigate to the Azure portal by opening `https://portal.azure.com`.
2. In the left menu, select **Azure Active Directory**.
3. In the Azure AD overview blade, under **Manage**, select **Devices**, as follows:

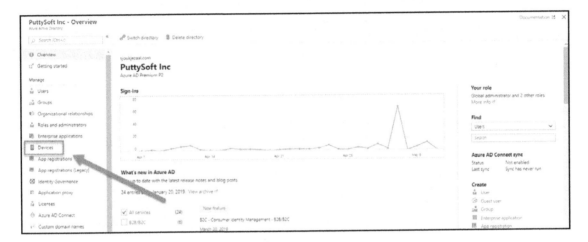

Selecting Devices from the menu

4. The Device management blade will open. Here, you can configure your device management settings, locate your devices, perform device management tasks, and review the device management-related audit logs.

5. To configure device settings, select **Device settings** from the left menu. In here, you can configure the following settings, which are shown in the following screenshot:

- **Users may join devices to Azure AD**: Here, you can set which users can join their devices to Azure AD. This setting is only applicable to Azure AD Join on Windows 10.

- **Additional local administrators on Azure AD joined devices**: Here, you can select the users that are granted local administrator permissions on a device. The users that are selected here are automatically added to the device administrator's role in Azure AD. Global administrators in Azure AD and device owners are granted local administrator rights by default (this is an Azure AD Premium option).

- **Users may register their devices with Azure AD**: This setting needs to be configured to allow devices to be registered with Azure AD. There are two options here: **None**, that is, devices are not allowed to register when they are not Azure AD joined or hybrid Azure AD joined, and **All**, that is, all devices are allowed to register. Enrolment with Microsoft Intune or **Mobile Device Management (MDM)** for Office 365 requires registration. If you have configured either of these services, **All** is selected and **None** is not available.

- **Require Multi-Factor Auth to join devices**: Here, you can set that users are required to perform multi-factor authentication when registering a device. Before you can enable this setting, MFA needs to be configured for the users that register their devices.

- **Maximum number of devices**: This setting allows you to select the maximum number of devices that a user can have in Azure AD:

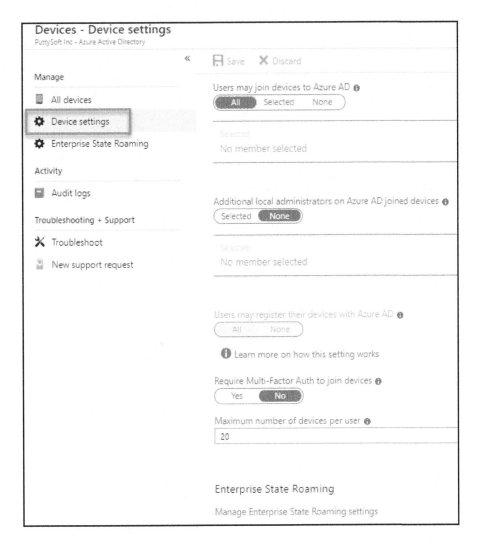

Device settings overview

6. To locate your devices, under **Manage**, select **All devices**. In this overview, you will see all the joined and registered devices, as follows:

Located devices

7. You can also select the different devices from the list to get more detailed information about the device. In here, global administrators and cloud device administrators can **Disable** or **Delete** the device, as follows:

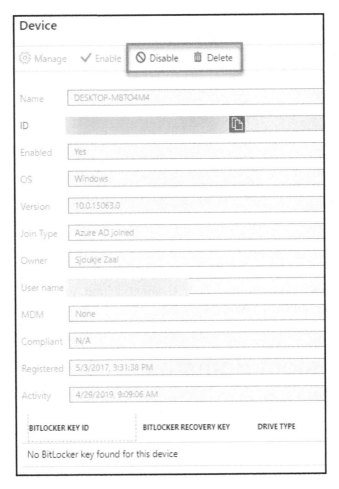

Device information

8. For audit logs, under **Activity**, select **Audit logs**. From here, you can view and download the different log files. You can also create filters to search through the logs, as follows:

Audit logs

We have now looked at all the different management and configuration options for devices that are registered or joined to Azure AD. In the next section, we are going to cover how you can add custom domains to Azure AD.

Adding custom domains

Azure creates an initial domain for every Azure AD tenant that is created in a subscription. This domain name consists of the tenant name, followed by `onmicrosoft.com` (`packtpub.onmicrosoft.com`). You cannot change or delete the initial domain name, but you can add custom domains to your Azure AD tenant.

This custom domain name can be registered at a third-party domain registrar and, after registration, you can add it to the Azure AD tenant.

To add a custom domain to Azure AD from the Azure portal, you have to perform the following steps:

1. Navigate to the Azure portal by opening `https://portal.azure.com`.
2. In the left menu, select **Azure Active Directory**.
3. In the Azure AD overview blade, under **Manage**, select **Custom domain names**. To add a custom domain, select the **+ Add custom domain** button in the top menu, as follows:

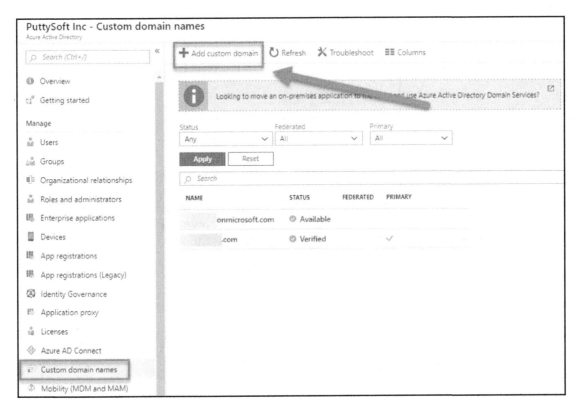

Adding a custom domain

4. Type the custom domain name in the **Custom domain name** field (for example, `packtpub.com`) and select **Add domain**, as follows:

Providing a custom domain name

5. After you add your custom domain name to Azure AD, you need to create a **TXT** record inside the DNS settings of your domain registrar. Go to your domain registrar and add the Azure AD DNS information from your copied TXT file. Creating this TXT record for your domain *verifies* ownership of your domain name. After creating the TXT file, click **Verify**, as follows:

packtpub.com
Custom domain name

🗑 Delete

ℹ To use packtpub.com with your Azure AD, create a new TXT record with your domain name registrar using the info below.

RECORD TYPE   (TXT   MX)

ALIAS OR HOST NAME   @

DESTINATION OR POINTS TO ADDRESS   MS=ms19059692

TTL   3600

Share these settings via email

Verify domain
Verification will not succeed until you have configured your domain with your registrar as described above.

Verify

Verifying the ownership of the domain

6. After you've verified your custom domain name, you can delete your verification TXT or MX file.

We have now configured a custom domain for our Azure AD tenant. Your users can now use this domain name to log in to the various Azure resources they have access to.

Summary

In this chapter, we covered the first part of the *Managing Identities* objective. We covered the various aspects of Azure AD. You've learned how to add users and groups, how to add guest users, and how to manage your devices in Azure AD. We also covered how to add custom domain names to our Azure AD tenant from the Azure portal.

In the next chapter, we will cover the second part of this exam objective. In this chapter, we will cover how to implement and manage hybrid identities.

Questions

Answer the following questions to test your knowledge of the information in this chapter. You can find the answers in the *Assessments* section at the end of this book:

1. If you want to create a guest user using PowerShell, you have to use the `New-AzureADMSInvitation` cmdlet.
   - Yes
   - No

2. If you want to use Azure AD Join for your devices, you first need to configure your on-premises AD environment in a hybrid environment, together with Azure AD.
   - Yes
   - No

3. When you add a custom domain to Azure AD, you need to verify it by adding a TXT record to the DNS settings of your domain registrar.
   - Yes
   - No

Further reading

You can check out the following links for more information about the topics that were covered in this chapter:

- *Azure Active Directory Documentation:* `https://docs.microsoft.com/en-us/azure/active-directory/`
- *Add or delete users using Azure Active Directory:* `https://docs.microsoft.com/en-us/azure/active-directory/fundamentals/add-users-azure-active-directory`
- *Azure Active Directory version 2 cmdlets for group management:* `https://docs.microsoft.com/en-us/azure/active-directory/users-groups-roles/groups-settings-v2-cmdlets`
- *Quickstart: Add a guest user with PowerShell:* `https://docs.microsoft.com/en-us/azure/active-directory/b2b/b2b-quickstart-invite-powershell`
- *Quickstart: Self-service password reset:* `https://docs.microsoft.com/en-us/azure/active-directory/authentication/quickstart-sspr`
- *How to: Plan your Azure Active Directory join implementation:* `https://docs.microsoft.com/en-us/azure/active-directory/devices/azureadjoin-plan`
- *What is device management in Azure Active Directory?:* `https://docs.microsoft.com/en-us/azure/active-directory/devices/overview`
- *Add your custom domain name using the Azure Active Directory portal:* `https://docs.microsoft.com/en-us/azure/active-directory/fundamentals/add-custom-domain`

15
Implementing and Managing Hybrid Identities

In the previous chapter, we've covered how to manage **Azure Active Directory (Azure AD)**. This chapter proceeds with the *Managing Identities* objective. In this chapter, we are going to cover how to implement and manage hybrid identities. We are going to install and configure Azure AD Connect to synchronize the identities from your on-premises Active Directory to Azure AD. Then you will learn how to manage Azure AD Connect. In the last part of this chapter, we will dive into password sync and password writeback. You will learn how to enable password sync in Azure AD Connect and the Azure portal. At lastly, you will learn how to manage password sync.

The following topics will be covered in this chapter:

- Azure AD Connect
- Installing Azure AD Connect
- Managing Azure AD Connect
- Managing password sync and password writeback

Azure AD Connect

Azure AD Connect is a service that you can use to synchronize your on-premises Active Directory identities with Azure. This way, you can use the same identities for authentication on your on-premises environment as well as in the cloud, and other **software as a service (SaaS)** applications.

The Azure AD Connect sync service consists of two parts, the Azure AD Connect sync component, which is a tool that is installed on a separate server inside your on-premises environment, and the Azure AD Connect sync service, which is part of Azure AD. The sync component can sync data from Active Directory and SQL Servers to Azure. There is also a third component named the **Active Directory Federation Services** (**ADFS**) component, which can be used in a scenario where ADFS is involved. To monitor the on-premises identity infrastructure and the different Azure AD components, you can use a tool named Azure AD Connect Health. The following diagram illustrates the architecture of Azure AD Connect:

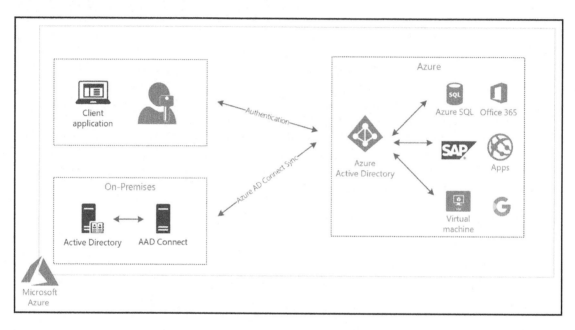

Azure AD Connect architecture

Azure AD Connect offers support for your users to sign in with the same passwords to both on-premises and cloud resources. It provides three different authentication methods for this, the password hash synchronization method, the pass-through authentication method, and the Federated SSO method (in conjunction with ADFS).

Azure AD password hash synchronization

Most organizations only have a requirement to enable user sign in to Office 365, SaaS applications, and other Azure AD-based resources. The password hash synchronization method is well suitable for those scenarios.

Using this method, hashes of the user's password are synced between the on-premises Active Directory and Azure AD. When there are any changes to the user's password, the password is synced immediately, so users can always log in with the same credentials on-premises as well as in Azure.

This authentication method also provides Azure AD Seamless **Single Sign-On (SSO)**. This way, users are automatically signed in when they are using a domain-joined device on the corporate network. Users only have to enter their username when using Seamless SSO. To use Seamless SSO, you don't have to install additional software or components on the on-premises network. You can push this capability to your users using group policies.

Azure AD pass-through authentication

Azure AD pass-through authentication offers the same capability as Azure AD password hash synchronization. Users can log in to their Azure resources as well as on-premises resources using the same credentials. The difference is that the passwords don't sync with Azure AD using pass-through authentication. The passwords are validated using the on-premises Active Directory and are not stored in the Azure AD at all.

This method is suitable for organizations that have security and compliance restrictions and aren't allowed to send usernames and passwords outside the on-premises network. Pass-through authentication requires an agent to be installed on a domain-joined Windows server that resides inside the on-premises environment. This agent then listens for password validation requests and only makes an outbound connection from within your network. It also offers support for **Multi-Factor Authentication (MFA)** and Azure AD conditional access policies.

Azure AD pass-through authentication offers Azure AD Seamless SSO as well.

In the next section, we are going to install Azure AD Connect and synchronize some on-premises users to Azure.

Installing Azure AD Connect

Azure AD Connect is installed on an on-premises server with Active Directory installed and configured on it. The first step is to download Azure AD Connect. After downloading, we can install it on a domain controller.

For this demonstration, I have already deployed a Windows Server 2016 virtual machine in Azure and installed and configured Active Directory on it. Configuring Active Directory is beyond the scope of the exam and this book. Make sure that when you configure Active Directory Domain Services, the Forest name matches one of the existing verified custom domains in Azure AD. Otherwise, you will receive a warning message when you install Azure AD Connect on your domain controller, that SSO is not enabled for your users. For installing Active Directory on a Windows Server 2016 machine, you can refer to the following website: `https://blogs.technet.microsoft.com/canitpro/2017/02/22/step-by-step-setting-up-active-directory-in-windows-server-2016/`.

Therefore, take the following steps:

1. Before downloading Azure AD Connect, add at least one user to your on-premises Active Directory.
2. To download Azure AD Connect, you can refer to the following website: `https://www.microsoft.com/en-us/download/details.aspx?id=47594`. Store it on a local drive on your domain controller and run `AzureADConnect.msi` after downloading.

3. The installation wizard starts with the welcome screen. Select the checkbox to agree with the license terms:

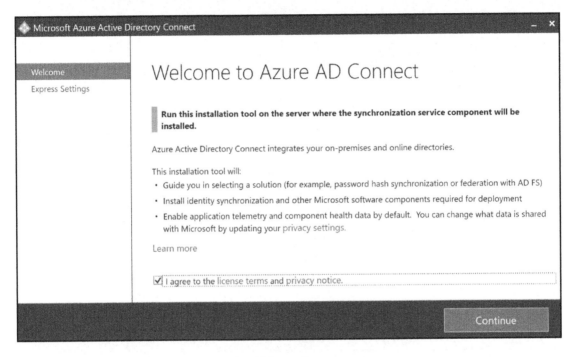

Azure AD Connect welcome screen

4. Select **Use express settings** in the next screen:

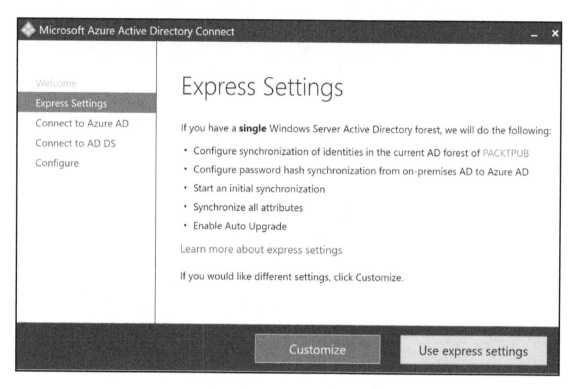

Installing Azure AD Connect using express settings

5. On the next screen, provide the username and password of a global administrator account (This account must be a school or organization account and cannot be a Microsoft account or any other type of account) for your Azure AD and click **Next**:

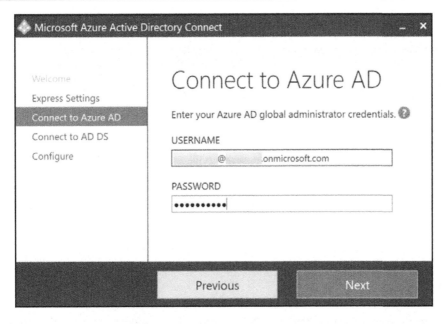

Provide global administrator credentials

6. On the **Connect to AD DS** screen, enter the username and password for an enterprise administrator account and click **Next** as follows:

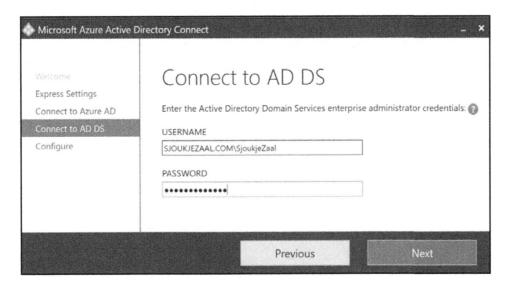

Enter enterprise administrator account

The last screen will give an overview of what is going to be installed, as follows:

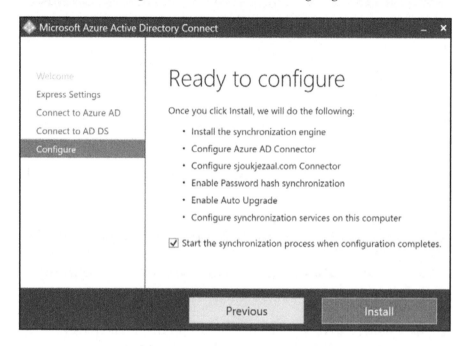

Ready to configure

7. Click **Install.**
8. This will install Azure AD Connect on your domain controller. The synchronization process of user accounts to Azure AD will automatically be started after configuration.

9. After successful configuration, you will see the following outcome:

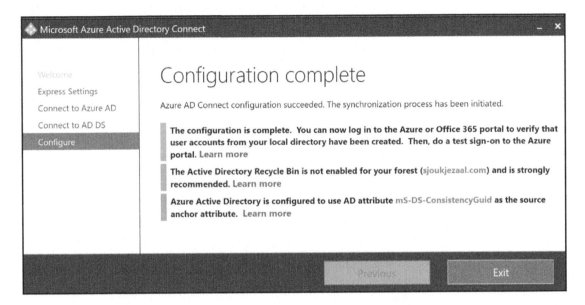

Configuration complete

10. Click **Exit** to close the installer.

In this demonstration, we installed Azure AD Connect on an on-premises domain controller. In the next section, we are going to manage it from the Azure portal.

Managing Azure AD Connect

Azure AD Connect can be managed from the Azure portal after installation and configuration on the on-premises domain controller. To manage it, you have to take the following steps:

1. Navigate to the Azure portal by opening `https://portal.azure.com`.
2. In the left menu, select **Azure Active Directory**.

3. Under **Manage**, select **Azure AD Connect**. In the **Azure AD Connect** blade, as shown in the following screenshot, you can see that sync is enabled, that the last sync was less than an hour ago, and that **Password Hash Sync** is enabled:

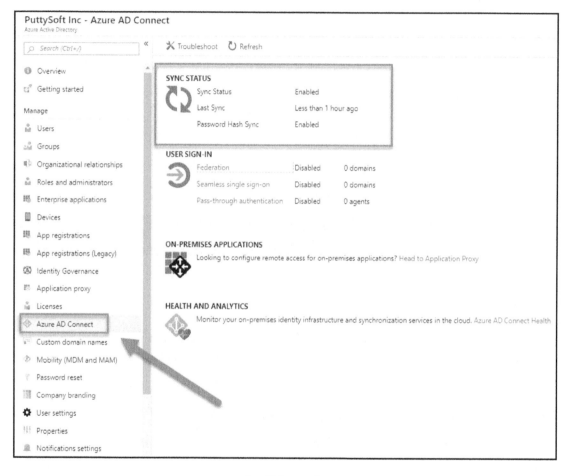

Azure AD Connect settings

4. You can also set the three authentication methods under **USER SIGN-IN**. Here, you can set the authentication method to **Federation, Seamless single sign-on**, or **Pass-through authentication**. You can monitor the health of your on-premises infrastructure and synchronization services under **Health and Analytics**.

5. To check if the users are synced, you can go to the **user overview** blade. Here, you will find your synced users, as in the following screenshot:

Synced users

 Azure AD Connect sync synchronizes changes in your on-premises directory using a scheduler. There are two scheduler processes, one for password sync and another for object/attribute sync and maintenance tasks. For more information on how to configure this or creating a custom scheduler using PowerShell, you can refer to the following tutorial: `https://docs.microsoft.com/en-us/azure/active-directory/hybrid/how-to-connect-sync-feature-scheduler`.

In this demonstration, we managed Azure AD Connect from the Azure portal. In the next section, we are going to cover how to manage password writeback in more detail.

Password writeback

Password writeback is used for synchronizing password changes in Azure AD back to your on-premises Active Directory environment. This setting is enabled as part of Azure AD Connect, and it provides a secure mechanism to send password changes from Azure AD back to an on-premises Active Directory.

It provides the following features and capabilities:

- **Enforcement of on-premises Active Directory password policies**: When a user resets their password, the on-premises Active Directory policy is checked to ensure it meets the password requirements before it gets committed to the directory. It checks the password complexity, history, password filters, age, and other password restrictions that are defined in the on-premises Active Directory.
- **Zero-delay feedback**: Users are notified immediately after changing their password, if their password doesn't meet the on-premises Active Directory policy requirements. This is a synchronous operation.
- **Supports password writeback when an administrator resets them from the Azure portal**: When an administrator resets the password in the Azure portal, the password is written back to the on-premises Active Directory (when a user is federated or password hash synchronized). This functionality doesn't work from the Office admin portal.
- **Doesn't require any inbound firewall rules**: Password writeback uses the Azure Service Bus for communicating with the on-premises Active Directory, so there is no need to open the firewall. All communication is outbound and goes over port 443.
- **Supports password changes from the access panel and Office 365**: When federated or password hash synchronized users change their password, those passwords are written back to your on-premises Active Directory as well.

In the next demonstration, we are going to enable password writeback.

Managing password writeback

To enable password writeback, we need to make some changes to both the configuration of Azure AD Connect on the on-premises domain controller, and from the Azure portal.

Enabling password writeback in Azure AD Connect

To enable password writeback in Azure AD Connect, we have to take the following steps:

1. Log in to your on-premises domain controller using **Remote Desktop (RDP)** and start the Azure AD Connect wizard again.
2. On the **Welcome to Azure AD Connect** page, select **Configure** as follows:

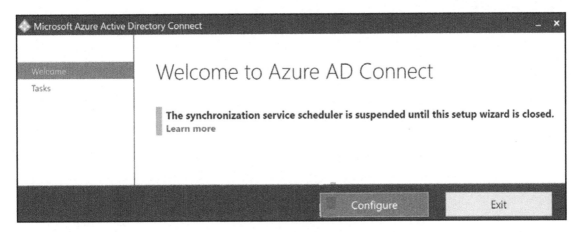

Welcome screen

3. In the **Additional tasks** screen, select **Customize synchronization options**, and select **Next** as follows:

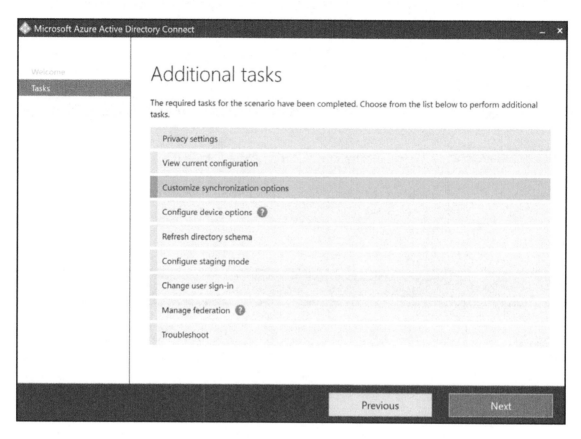

Additional tasks screen

4. Provide Azure AD global administrator credentials and select **Next** as follows:

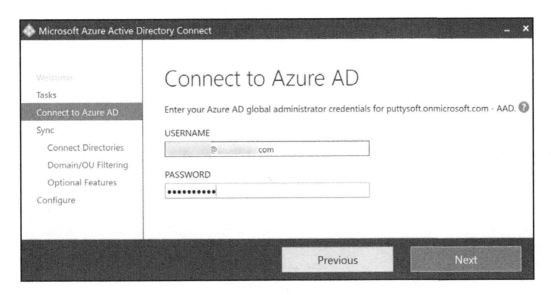

Providing administrator credentials

5. On the **Connect your directories** screen, select **Next** as follows:

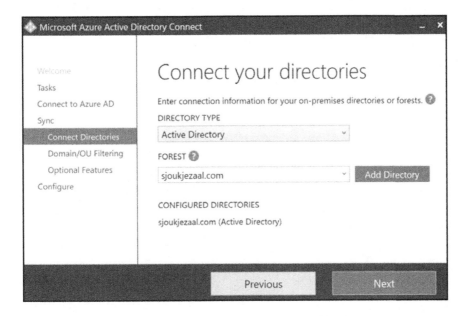

Connecting your directories

6. On the **Domain and OU filtering** screen, select **Next** again as follows:

Domain and OU filtering screen

7. On the **Optional features** screen, select the box next to **Password writeback** and select **Next** as follows:

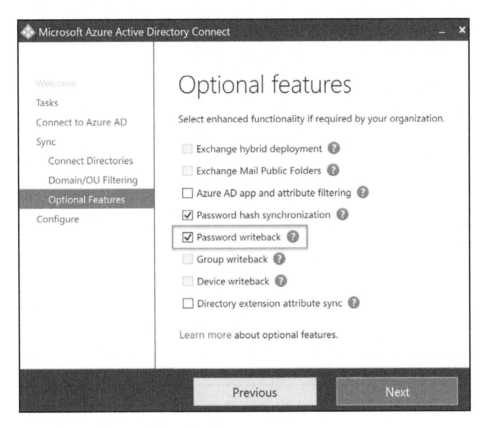

Enabling password writeback

8. On the **Ready to configure** page, select **Configure**.
9. When the configuration is finished, select **Exit**.

We have now enabled password writeback on the domain controller. In the next section, we are going to enable it in the Azure portal as well.

Enabling password writeback in the Azure portal

To enable password writeback in the Azure portal, we have to take the following steps:

1. Navigate to the Azure portal by opening `https://portal.azure.com`.
2. In the left menu, select **Azure Active Directory**.
3. Under **Manage**, select **Password reset** as follows:

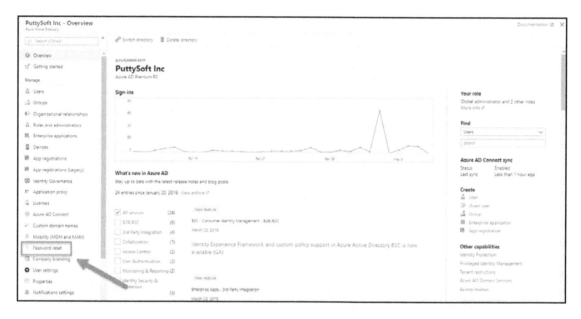

Password reset in the Azure portal

4. In the **password reset** blade, under **Manage**, select **On-premises integration**. Set the option for **Write back passwords to your on-premises directory?** to **Yes** and set the option for **Allow users to unlock accounts without resetting their password?** to **Yes** as follows:

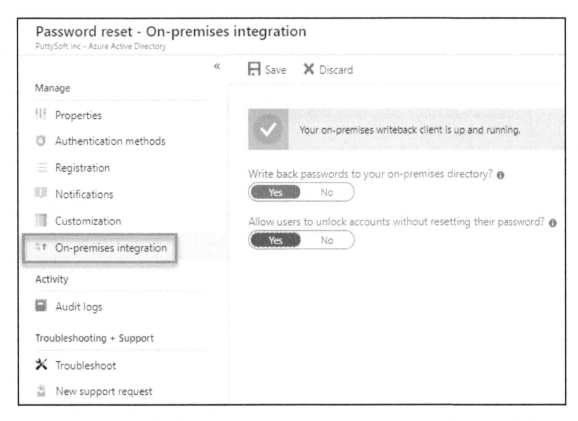

Enabling password writeback

5. Click **Save**.

We have now completely configured password writeback in Azure AD Connect and the Azure portal. In the next section, we are going to cover how to manage password sync.

Password sync

In this last section of this chapter, we are going to cover password sync. We installed Azure AD Connect using the **Express Settings** option. Password hash synchronization is automatically enabled if you use this option.

If you install Azure AD Connect using the custom settings, password hash synchronization is available on the **User sign-in** screen and you can enable it there, as shown in the following screenshot:

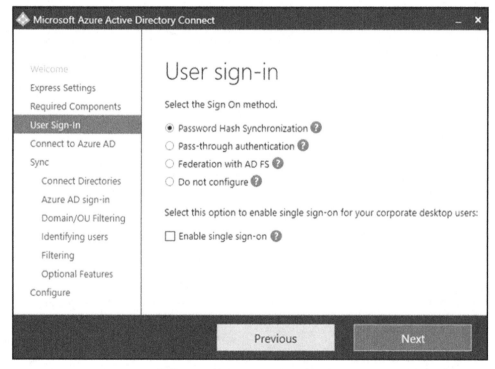

Enabling password hash synchronization during installation

Summary

In this chapter, we covered the second part of the *Managing Identities* objective. We covered Azure AD Connect and you've learned how to install and manage it after installation. We also covered how to enable password writeback and password hash synchronization.

In the next chapter, we will cover the third and final part of this exam objective. In this chapter, we will cover how to implement **Multi-Factor Authentication (MFA)** in Azure.

Questions

Answer the following questions to test your knowledge of the information in this chapter. You can find the answers in the *Assessments* section at the end of this book:

1. If you use the **Express Settings** when installing Azure AD Connect, password hash synchronization is disabled by default.
   - Yes
   - No

2. When you want to enable password sync, you only have to do this inside the Azure portal.
   - Yes
   - No

3. If the on-premises Forest name doesn't match one of the Azure AD custom domain names, you cannot install Azure AD Connect.
   - Yes
   - No

Further reading

You can check out the following links for more information about the topics that were covered in this chapter:

- *What is hybrid identity with Azure Active Directory?*: `https://docs.microsoft.com/en-us/azure/active-directory/hybrid/whatis-hybrid-identity`
- *What is federation with Azure AD?*: `https://docs.microsoft.com/en-us/azure/active-directory/hybrid/whatis-fed`
- *What is password hash synchronization with Azure AD?*: `https://docs.microsoft.com/en-us/azure/active-directory/hybrid/whatis-phs`
- *User sign-in with Azure Active Directory Pass-through Authentication*: `https://docs.microsoft.com/en-us/azure/active-directory/hybrid/how-to-connect-pta`
- *Azure AD Connect sync: Understand and customize synchronization*: `https://docs.microsoft.com/en-us/azure/active-directory/hybrid/how-to-connect-sync-whatis`
- *Azure AD Connect user sign-in options*: `https://docs.microsoft.com/en-us/azure/active-directory/hybrid/plan-connect-user-signin`
- *Tutorial: Enabling password writeback*: `https://docs.microsoft.com/en-us/azure/active-directory/authentication/tutorial-enable-writeback`
- *Implement password hash synchronization with Azure AD Connect sync*: `https://docs.microsoft.com/en-us/azure/active-directory/hybrid/how-to-connect-password-hash-synchronization`

16
Implementing Multi-Factor Authentication

In the previous chapter, we covered the second part of the *Managing Identities* objective. You've learned how to install Azure AD Connect and how to manage it.

This chapter covers the last part of this objective and is the last chapter of this book. In this chapter, we are going to focus on **Multi-Factor Authentication (MFA)** in Azure, so you can add a second layer of security to sign-up and sign-in experiences for your Azure resources. We are going to look at the different verification methods and how you can configure this. We are also going to configure fraud alerts, so users can report fraudulent attempts to access their resources. And to finish this chapter, we are going to configure trusted IPs to bypass MFA.

The following topics will be covered in this chapter:

- Azure MFA
- Configuring user accounts for MFA
- Configuring verification methods
- Configuring fraud alerts
- Configuring bypass options
- Configuring trusted IPs

Azure MFA

MFA is a security feature that requires more than one method of authentication. You can use it to add an additional layer of security to the sign in of users. It enables two-step verification, where the user first signs in using something they know (such as a password), and then signs in with something they have (such as a smart phone), or some human characteristic (such as biometrics).

Azure MFA maintains the simplicity for the users, but also helps to keep data and applications safe by providing additional security by requiring a second form of authentication. It offers a variety of configuration methods made by an administrator that determines whether users are challenged for MFA or not.

Azure MFA is part of the following offerings:

- **Azure Active Directory Premium license**: With this license, you can use Azure MFA Service (cloud) and Azure MFA Server (on-premises). The latter is most suitable in scenarios where an organization has **Active Directory Federation Services** (**ADFS**) installed and needs to manage infrastructure components.
- **Azure Active Directory Global Administrators**: A subset of the MFA features is available for administrator accounts in Azure.
- **MFA for Office 365**: A subset of the MFA features is available for Office 365 users.

With Azure MFA, you can use the following verification methods:

Verification method	Description
Voice call	A call is made to the registered phone of the user. The user needs to enter a PIN for verification.
Text message	A text message is sent to the user's mobile phone containing a six digit code. The user needs to fill in this code on the sign-in page.
Mobile app notification	A request for verification is sent to the user's smart phone. When necessary, the user will enter a PIN and then select **Verify**.
Mobile app verification code	The mobile app on the user's smart phone will display a verification code, which will refresh every 30 seconds. The user will select the most recent code and will enter it in the sign-in page.
Third-party tokens	Azure MFA Server can be configured to accept third-party security tokens.

In the upcoming sections, we will enable MFA for the Azure AD tenant, configure user accounts, configure fraud alerts, and configure bypass options.

 For the demos in this chapter, I will use an Azure Active Directory Premium P2 license.

Enabling MFA for an Azure AD tenant

The following are the three different options for enabling MFA for your users, data, and applications:

- **Using a conditional access policy**: You can use conditional access policies to enable MFA. This can be enabled at the user or application level. You can also enable MFA for security groups or for all external users using a conditional access policy. This is available for premium Azure AD licenses.
- **At the user level**: This option is covered in more detail in the next section of this chapter. This is the traditional method for enabling MFA. With this method, the user needs to perform MFA every time they sign in. This will override conditional access policies when these are set.
- **Using Azure AD Identity Protection**: With this option, you will create an Azure AD Identity Protection risk policy based on sign-in risk for all of your cloud applications. This will also override conditional access policies, if created. This option requires an Azure Active Directory P2 license.

Configuring user accounts for MFA

Azure MFA is enabled in Azure AD at the user level. To enable MFA for a user account in Azure AD, take the following steps:

1. Navigate to the Azure portal by opening `https://portal.azure.com/`.
2. Go to **All services**, then type `Azure Active Directory` and open the Azure AD resource.

3. In the Azure AD blade, under **Manage**, select **Users** as follows:

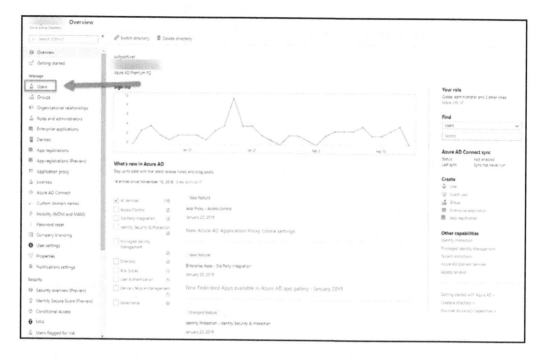

Azure AD user settings

4. In the **All users** blade, select **Multi-Factor Authentication** in the top menu as follows:

Selecting Multi-Factor Authentication

5. You then will be redirected to the **multi-factor authentication** portal. In there, select a user and click **Enable** at the right side of the screen as follows:

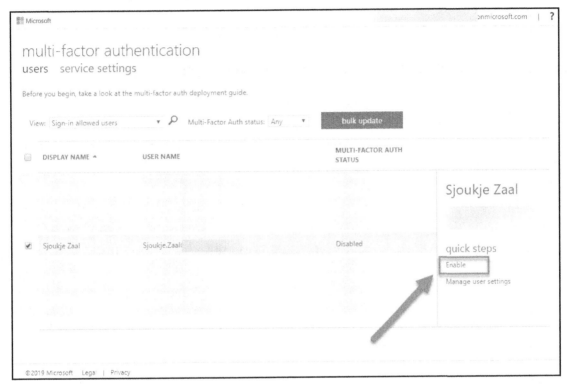

Enabling MFA for a user

6. After clicking the link, you will receive the following warning:

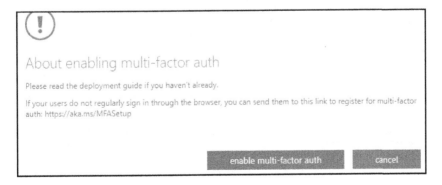

Warning window

7. Click **enable multi-factor auth** to activate MFA for this user.

Now that we have enabled MFA for the user, we can look at how to configure the verification methods.

Configuring the verification methods

Verification methods are also configured in the Azure MFA portal, just as you enabled MFA for the user account in the previous step. Take the following steps:

1. With the MFA portal still open, select **service settings** in the top menu as follows:

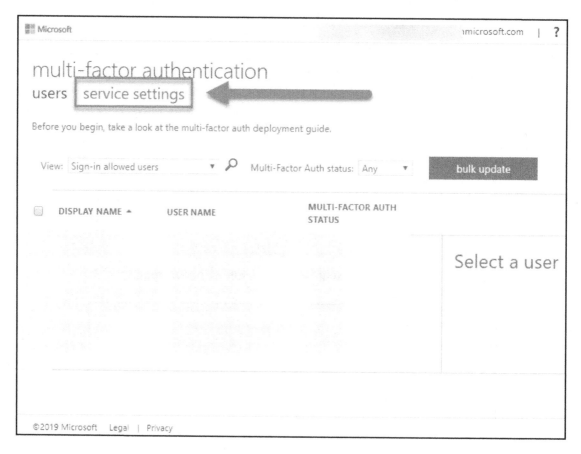

MFA portal service settings

2. Under **verification options**, you can select the methods that you want to enable for your users. By default, all verification options are enabled, as follows:

MFA verification options

3. If you want to disable options, uncheck the checkbox and click the **Save** button.

We have seen how to configure the verification methods that users are allowed to use for using MFA in Azure. In the next section, we are going to look at how to configure trusted IPs.

Configuring trusted IPs

Trusted IPs are used by administrators of an Azure AD tenant. This option will bypass the MFA for users that sign in from a trusted IP, such as the company intranet.

Trusted IPs can be configured from the **service settings** page from the MFA portal. Take the following steps:

1. With the **server settings** page still open from the previous demonstration, under **trusted ips**, check the checkbox that says **Skip multi-factor authentication for requests from federated users on my intranet**. Then, add an IP address or a range of IP addresses in the list as follows:

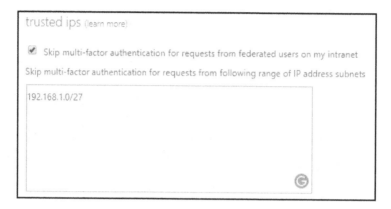

Trusted IP settings

2. Click the **Save** button to save your settings.

In the next section, we are going to cover how to configure fraud alerts in the Azure portal.

Configuring fraud alerts

With the fraud alert feature, users can report fraudulent attempts to access their resources using their phone or the mobile app. This is an MFA Server (on-premises) feature.

Fraud alerts are configured from the Azure portal, in the Azure Active Directory settings. Take the following steps:

1. Navigate to the Azure portal by opening `https://portal.azure.com`.
2. Select **All services**, then type `Azure Active Directory` in the search bar and open the settings.

3. Under **Security**, select **MFA** as follows:

MFA in Azure AD

4. The **Getting started** blade is automatically opened. Under **Settings**, select the **Fraud alert**.

5. The **Fraud alert** settings page is opened. In here, you can enable users to submit fraud alerts as follows:

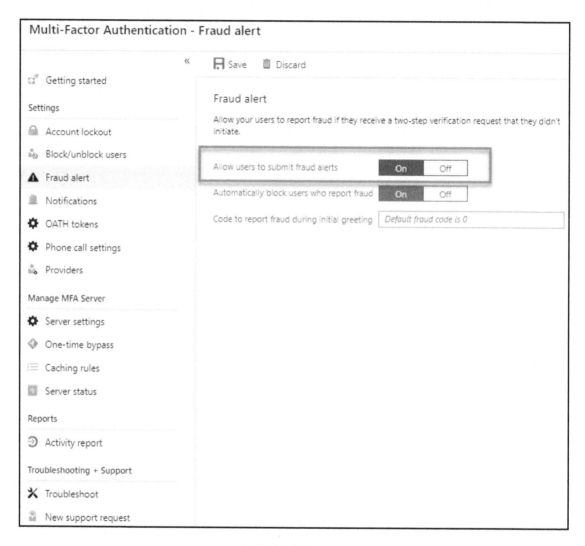

Enable submitting fraud alerts

6. Click the **Save** button to save the settings.

We've now seen how we can allow users to submit fraud alerts. In the next section, we are covering how to configure bypass options.

Configuring bypass options

With the one-time bypass feature, users can authenticate once and bypass the MFA. This setting is temporary, and after a specified number of seconds, it will expire automatically. This can be a solution in cases when a phone or mobile app doesn't receive a phone call or a notification.

This setting is also configured from the **Azure Active Directory** settings in the Azure portal as follows:

1. Navigate to the Azure portal by opening `https://portal.azure.com`.
2. Select **All services**, then type `Azure Active Directory` in the search bar and open the settings.
3. Under **Manage MFA Server**, select **One-time bypass** as follows:

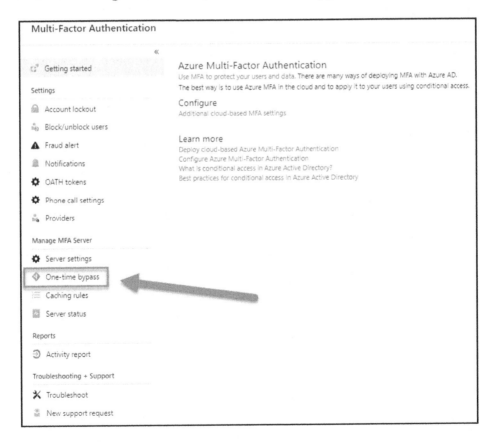

One-time bypass

4. In the settings page, enter the username, including the full domain name, such as `username@domain.com`. Specify the number of seconds that the bypass should last and the reason for the bypass.

5. Click the **Add** button. The time limit will go in immediately.

We've now covered how to authenticate once and bypass the MFA using the one-time bypass feature.

Summary

In this chapter, we covered the last part the *Managing Identities* objective by looking at how to configure user accounts for MFA in Azure. We covered different authentication methods and enabled it for our users. Lastly, we looked at the various ways to bypass MFA, such as trusted IP addresses.

With the knowledge gained throughout the chapters, you should be able to pass the AZ-103 exam. Don't forget to look at the *Further reading* sections at the end of each chapter, because there is a lot of extra information there that could be covered in the exam as well.

Questions

Answer the following questions to test your knowledge of the information in this chapter. You can find the answers in the *Assessments* section at the end of this book:

1. Can you add trusted IP addresses for bypassing MFA for certain IPs?
    - Yes
    - No

2. MFA cannot be enabled using conditional access policies.
    - Yes
    - No

3. Are fraud alerts part of the MFA Server (on-premises) offering?
    - Yes
    - No

Further reading

You can check the following links for more information about the topics that are covered in this chapter:

- *How it works: Azure Multi-Factor Authentication:* `https://docs.microsoft.com/en-us/azure/active-directory/authentication/concept-mfa-howitworks`
- *Planning a cloud-based Azure Multi-Factor Authentication deployment:* `https://docs.microsoft.com/en-us/azure/active-directory/authentication/howto-mfa-getstarted`
- *Configure Azure Multi-Factor Authentication settings:* `https://docs.microsoft.com/en-us/azure/active-directory/authentication/howto-mfa-mfasettings`
- *What is conditional access in Azure Active Directory?:* `https://docs.microsoft.com/en-us/azure/active-directory/conditional-access/overview`
- *Quickstart: Require MFA for specific apps with Azure Active Directory conditional access:* `https://docs.microsoft.com/en-us/azure/active-directory/conditional-access/app-based-mfa`

17
Mockup Test Questions

Chapter 1, Managing Azure Subscriptions and Resource Groups Access Control

1. You have an Azure subscription named Subscription1, which contains two resource groups named ResourceGroup1 and ResourceGroup2. You need to ensure that all global administrators can manage all the resources inside both resource groups. You enable access management for the Azure resources from the Azure Active Directory properties blade. Does this solution meet your goal?
   1. Yes
   2. No

2. You are creating a Windows Server **Virtual Machine (VM)** that you plan to use as an image for future deployments. You need to ensure that other administrators cannot make any changes to it until you complete the image. What should you do?
   1. Edit the **role-based access control (RBAC)** permissions on the VM level.
   2. Edit the RBAC permissions on the resource group level.
   3. Set a delete lock at the VM level.
   4. Set a read-only lock on the resource group level.

3. You determine that business units inside your organization have Azure resources spread across different Azure resource groups. You need to make sure that the resources are assigned to proper cost centers. What should you do?
    1. Deploy an Azure policy
    2. Create taxonomic tags and assign them at the resource level
    3. Create taxonomic tags and assign them at the resource group level
    4. Use queries to obtain the right resources and create a report from this outcome

Chapter 2, Analyzing Resource Utilization and Consumption

1. You have an Azure subscription that has eight VMs deployed in it. You need to configure monitoring for this, and want to receive a notification when the **Central Processing Unit (CPU)** or available memory reaches a certain threshold value. The notification needs to be sent using an email and needs to create a new issue in the corporate issue tracker. What is the minimum number of action groups and alerts that you need to create to meet these requirements?
    1. Eight alerts and one action group
    2. Two alerts and two action groups
    3. One alert and two action groups
    4. One alert and one action group

2. You have two Azure resource groups named `ResourceGroup1` and `ResourceGroup2`. The `ResourceGroup1` resource group contains 20 Windows Server VMs and all the VMs are connected to an Azure Log Analytics workspace named `Workspace1`. You need to write a log search query that collects all security events with the following properties: all security levels other than 8 and with Event ID 4672. How should you write your query?
    1. `SecurityEvent | where Level == 8 | and EventID == 4672`
    2. `SecurityEvent | where Level <> 8 | where EventID == 4672`
    3. `SecurityEvent | where Level == 8 | summarize EventID == 4672`
    4. `SecurityEvent | where Level <> 8 | and EventID == 4672`

3. Your company has an application that uses an Azure SQL Database for storing information. The company has also deployed System Center Service Manager. You need to configure an alert when the database reaches 80% of CPU usage. When this alert rises, you want your administrator to be notified using email and SMS. You also need to create a ticket in the corporate issue tracker automatically when the alert arises. Which two actions should you perform?
    1. Configure System Center Service Manager with Azure Automation
    2. Configure one action group with three actions: one for email, one for SMS, and one for creating the ticket
    3. Configure an IT Service Management Connector
    4. Configure two actions groups: one for email and SMS and one for creating the ticket

Chapter 3, Managing Role-Based Access Control

1. You need to delegate some of the global administrator privileges to a new cloud engineer in your office. You decide to create a custom role using a JSON file and the following PowerShell cmdlet to add the custom role: `New-AzureRmRoleDefinition -InputFile "C:\ARM_templates/customrole.json"`. Is this correct?
    1. Yes
    2. No

2. Your company has an Azure AD tenant and an on-premises AD that are synced using Azure AD Connect. You have one subscription called `Packt_Main`. The helpdesk administrators are members of the `Packt_HD` group. You need to grant the helpdesk group the permissions to reset user passwords using the Azure portal, while using the least amount of permissions. What should you do?
    1. Grant the `Packt_HD` group the password administrator role in Azure administrator
    2. Delegate password reset privileges to the `Packt_HD` group on the user's **Organizational Unit (OU)** in Azure Directory users and computers
    3. Add the `Packt_HD` group to the domain admins user group
    4. Grant the `Packt_HD` group the ownership role on the `Packt_Main` subscription

3. You want to create a group of resource group managers in the Azure portal. Which RBAC role do you need to assign to them to manage all the resource groups in the Azure subscription?
    1. Contributor
    2. Reader
    3. Owner
    4. Monitoring reader

Chapter 4, Creating and Configuring Storage Accounts

1. Your company is developing a .NET application that stores information in an Azure storage account. You need to ensure that the information is stored in a secure way. You ask the developers to use a **shared access signature (SAS)** when accessing the information. You need to make the required configurations on the storage account to follow security best practices. Which statement is true?
    1. You need to configure a stored access policy.
    2. To revoke a SAS, you can delete the stored access policy.
    3. You should set the SAS start time to now.

2. Your company has an application that requires data from a blob storage to be moved from the hot access tier to the archive access tier to reduce costs. Which type of storage account do you need to create?
    1. General Purpose V2 storage account
    2. General Purpose V1 storage account
    3. Azure File storage
    4. Azure Blob storage

3. Your company wants to deploy a storage account. You need to ensure that the data is available in the case of the failure of an entire data center. The solution must be the most cost effective. What should you do?
    1. Configure geo redundant storage
    2. Configure local redundant storage
    3. Configure read-access geo redundant storage
    4. Configure zone redundant storage

Chapter 5, Importing and Exporting Data to Azure

1. Your company has developed a web application that uses dynamic and static content. The application is deployed in multiple regions to achieve the best performance. Users complain about the performance of the web application and report that it takes a lot of time before the images are loaded. You decide to configure a **Content Delivery Network (CDN)**. Which two actions should you perform?

    1. Implement custom caching rules on the CDN
    2. Implement cross-origin sharing on the website
    3. Implement general web delivery on the CDN
    4. Implement dynamic site acceleration on the CDN

2. Your company has developed a web application that uses dynamic and static content. The application is deployed in multiple regions to achieve the best performance. Users complain about the performance of the web application and report that it takes a lot of time before the images are loaded. You decide to configure a CDN. What are two possible ways to configure the CDN?

    1. Configure a single Azure CDN Premium Verizon endpoint, configure dynamic site acceleration, and configure caching rules
    2. Configure a single Azure CDN Standard Akamai endpoint, configure dynamic site acceleration, and configure caching rules
    3. Configure a single Azure CDN Standard Verizon endpoint, configure dynamic site acceleration, and configure caching rules
    4. Configure a single Azure CDN Standard Microsoft endpoint, configure dynamic site acceleration, and configure caching rules

3. Your company has a large amount of data stored inside on-premises databases and file servers (120 TB). This data needs to be uploaded to Azure. What is the fastest way to upload it to Azure?

    1. Using Azure Data Box
    2. Using Azure Storage Explorer
    3. Uploading it manually from the Azure portal
    4. Creating an Azure file share

Chapter 6, Configuring Azure Files and Implementing Azure Backup

1. Your company has eight on-premises file servers and an Azure subscription, which includes a storage account. You are planning to implement an Azure file share in a hybrid configuration using Azure file share sync. Which of the following statements is true?
    1. Azure file share sync secures the hybrid connection using IPSec
    2. Azure file share sync reduces the storage footprint of the on-premises file servers
    3. Azure file share sync provides fault tolerance for the on-premises file shares

2. You are configuring Azure file sync to sync on-premises file shares with Azure File storage. Which two actions must be complete to ensure that the service will operate successfully on your servers?
    1. Disable Internet Explorer Enhanced Security for both administrators and users
    2. Disable Internet Explorer Enhanced Security for administrators only
    3. Ensure that PowerShell version 5.1 or higher is deployed on the servers
    4. Ensure that Azure AD Connect is installed on your servers

3. You are setting up backup and restore for your Azure file shares. To create a backup policy in PowerShell, which of the following cmdlets should you use?
    1. `New-AzRecoveryServicesBackupProtectionPolicy`
    2. `Get-AzRecoveryServicesBackupSchedulePolicyObject`
    3. `Get-AzRecoveryServicesVault`
    4. `Enable-AzRecoveryServicesBackupProtection`

Chapter 7, Creating and Configuring VMs for Windows and Linux

1. You have an Azure resource group named `PacktResourceGroup1` that contains a Linux VM named `PacktVM1`. You need to automate the deployment of 30 additional Linux machines. The VMs should be based on the configuration of the `PacktVM1` VM. Which of the following solutions will meet the goal?

    1. From the VM Automation's script blade, you click **Deploy**
    2. From the **Templates** blade, you click **Add**
    3. From the resource group's policy blade, you click **Assign policy**

2. Your company has a VM that is stored inside a resource group. You need to deploy additional VMs in the same resource group. You are planning to deploy them using an ARM template. You need to create a template from the original VM using PowerShell. Which cmdlet should you use?

    1. Use the `Export-AzResourceGroup`
    2. Use the `Get-AzResourceGroupDeployment`
    3. Use the `Get-AzResourceGroupDeploymentOperation`
    4. Use the `Get-AzResourceGroupDeploymentTemplate`

3. You have a Windows Server 2016 machine deployed inside an availability set. You need to change the availability set assignment for the VM. What will you do?

    1. Migrate the VM to another Azure region
    2. Assign the VM to a new availability set
    3. Redeploy the VM from a recovery point
    4. Move the VM to a different availability set

Chapter 8, Managing Azure VMs and VM Backups

1. Your company has two different Azure subscriptions named PacktSubscription1 and PacktSubscription2, which both have their own Azure Active Directory assigned. You have a VM deployed in a resource group called PacktResourceGroup1 in the PacktSubscription1 subscription. You want to move this VM to another resource group, which is deployed in PacktSubscription2. You get an error when you try to move the VM. What is most likely causing this error?
   1. The VM has managed disks configured
   2. The VM is a classic VM
   3. The destination resource group is in a different subscription
   4. The subscriptions are in different Azure AD tenants

2. You need to move a VM using PowerShell. Which cmdlet should you use?
   1. Set-AzVM
   2. Get-AzVM
   3. Update-AzVM
   4. Redeploy-AzVM

3. You have a VM deployed in a resource group and want to add an additional data disk to it to increase storage. You want to add the disk using PowerShell. Which cmdlet should you use?
   1. Set-AzVMDataDisk
   2. New-AzVMDataDisk
   3. Add-AzVMDataDisk
   4. New-AzDisk

Chapter 9, Implementing and Managing Virtual Networking

1. Your company has two **Virtual Networks (VNets)** deployed, VNet1 and VNet2. You need to connect both VNets together. What is the most cost effective solution?

   1. VNet-to-VNet
   2. Site-to-site
   3. User-defined Routes
   4. VNet peering

2. A VM named PacktVM1 is deployed in a resource group named PacktResourceGroup1. The VM is connected to a VNet named PacktVNet1. You plan to connect the PacktVM1 VM to an additional VNet named PacktVNet2. You need to create an additional **network interface** on the PacktVM1 VM and connect it to the PacktVNet2 VNet. Which two Azure **Command-line Interface (CLI)** commands should you use?

   1. `az vm nic add`
   2. `am vm nic create`
   3. `az network update`
   4. `az network nic create`

3. You need to assign a static IPv4 address for a Windows Server VM named PacktVM1 running in a VNet named PacktVNet1. What should you do?

   1. Modify the IP configuration of the VNet interface associated with the PacktVM1 VM
   2. Edit the address range of the PacktVNet1 VNet
   3. Connect to the PacktVM1 VM by using WinRM and run the Set-NetIPAddress cmdlet
   4. Connect to the PacktVM1 VM by using Remote Desktop Protocol and edit the VM's virtual network connection properties

Chapter 10, Integrating On-Premise Networks with Azure Virtual Networks

1. You are managing the network of your organization. The on-premises infrastructure consists of multiple subnets. A new branch office was recently added. The network devices in the new office are assigned to a 192.168.22.0/24 subnet. You need to configure the Azure VPN Gateway to make sure that all the network devices in the branch office are accessible from the Azure network as well. Which PowerShell cmdlet should you use?
   1. Add-AzureRmVirtualNetworkSubnetConfig
   2. Set-AzureRmLocalNetworkGateway
   3. Set-AzureRmNetworkInterface
   4. Add-AzureRmNetworkInterfaceIpConfig

2. You have an application running on an Azure VM. Your on-premises network connects to the Azure Virtual Network using an Azure VPN Gateway. The application cannot be exposed directly to the internet due to security requirements. Users of the marketing department should be able to access the application when they are traveling and are using their company laptop. Which kind of connection should you configure?
   1. ExpressRoute
   2. Point-to-site
   3. Site-to-site
   4. VNet-to-VNet

3. Your organization has Azure resources deployed in the West US, West Europe, and East Australia regions. The company has four offices located in these regions. You need to provide connectivity between all the on-premises networks and all the resources in Azure using a private channel. You configure a VPN gateway for each Azure region and configure a site-to-site VPN for each office and connect to the nearest VPN gateway. You then configure virtual network peering. You need to ensure that users have the lowest traffic latency. Does this solution meet your goal?
   1. Yes
   2. No

Chapter 11, Monitoring and Troubleshooting Virtual Networking

1. You have a Windows Server that is deployed in Azure and uses an ExpressRoute connection. After two months of normal use without any issues, suddenly you receive feedback from the users that they are experiencing network issues when they attempt to connect to the server. What tool do you need to use to monitor the network traffic to the server?
    1. Network Performance Monitor
    2. Application Insights
    3. Azure Monitor
    4. Network Watcher

2. You have several VNets configured in several Azure regions. Your on-premises infrastructure is based in the East US region and has four subnets configured. You are experiencing network performance issues in your on-premises infrastructure and decide to use the Network Performance Monitor for troubleshooting. Do you need to install the Log Analytics agent on all on-premises servers?
    1. Yes
    2. No

3. Your organization has Azure resources deployed in the West US, West Europe, and East Australia regions. The company has four offices located in these regions. Each office is connected to the nearest available Azure region using a site-to-site VPN connection. The VNets from each region are connected using virtual network peering. You need to monitor the traffic between the networks. You configure the connection troubleshoot capability of Azure Network Watcher. Does this solution meet your goal?
    1. Yes
    2. No

Chapter 12, Azure Security Groups and Azure DNS

1. Your company plans to release a new web application. This application is deployed using an App Service in Azure and will be available for all users of the `packtpub.com` domain. You have already purchased the `packtpub.com` domain name. You configure the `packtpub.com` Azure **Domain Name System (DNS)** zone and delegate it to the Azure DNS. You need to ensure that the web application can be accessed by using the `packtpub.com` domain name. You decide to use PowerShell to accomplish this. Which command should you use?

   1. ```
      New-AzDnsRecordSet -Name "packtpub.com" -RecordType
      "AAAA" -ZoneName "packtpub.com" `
      -ResourceGroupName "MyAzureResourceGroup" -Ttl 600 `
      -DnsRecords (New-AzDnsRecordConfig -IPv4Address "<your
      web app IP address>")

      New-AzDnsRecordSet -ZoneName packtpub.com -
      ResourceGroupName PacktAzureResourceGroup `
      -Name "applicationscs.azurewebsites.net" -RecordType
      "CNAME" -Ttl 600 `
      -DnsRecords (New-AzDnsRecordConfig -Value
      "packtpub.azurewebsites.net")
      ```

   2. ```
      New-AzDnsRecordSet -Name "@" -RecordType "A" -ZoneName
      "packtpub.com" `
      -ResourceGroupName "MyAzureResourceGroup" -Ttl 600 `
      -DnsRecords (New-AzDnsRecordConfig -IPv4Address "<your
      web app IP address>")

      New-AzDnsRecordSet -ZoneName packtpub.com -
      ResourceGroupName PacktAzureResourceGroup `
      -Name "@" -RecordType "txt" -Ttl 600 `
      -DnsRecords (New-AzDnsRecordConfig -Value
      "packtpub.azurewebsites.net")
      ```

   3. ```
      New-AzDnsRecordSet -Name
      "applicationscs.azurewebsites.net" -RecordType "AAAA" -
      ZoneName "packtpub.com" `
      -ResourceGroupName "MyAzureResourceGroup" -Ttl 600 `
      -DnsRecords (New-AzDnsRecordConfig -IPv4Address "<your
      web app IP address>")
      ```
      ```

```
New-AzDnsRecordSet -ZoneName packtpub.com -
ResourceGroupName PacktAzureResourceGroup `
-Name "www.packtpub.com" -RecordType "AAAA" -Ttl 600 `
-DnsRecords (New-AzDnsRecordConfig -Value
"packtpub.azurewebsites.net")
```

2. Your company plans to release a new web application and it needs to be available for all users on the `packtpub.com` domain. You decide to configure a DNS zone in Azure and check whether the domain is still available. What is the first step that you have to take to configure Azure DNS for this web application?

1. Create a Start of Authority record in your Azure DNS zone that points to Azure DNS servers

2. Configure a forward DNS zone in Azure

3. Configure a private DNS zone in Azure

4. Purchase the `packtpub.com` domain from a third-party domain registrar

3. You design a virtual network topology with the following characteristics: web subnet: 3 web frontend VMs, app subnet: 3 application server VMs, data subnet: 3 database server VMs. Your company requires that inter-subnet network traffic be strictly controlled with **Network Security Groups** (**NSGs**). You need to design a solution that minimizes NSG rule creation and maintenance. What should you do?

1. Enable the built-in rules in each NSG

2. Bind a route table to each subnet

3. Define application security groups that align to each application tier

4. Enable the Virtual Network NSG Service Tag in each NSG

Chapter 13, Implementing Azure Load Balancer

1. You have deployed an Azure Load Balancer, which is using the Basic tier and is load balancing a set of VMs in an availability set that is called `PacktSet1`. You now need to load balance a set of VMs that are deployed to an availability set called `PacktSet2`. What should you do?

1. Replace the existing Load Balancer with a new one that is created in the Standard tier and use this Load Balancer for both of the availability sets

2. Edit the existing Load Balancer and add an additional backend pool to it

3. Edit the existing Load Balancer and add a new frontend IP configuration to it that will load balance the traffic to the new availability set

4. Deploy a second Load Balancer using the Basic tier and configure this one to load balance the traffic to the new availability set

2. You deploy an Azure public Load Balancer to load balance traffic to six virtual machines. You want to remotely access VM1 from the internet through the public Load Balancer using the **Remote Desktop Protocol** (RDP). What should you do?

1. Set a frontend IP configuration that maps the public IP address to the private IP address of VM1

2. Configure an inbound network address translation rule that maps the **Transmission Control Protocol** (TCP) port 3389 to VM1

3. Configure a new internal Load Balancer and configure it to allow the TCP port 3386 from the internet to VM1

4. Configure a load balancing rule that uses the TCP port 3386 to forward traffic to VM1

3. You deploy an Azure internal Load Balancer to load balance traffic to the internal corporate portal. You want to ensure that users only view the most recent copy of the portal. You created a file called NewVersion.html and want to configure the Load Balancer to direct the traffic only to the VMs that contain these files. What should you do?

1. Create a new health probe that uses HTTP as the protocol and includes the path to the NewVersion.html file.

2. Create a new health probe that uses TCP as the protocol and includes the path to the NewVersion.html file.

3. Create a new load balancing rule that includes the path to the NewVersion.html file. This rule will only load balance traffic if the file exists.

4. Use the Set-AzureRmLoadBalancerProbeConfig PowerShell cmdlet to create a new health probe that uses HTTP as the protocol and includes the path to the NewVersion.html file.

Chapter 14, Managing Azure Active Directory

1. You are asked to create a new set of Azure **Active Directory (AD)** security groups that represent the entire hierarchy of a manager's team. This includes people that are managed by the manager. You need to implement the request using the least amount of administrative effort. What should you do?
   1. Create new groups using the Direct Reports rule
   2. Create new Azure AD groups for each manager and use a custom script to detect the `ManagerID` attribute changes and modify the group membership when needed
   3. Create dynamic groups and Azure AD using a ruleset, including the `ManagerID` attribute
   4. Create multiple Azure AD groups and add the members with the same `ManagerID` attribute value to each group

2. You need to grant access to an external consultant to some resources inside your Azure subscription. You plan to add this external user using PowerShell. Which cmdlet should you use?
   1. `New-AzADUser`
   2. `New-AzureADMSInvitation`
   3. `Get-AzADUser`
   4. `Get-AzureADMSInvitation`

3. You need to add another administrator who will be responsible for managing all **Infrastructure-as-a-Service (IaaS)** deployments in your Azure subscription. You create a new account in Azure AD for the user. You need to configure the user account to meet the following requirements: read and write access to all Azure IaaS deployments, read-only access to Azure AD, and no access to Azure subscription metadata. The solution must also minimize your access maintenance in the future. What should you do?
   1. Assign the owner role at the resource level to the user account
   2. Assign the global administrator directory role to the user account
   3. Assign the virtual machine operator role at the subscription level to the user account
   4. Assign the contributor role at the resource group level to the user account

Chapter 15, Implementing and Managing Hybrid Identities

1. You are asked to configure a solution that allows users to log into Office 365 applications without providing their passwords. Your company also wants to deploy cloud-based two-factor authentication for some user profiles. What should you do?

    1. Enable password hash synchronization
    2. Enable pass-through authentication
    3. Install Azure AD Connect
    4. Enable Azure Multi-Factor Authentication

2. You use Azure AD Connect to synchronize all AD domain users and groups with Azure AD. As a result, all users can use **Single Sign-on** (**SSO**) to access applications. You should reconfigure the directory synchronization to exclude domain services accounts and user accounts that shouldn't have access to the application. What should you do?

    1. Re-run Azure AD Connect
    2. Stop the synchronization service
    3. Remove the domain services and user accounts manually
    4. Configure conditional access rules in Azure AD

3. Your company wants to enable all user accounts to use SSO to log in to applications and Office 365. The company has an on-premises AD and uses smartcard authentication. Which solution do you need to deploy to allow users to login without providing a password?

    1. Azure AD Connect with pass-through authentication and SSO
    2. Azure AD Connect with pass hash synchronization and SSO
    3. Azure AD Connect with pass hash synchronization
    4. Active Directory Federation Services

Chapter 16, Implementing Multi-Factor Authentication

1. You deploy **Multi-Factor Authentication (MFA)** in your Azure AD tenant. You don't want your users to be required to enter any additional passwords or code in the browser when using MFA. Which two methods should you make available?
    1. Call to phone
    2. Text message to phone
    3. Notification through the mobile app
    4. Verification code from hardware token

2. Your company has an Azure AD tenant and an on-premises AD that are synced using Azure AD Connect. Your on-premises environment is running a mix of Windows Server 2012 and Windows Server 2016 servers. You use Azure MFA for multi-factor authentication. Users report that they are required to use MFA while using company devices. You need to turn MFA off for domain-joined devices. What should you do?
    1. Enable SSO on Azure AD Connect
    2. Create a conditional access rule to allow users to use either MFA or a domain-joined device when accessing applications
    3. Configure Windows Hello for Business on all domain-joined devices
    4. Add the company external IP address to the Azure MFA Trusted IPs list

3. Your company has an Azure AD tenant and an on-premises AD that are synced using Azure AD Connect. The security department notices a high number of logins from various public IP addresses. What should you do to reduce these logins?
    1. Enable Azure AD smart lockout
    2. Add all the public IP addresses to conditional access and use location blocking to deny all login attempts
    3. Create a conditional access rule to require MFA for all risky logins labeled medium risk and above
    4. Turn on Azure MFA fraud alerts

18
Mockup Test Answers

Chapter 1, Managing Azure Subscriptions and Resource Groups

1. **1**—Yes, this does meet your goal. The access management setting from the Azure Active Directory **Properties** blade ensures that Azure AD users assigned to the global administrator role maintain full control over all subscription resources.
2. **4**—You need to set a read-only lock on the resource group level. This will ensure that administrators and all other users can't make changes to all the different Azure resources that are created for your VM, such as changes to virtual networks, disks, and more.
3. **2**—You should create taxonomic tags and assign them to the resource level; because Azure resources are spread over different resource groups, you can't apply them to the resource group level.

Chapter 2, Analyzing Resource Utilization and Consumption

1. **4**—You should create one alert and one action group for this. One alert can contain multiple metrics-based conditions and a single action group can contain more than one notification or remediation step. So, you can create the metrics for both the CPU and memory in one alert. You can use one action group for sending out the email and creating an issue in the corporate issue tracker.

2. **2**—The right query should be `SecurityEvent | where Level <> 8 | where EventID == 4672`.

3. **2 and 3**—You need to create one action group and you need to configure the **IT Service Management Connector (ITSMC)**. This connector connects System Center Service Manager with Azure.

Chapter 3, Managing Role-Based Access Control

1. **1**—Yes, this is the right way to create a custom role using PowerShell.

2. **1**—You should grant the `Packt_HD` group the password administrator role in Azure AD. This role grants the right to reset non-admin passwords, which are the minimal permissions that are required.

3. **3**—You should assign the owner role to the group of resource group managers.

Chapter 4, Creating and Configuring Storage Accounts

1. **1**—True, you need to configure a stored access policy. **2**—True, to revoke an SAS, you can delete the stored access policy. **3**—False, when you set the timer to now, there can be differences in the clock of the servers hosting your storage account. This can lead to access problems for a short period of time.

2. **1**—You need to configure a general-purpose V2 storage account to move data between different access tiers.

3. **4**—You should configure a storage account with **Zone Redundant Storage (ZRS)** replication. This makes a synchronous copy of the data between three different zones in the same region.

Chapter 5, Importing and Exporting Data to Azure

1. **1 and 4**—You should implement custom caching and dynamic site acceleration on the CDN. Dynamic site acceleration improves performance when delivering dynamic content. You can configure caching rules for static content.

2. **2 and 3**—You can configure an Azure CDN Standard Akamai and an Azure CDN Standard Verizon endpoint, configure dynamic site acceleration, and configure caching rules. Dynamic site acceleration improves performance when delivering dynamic content. You can configure caching rules for static content. You should not create an Azure CDN Standard Microsoft endpoint, because this doesn't support dynamic site acceleration. You also should not create an Azure CDN Premium Verizon endpoint, because caching is configured using a rule engine instead of caching rules.

3. **1**—You should order an Azure Data Box. You can copy all the data to it, and ship it back to Microsoft. Microsoft will then upload this data into the Azure data center directly from the device.

Chapter 6, Configuring Azure Files and Implementing Azure Backup

1. **2 and 3**—Azure File Share Sync reduces the storage footprint of the on-premise file servers by using cloud tiering. This generates a heat map on the on-premise file share and archives infrequently accessed files to Azure. It also provides fault tolerance for on-premise file shares. If a file server goes offline, you can easily restore its file shares to another file server.

2. **1 and 3**—You need to make sure that Internet Explorer Enhanced Security is disabled for both administrators and users and you need to make sure that PowerShell version 5.1 or higher is deployed on the servers.

3. **1**—When you create a new policy in PowerShell, you should use the `New-AzRecoveryServicesBackupProtectionPolicy` cmdlet. The `Get-AzRecoveryServicesBackupSchedulePolicyObject` cmdlet gets a reference to a base policy item. The `Get-AzRecoveryServicesVault` cmdlet gets a reference to the Recovery Services Vault and the `Enable-AzRecoveryServicesBackupProtection` cmdlet enables the backup policy after creation.

Chapter 7, Creating and Configuring VMs for Windows and Linux

1. **1** and **2**—You can deploy the ARM template of the virtual machine from the virtual machine's **Automation script** blade and you can deploy the template from the **Templates** blade in the Azure portal.
2. **1**—You should use the `Export-AzResourceGroup` cmdlet. This captures the specified resource group as a template and saves it to a JSON file.
3. **3**—You should redeploy the VM from a recovery point. VMs can only be assigned to an availability set during initial deployment.

Chapter 8, Managing Azure VMs and VM Backups

1. **4**—You cannot move the VM because the subscriptions are in different Azure AD tenants. One of the prerequisites for moving VMs is that the source and the destination subscriptions remain in the same Azure AD tenant.
2. **1**—You should use the `Set-AzVM` cmdlet, followed by the `-Redeploy` method.
3. **3**—The `Add-AzVMDataDisk` cmdlet adds a data disk to a virtual machine. You can add a data disk when you create a virtual machine, or you can add a data disk to an existing virtual machine.

Chapter 9, Implementing and Managing Virtual Networking

1. **4**—VNet peering is the most cost-effective solution to connect different VNets.
2. **1** and **4**—You should use `az vm nic add` to create a new NIC. Then you should use `az network nic create` to attach the NIC to `PacktVM1`.
3. **1**—You should modify the IP configuration of the virtual network interface associated with `PacktVM1`.

Chapter 10, Integrating on-Premise Networks with Azure Virtual Networks

1. **2**—You should use the `Set-AzureRmLocalNetworkGateway` cmdlet. You need to reconfigure the local network gateway for this.
2. **2**—You should configure an Azure VPN gateway to accept point-to-site VPN connections from users' laptops.
3. **1**—Yes—because you configure a VPN gateway for each region, this solution meets the goals. This will result in the lowest traffic latency for your users.

Chapter 11, Monitoring and Troubleshooting Virtual Networking

1. **1**—You should use Network Performance Monitor to monitor network traffic. You can also use this to monitor network traffic across an ExpressRoute connection.
2. **2**—You don't need to install the Log Analytics agent on all the on-premise servers. You only need to install the agent for each network subnet, so you need to install at least four agents.
3. **2**—No—the network monitor is only capable of monitoring traffic generated from Azure to the on-premise network and not the other way around. You need to monitor all of the traffic on all of your networks.

Chapter 12, Azure Security Groups and Azure DNS

1. **2**—You should use the following commands to add the DNS:
```
New-AzDnsRecordSet -Name "@" -RecordType "A" -ZoneName
"packtpub.com" `
-ResourceGroupName "MyAzureResourceGroup" -Ttl 600 `
-DnsRecords (New-AzDnsRecordConfig -IPv4Address "<your web app
IP address>")

New-AzDnsRecordSet -ZoneName packtpub.com -ResourceGroupName
```

```
PacktAzureResourceGroup `
-Name "@" -RecordType "txt" -Ttl 600 `
-DnsRecords (New-AzDnsRecordConfig -Value
"packtpub.azurewebsites.net")
```

2. **4**—You should purchase the `packtpub.com` domain from a third-party domain registrar first, before taking any other steps.

3. **3**—You should define **application security groups (ASGs)** that align to each application tier. This simplifies network administration in Azure and makes rule maintenance more straightforward.

Chapter 13, Implementing Azure Load Balancer

1. **1 and 4**—You should deploy a second Load Balancer using the Basic tier and use this one to route traffic to the new availability set or delete the old Load Balancer and create a new one using the Standard tier. Only the Standard tier is allowed to route traffic to different availability sets.

2. **2**—You should configure an inbound **network address translation (NAT)** rule that maps TCP port 3389 to VM1. Inbound NAT rules are designed to map a port to an internal IP address of a VM.

3. **1**—You should create a new health probe that uses HTTP as the protocol and include the path to the `NewVersion.html` file. Health probes are designed to test whether a port or file is accessible.

Chapter 14, Managing Azure Active Directory

1. **1**—You should create new groups using the Direct Reports rule. This will create a dynamic group, including all members who have the same `ManagerID` attribute. This will also handle updates to the group accordingly.

2. **2**—You should use the `New-AzureADMSInvitation` cmdlet to add an external user to your Azure AD tenant using PowerShell.

3. **4**—You should assign the Contributor role at the resource group level to the user account. This provides the user with full read/write access at the resource group level, but doesn't grant the user any permissions in the subscription or Azure AD levels.

Chapter 15, Implementing and Managing Hybrid Identities

1. **2**—You should enable pass-through authentication. This enables SSO for users and enables the company to implement two-factor authentication using Azure MFA.
2. **1**—You should rerun Azure AD Connect. This will perform OU filtering and refreshes the directory schema.
3. **4**—You should deploy ADFS. Using this solution, users can log in using SSO and use smartcard authentication. Smartcard authentication is not supported for Azure AD Connect.

Chapter 16, Implementing Multi-Factor Authentication

1. **1 and 3**—Both, call to phone and notification via mobile apps don't require the user to enter a code in a browser.
2. **2**—You should create a conditional access rule to allow users to use either MFA or a domain-joined device when accessing applications. The rule will not force MFA when using a domain-joined device.
3. **3**—You should create a conditional access rule to require MFA authentication for all risky logins labeled medium-risk and above. Azure AD can apply risk levels to all sign-in attempts using a selection of parameters. You can use conditional access to enforce sign-in requirements based on those levels.

Assessments

Chapter 1, Managing Azure Subscriptions and Resource Groups

1. No—you can't move a VM using managed disks that are deployed inside an availability set. This is one limitation.
2. Yes—you can create resource groups from the Azure portal, PowerShell, CLI, and the REST API.
3. Yes—you can delete resource groups from the Azure portal, PowerShell, CLI, and the REST API as well.

Chapter 2, Analyzing Resource Utilization and Consumption

1. Yes—Log Analytics is integrated in Azure Monitor. However, the data is still stored inside the Log Analytics Workspace.
2. No—you can't use SQL. You need to use the Kusto Query Language to query the data.
3. No— Action Groups are unique sets of recipients and actions that can be shared across multiple alert rules.

Chapter 3, Managing Role-Based Access Control

1. No—to assign permissions to users, you need to use role-based access control.
2. Yes—you can use the Azure policy to check whether all of the virtual machines inside your Azure subscription use managed disks.
3. No—custom policies are created in JSON.

Chapter 4, Creating and Configuring Storage Accounts

1. No—you can also download the Azure Storage Explorer for Linux and macOS.
2. No—you can also configure storage accounts to be accessed from from on-premise networks as well.
3. No—you can change the replication type of your storage account later as well, from the Azure portal, PowerShell, or CLI.

Chapter 5, Importing and Exporting Data to Azure

1. Yes—the disk needs to be encrypted before you can copy the data to it.
2. No—Azure CDN does support HTTPS on a CDN endpoint hostname by default.
3. Yes—an Azure Data Box is a physical device which can be used to upload large amounts of data. This box is then shipped to Azure, where Microsoft will upload the data inside an Azure data center.

Chapter 6, Configuring Azure Files and Implementing Azure Backup

1. Yes—Azure backup can be used to backup Azure files as well.
2. Yes—Azure backup supports backing up machines that are protected by MABS and DPM.
3. No—the Azure File Share Sync Service is used to sync data from on-premise file shares to Azure.

Chapter 7, Creating and Configuring VMs for Windows and Linux

1. Yes— you use VM Scale Sets to automate the deployment of multiple VMs.
2. Yes— by using Availability Sets, you can spread VMs across different fault and update domains.
3. Yes—you use Resource Providers to deploy different artifacts in Azure using ARM templates.

Chapter 8, Managing Azure VMs and VM Backups

1. Yes—you can use both PowerShell and CLI to move, redeploy, and resize your Windows and Linux VMs. You can also move them from the Azure portal.
2. No— you can add data disks and network interfaces from the Azure portal, PowerShell, and CLI.
3. No—Custom Script Extensions are for configuring Windows machines after deployment. If you need to configure macOS machines, Chef is a better option.

Chapter 9, Implementing and Managing Virtual Networking

1. No—VNet peering uses the backbone infrastructure of Azure; there is no need to create gateways.
2. Yes—by defining User Defined Routes, you can adjust the routing between the different resources in your VNet, according to your needs.
3. No—you can only assign IPv6 addresses to external Load Balancers.

Chapter 10, Integrating On-Premise Networks with Azure Virtual Networks

1. No—traffic over an ExpressRoute circuit is not encrypted by default. However, you can create a solution that encrypts the traffic that goes over the ExpressRoute circuit.
2. Yes—a point-to-site VPN connection is designed to create a secure connection between an individual client and your virtual network over the internet. This connection type is most suitable for employees who work from other locations.
3. Yes—it is not allowed to host the server behind a NAT.

Chapter 11, Monitoring and Troubleshooting Virtual Networking

1. No—Azure Network Watcher can be used to monitor and diagnose network connectivity in Azure, on-premise, and in hybrid configurations.
2. Yes—IP Flow Verify can be used to verify outbound connections.
3. Yes—IP Flow Verify can be used to verify connections between different VMs hosted inside Azure.

Chapter 12, Azure Security Groups and Azure DNS

1. Yes—you can associate a Network Security Group with both a subnet and a network interface.
2. No—you can't use Azure DNS to register a domain name. You can redirect an existing domain name to Azure DNS.
3. Yes—at the time of writing, private DNS zones can only be configured from PowerShell and CLI.

Chapter 13, Implementing Azure Load Balancer

1. No—a basic load balancer can be created from the Azure portal, PowerShell, and CLI.
2. Yes—for a standard load balancer, the VMs in the backend are required to have NICs that are placed in a network security group.
3. Yes—a standard Load Balancer needs a standard public IP address to function properly.

Chapter 14, Managing Azure Active Directory

1. Yes—you need to use the `New-AzureADMSInvitation` to add a guest user to your Azure AD tenant.
2. No—Azure AD Join can be used without connecting an on-premise Active Directory to Azure AD.
3. Yes—When you add a custom domain to Azure AD, you need to verify it by adding a TXT record to the DNS settings of your domain registrar. After adding this record, you can verify the domain in the Azure portal.

Chapter 15, Implementing and Managing Hybrid Identities

1. No—password hash synchronization is enabled by default if you use the Express settings during Azure AD Connect installation.
2. No—password sync needs to be enabled on the on-premise domain controller and in the Azure portal.
3. No—you can install Azure AD Connect when the on-premise Forest name doesn't match one of the Azure AD custom domain names, but you will receive a warning during installation that SSO is not enabled for your users.

Chapter 16, Implementing Multi-Factor Authentication

1. Yes—trusted IP addresses are meant for bypassing multi-factor authentication for certain IPs. This way, you can disable MFA for users who log in from the company intranet, for instance.
2. No—you can use conditional access policies to enable MFA for users and applications.
3. Yes—fraud alerts can only be enabled for MFA Server deployments.

Other Books You May Enjoy

If you enjoyed this book, you may be interested in these other books by Packt:

Hands-On Cloud Administration in Azure

Mustafa Toroman

ISBN: 978-1-78913-496-4

- Understand the concepts of IaaS and PaaS
- Learn design patterns for Azure solutions
- Design data solutions in Azure
- Explore concepts of hybrid clouds with Azure
- Implement Azure Security in cloud
- Create and manage Azure resources with script-based tools

Hands-On Linux Administration on Azure
Frederik Vos

ISBN: 978-1-78913-096-6

- Understand why Azure is the ideal solution for your open source workloads
- Master essential Linux skills and learn to find your way around the Linux environment
- Deploy Linux in an Azure environment
- Use configuration management to manage Linux in Azure
- Manage containers in an Azure environment
- Enhance Linux security and use Azure's identity management systems
- Automate deployment with Azure Resource Manager (ARM) and Powershell
- Employ Ansible to manage Linux instances in an Azure cloud environment

Leave a review - let other readers know what you think

Please share your thoughts on this book with others by leaving a review on the site that you bought it from. If you purchased the book from Amazon, please leave us an honest review on this book's Amazon page. This is vital so that other potential readers can see and use your unbiased opinion to make purchasing decisions, we can understand what our customers think about our products, and our authors can see your feedback on the title that they have worked with Packt to create. It will only take a few minutes of your time, but is valuable to other potential customers, our authors, and Packt. Thank you!

Index